Cartwheels in a Sari

Cartwheels in a Sari

A Memoir of Growing Up Cult

JAYANTI TAMM

HARMONY BOOKS

NEW YORK

Library of Congress Cataloging-in-Publication Data
Tamm, Jayanti.
Cartwheels in a sari / Jayanti Tamm.—1st ed.
1. Chinmoy, Sri, 1931–2007—Cult. 2. Tamm, Jayanti. 3. Spiritual
biography. I. Title.
BP610.C552T36 2009
294.5092—dc22
[B]
2008036450

ISBN 978-0-307-39392-0

Printed in the United States of America

Design by Lauren Dong

10 9 8 7 6 5 4 3 2 1

First Edition

For all those who dare examine their faith,
be it past or present

Most of all,
for Duane,
my best friend and husband

Author's Note

SINCE SRI CHINMOY's arrival in America in 1964, thousands of sincere seekers and curious onlookers sought his presence. Some remained only for a few hours, others for decades. No doubt that all those who encountered Sri Chinmoy have their own experiences, their own understanding of him. This memoir isn't the definitive account of Sri Chinmoy; it is my own remembrance. Although all the events within these pages are true, the names and identifying characteristics of most people mentioned in the book have been altered in an effort to honor the privacy of those involved.

ACKNOWLEDGMENTS

MUCH GRATITUDE goes out to my friends and colleagues for their support in this endeavor. For sharing their remembrances of former times, I thank my family. In particular, I am extremely grateful to Samarpana for her constant encouragement and her willingness to unearth her past.

I thank my superb agent, Adam Chromy, and my perceptive and insightful editor, Julia Pastore, for their vision.

Finally, for his tireless belief and love, I am forever in debt to my husband, Duane.

CONTENTS

Cartwheels in a Sari

Prologue

THE LAST TIME I RECEIVED A MESSAGE FROM GURU, THE
self-proclaimed spiritual master Sri Chinmoy, six years
had passed since his personal envoy called to inform
me that my discipleship was officially and permanently ter-
minated and all contact and association with his headquarters in Queens, New York, was forbidden. Now, after years
of struggling to shed all outer remnants of my former life, I
listened with muted curiosity and suspicion as the same
breathless disciple carefully conveyed Guru's unexpected and
urgent message. His words foretold of a "dangerous destructive force" trying to physically attack me, and, in order to protect myself, for the next two months, every hour on the hour,
I needed to pray ceaselessly to Guru for protection.

I was livid.

I knew Guru's masterful tactics of manipulation to lure
me back into his fold. It had worked countless times in the
past. Since birth, as his chosen devotee, I witnessed Guru lovingly warn of the vicious karmic punishments in store for
disciples who did not strictly adhere to his teachings. Whether
it was dread of the massive wheel of karma, or weakness for

his doe-eyed charms, it had been enough to keep me beholden to him.

I couldn't hang up the phone.

Captured by his honey-coated appeal that promised his eternal concern and compassion, in an instant, all of my years of struggling to separate myself from his hold dissolved. I still possessed enough faith to fear that his prophecy might be true.

I held vigil, clocking protective prayer sessions by the hour. Two months later, when the supposed witching hour came and passed without incident, I was enraged and mortified that Guru still retained the power to control me, despite all I had experienced living as his chosen disciple for more than a quarter of a century.

That was it, my final act of belief in the cult of the short, bald man in the flowing robes who declared himself to be God.

1

The Myth Begins

M Y LIFE STORY CAN BE TRACED BACK TO AN AD-
dress scrawled across a matchbook directing my
mother to the place where she hoped her lifelong
search would end. She didn't have a phone number or contact name. Although it was just after dusk, the New York
neighborhood seemed empty. No one to ask, no clues. After
crisscrossing the street four times, she stood before the only
building on the block without a number. Wrought-iron bars
covered the cracked glass of the front door. Instead of a panel
of backlit doorbells, five chewed wires jutted from the brick.
The door was unlocked and sighed open at her touch.

The dank stairwell had one bare lightbulb. Cigarette butts
littered the floor like flattened cockroaches. She rechecked
the address clutched in her left hand. This was suddenly absurd. All of it—her exhausting journey, hitchhiking from San
Francisco with her two-year-old son, leaving behind her stray-
ing husband and all of the contents of her former life, bringing nothing other than one small satchel and a matchbook
with the address of Sri Chinmoy, a guru recently arrived from

Pondicherry, India. A drip of rusty water fell onto her shoulder from a brown-stained ring on the ceiling. This was not the place to find a holy man. They reside by the gardenia-soaked banks of the Ganges, or inside cavernous mountain dwellings, or shaded by boughs of the bodhi tree, not in dilapidated East Village tenements.

As she turned to leave, an ancient voice, gentle and lulling, drifted down to her.

"At last, at last. You have come, good girl. Bah."

She looked up. Dressed in traditional Indian garb, a pale blue dhoti, and matching kurta, Guru's gold-hued skin glowed, and he seemed to flood the stairwell with his radiance.

When she and her very first boyfriend fled Chicago, leaving behind her abusive alcoholic father, she actively began her search for spiritual fulfillment. In her earnest longing, she had wandered through San Francisco, the epicenter for alternative spiritual paths, kneeling in silent *zazen* at Zen temples, dancing and whirling with Sufi mystics, quietly reflecting in Quaker Meeting Houses, and clapping and chanting at the Hare Krishna temple, but everything, even the splashes of mysticism, felt too formal and processed, reminding her of dreaded days in Catholic school. Once, years ago, she had read that when the disciple was ready, the guru would appear.

And there he was, leaning over the railing from the floor above, as though he had been standing there, waiting for her, her entire life. Why had it taken her this long to arrive? And how could she possibly waste one more minute when her guru had finally appeared? At that moment she chose to surrender her entire existence to him. This guru was the answer to all of her questions and longings. He seemed to know her, and perhaps he could fill all the gaping holes that echoed inside.

He motioned for her to follow him inside his crowded apartment where the guests sat upon a bare wood floor in silence. Through swirls of sandalwood incense smoke, Guru instructed her to sit beside a young hippie, barefoot and with a sour odor. After hours of potent, silent meditation, Guru stated that if she wanted to "jump into the sea of spirituality," she would marry the long-haired man.

That, according to my mother, is how she met my father.

The blond mendicant, my father, was also at Guru's for the first time. He drove from Yale University, where he was a graduate fellow studying philosophy. Born in a refugee camp in Augsburg, Germany, to Estonian parents who had fled when Stalin's troops invaded their homeland, my father's family immigrated to America and settled in Bismarck, North Dakota. Thoroughly dissatisfied with Bismarck's status quo, by his late teens, my father devoured drugs along with sacred Sanskrit texts as he hitchhiked, journeying through communes and churches for answers to his questions on the meaning of existence. He found the ancient tradition of asceticism appealing. After arriving at Yale, he began his own intensive course of study to become a *sadhana,* which included renouncing all material objects and attachments. He welcomed personal discomfort and self-denial as important steps toward inner strength. He roamed the Yale campus barefoot, even in the midst of the New England winters, as part of his spiritual practice. According to my father, the night he entered Guru's apartment, he planned to take a vow as a *sanyassi,* a celibate monk, to learn about the realms of the inner world first-hand from a true Yogi.

The last thing he expected that night was acquiring a wife and stepson.

When Guru blessed them both, pressing his hands over their foreheads, they felt a river of warmth course through them, awakening their senses. With closed eyes, Guru chanted in Sanskrit, and in the incense haze and overheated space, his words felt familiar. He praised their inner aspiration, welcoming them into his "golden boat that will steer them safely through the ignorance-sea to the golden-shore of the Beyond." My mother and my father were both fatigued charting their own courses, and the guarantee of safe passage to the golden-shore of the Beyond was not something to pass up. This guru felt homespun, humble, and lacked the trappings of protocol, profits, and proselytizing over which other religious groups obsessed. This was different—just a small circle of devoted seekers guided by a simple sage. It was exactly what my mother and father yearned for. Though neither one had a desire for marriage, they were thoroughly entranced by the idea of a life with Guru. They bowed their heads, accepting Guru's wisdom.

And so on that night my mother and father became Sri Chinmoy's disciples.

ALMOST AS SOON as my parents committed themselves to Guru as full-time disciples, Guru rapidly changed his small informal meditation circle into a structured organization. Since Guru wanted all his disciples to expedite their spiritual growth, he prescribed a lifestyle that, according to him, would guarantee the quickest route toward self-perfection. He prohibited all activities he considered dangerous detours: alcohol, caffeine, smoking, drugs, TV, radio, movies, music, newspapers, magazines, books not written by Guru, meat, dancing, and pets. In addition, all disciples were to remain single. According to Guru, traditional families created insurmountable tangles and distractions that at best delayed, but more often derailed, true seekers in their quest for enlightenment.

There were, however, a few exceptions. Guru sanctioned certain unions that he arranged and labeled as "divine marriages." Created to encourage intensified spiritual practice to achieve "faster than the fastest progress in their inner lives," Guru paired a number of new disciples with the mandate that they marry but remain celibate. Shortly after my parents' "divine marriage" in 1969, my mother became pregnant, clearly violating Guru's policy. The problem of my mother's pregnancy drove an immediate thorny wedge between the newlyweds, who were still strangers to each other. Nervous to confess to Guru, they felt ashamed and embarrassed.

Guru scolded my parents for being undivine and indulging in "lower-vital forces" that threatened to eradicate all of their spiritual hunger. My parents were mortified and pleaded with Guru that their failing was due to weakness and not out of deliberate disobedience. Eventually, Guru's infinite compassion intervened. He pleaded with the "Supreme"—his preferred word for God—and told my parents that the Supreme was so moved by Guru's prayers that he decided to allow Guru to turn what he called this "undivine" episode into a spiritual boon. Guru then announced that he had contacted the "highest heaven" and arranged for a special soul to incarnate as his chosen disciple. My grateful parents humbly vowed to never again indulge in "lower-vital activities," and renewed their undying commitment to Guru to never permit the "trappings of family" to deter them from spiritual progress. They understood that what held them together was Guru and Guru alone. He served as the foundation of their marriage and lives.

As in all great faiths of the world, Guru, too, had stories to answer the unanswerable, to explain the unexplainable, to rationalize the irrational. His story was me—the miracle child. In the history of the Sri Chinmoy Center, from its humble beginnings in 1964 to its present-day expansion with more than seven thousand followers around the world and the hundreds of thousands of ex-disciples and seekers who, for however fleeting a time, came to experience Guru's presence, I, according to the legend originally told by Guru and then repeated endlessly by disciples around the world, am the *only* soul to have been personally invited, selected, or commanded to incarnate into his realm on earth. Though mine wasn't proclaimed a virgin birth, he announced that I descended from the highest heavens to be an exemplary disciple; I was to be the Ananda to Buddha, the Peter to Jesus, the Lakshmana to Rama, a devoted, sacrificial being, selfless and tireless, pleasing the master unconditionally.

The myth of my birth was one of Guru's favorite stories that he repeated over the years. Although it changed slightly depending on his mood, the standard version is the following: At 6:01 on a warm morning in September 1970, my soul entered the world, landing in a Connecticut hospital. My exhausted mother beamed and clutched me tightly to her breast, while my father was in the parking lot waiting for Guru. Guru was being chauffeured from Queens, New York, and as soon as he arrived, my father escorted Guru directly into the nursery.

According to Guru, my first *dharshan,* official blessing, occurred an hour after my birth. Guru walked up to the window and spotted me. I, like the other shriveled, stunned newborns, was asleep. Guru had brought with him my name. In Eastern traditions, a spiritual name means receiving a new life, a new identity. My mother, originally Kathleen, was given the name Samarpana by Guru, and my father, originally Tonis, was renamed Rudra. My parents would never have considered naming me themselves. I was Guru's. He picked out the name, Jayanti, meaning "the absolute victory of the highest Supreme."

Guru started meditating on me, sending me an inner message to wake up and respond to his presence. In the first of many of my great acts of disobedience and disappointment, I continued sleeping. Again, Guru intently concentrated on me, attempting to stir me, yet I offered no reply. Feeling frustrated, he inwardly told my soul, *Is this your gratitude? I specially chose you from the highest heavens to come to earth to be with me, and this is your gratitude? You do not acknowledge your Guru? Bah.* At this point, I uncurled my fingers and moved my hands together in a prayerful *pranam,* opened my eyes, and slightly bowed my head and neck into my chest. It was a perfect moment, an act of unconditional surrender, of pure *bhakti,* devotion. It was miraculous and yet expected. It was my first test, and I had passed it, cementing my status, cementing my bonds.

FOR THE FIRST six months of my life I was homebound because Guru told my mother that my special soul, so dazzlingly beatific, needed careful sanctuary while adjusting to the vibrations and consciousness of the chaotic world.

Unquestioning, my mother obeyed. That was the requirement necessary to be his true disciple: obey and please Guru
unconditionally, and, in return, he would deliver the disciple
to the golden-shore of perfection. It was his guarantee.

All of my childhood memories involve trying to obey and
please Guru. My earliest memory is of my third birthday
party in Queens. The meditation that night was at the house
of a disciple who lived a few blocks from Guru. My mother
dressed me in a sari of Guru's favorite color, a shade of light
blue the disciples officially dubbed "Guru-blue." Saris were
the required uniform for meditations—six yards of fabric,
carefully pleated and draped, that modestly concealed the
body. When worn well, saris produced goddess-like silhou-
ettes. The disciples' saris included many colors, from jewel-
toned silks that evoked the splendor of strutting peacocks
to pure white cotton that suggested nunlike severity. For my
mother, trying to keep six yards of slick blue polyester pinned
and tucked on a three-year-old determined to waddle around,
kicking and spinning, was a true challenge. I kept tripping
over the pleats, even though my mom had safety pinned my
goddess draping to my undershirt.

When Guru summoned me to the front of the room for
my birthday cake, a bus-wheel-size mound covered in sugar
icing and pink rosettes with three thick candles, I marched
over, anxious to blow out the flames. But, as always before
any activity, first came the meditation. Guru motioned for me
to stand still in front of him.

I started to squirm. I heard the flames lick the air, then
watched the candles melt into pink wax puddles on the icing.
I needed to get to those candles. I needed to lick off the pink

rosettes, but I was trapped. He wasn't done. I hadn't yet been thoroughly blessed. He smothered my folded hands with his left hand, capturing them, then pressed his right hand on my head, covering my entire skull, then he pushed harder, as if to ensure through force that the showering of love would be better received. I wiggled more, trying to turn my head to look for my mother. I was worried now. The candles were shrinking while people giggled and oowwd and aahhd behind me. Guru rotated me to face him. His blessing wasn't done.

Finally, with a large smile, he proclaimed, "Good girl, Jayanti, you are a good girl."

He let go. I took a step back, dazed from all the blessing, and again looked for my mother. Spotting her, with a huge smile, her eyes happily streaming with tears, was a relief. I was always relieved when I could see my mother. With both hands folded, she prompted me to do the same—keep those hands folded. I did. I brought my hands together and stood beside the cake. I then looked for my father and brother. My father was fidgeting with a camera, staring down at the lens cap, as if looking at himself in the reflection. My six-year-old brother, Ketan, glared at me with his arms squeezing his knees. He hated all birthdays that were not his own.

But then it was finally time—the big event—the sugar fortress awaited. The sheer bulk of the cake meant that I couldn't get close enough to blow out the candles properly. I tried with a faint puff and nothing happened. I looked up at Guru for my instructions. He always had answers.

"Blow, good girl. Bah, bah. Blow hard."

I tried again. Nothing happened. I didn't want to disappoint Guru. Disappointing Guru meant he did not smile at me, and my parents didn't either. More giggles and oowws and aahhs. I forced a burst of sloppy wind up from the bottom of my stomach. Again nothing.

"Oi," Guru said. "She cannot do it. Her mother, come, help her." Guru started reading a note on his side table.

I had failed. My eyes filled with tears. Guru did not look up at me again.

My mother stood up, ready as always to sacrifice herself for her family, but then, without any invitation, Ketan dashed up onto the stage, rammed his entire fist into the scripted lettering of *Beloved Jayanti,* and blew out my candles. So there, he glared at me. He had won.

"Oi," Guru said at the chaos before him.

Happy Birthday.

As the number of disciples quickly grew, the informal meditation group my parents joined disappeared. In its place, Guru established the groundwork for a booming organization. Guru invited my parents to be active pioneers in the process, and they were both honored and overjoyed to be part of what they viewed as an expanding movement with the potential to radically transform the world for the better. My father, in particular, wanted to be at the forefront of Guru's evolving mission. Although my parents longed to move permanently to Guru's new neighborhood in Queens, New York, Guru told them to remain in Connecticut to manage the Connecticut Center—the gathering place for potential and current disciples. One year after my birth, after consulting with Guru, my parents found a humble two-story ranch house in

Norwalk that had a fully finished basement to host the Connecticut Center. With plenty of parking, a separate entrance, and low rent, it was ideal. After Guru came to view the house, he gave his consent, and we packed up and moved. The Connecticut Center occupied the entire basement, and we inhabited the first floor of the house. I shared a room with Ketan, my parents had a room with separate beds, and there was a living room and small kitchen. Norwalk, in 1971, was closer to the country than the suburbs, and the house had a field on both sides with large woods stretching out behind it. The semi-seclusion worked well, for we were definitely unlike the other residents in the neighborhood.

It was made clear to me right away that the new house was not for us. We were just custodians; the house served the needs of the meditation group and Guru. Our living room had only one piece of furniture, a throne for Guru. Our kitchen cupboards stored the pots, utensils, and ingredients my mother used when cooking for Guru. Our bathroom shelf held special sponges and cleaners to be used before Guru's visits. The sole point of everything was Guru—and everything that belonged to Guru, including all his personal items—his cup, blanket, pens—items that had once belonged to Guru—used cups, blankets, and pens—or objects that had any faint relation to Guru, including candle holders, incense burners, and shrine cloths placed near his pictures, were sacred relics.

Our house felt like a Guru museum, replete with photo gallery—pictures of Guru occupied every single free space upon the wall—Guru with his hands folded, Guru laughing, Guru sniffing a gardenia, Guru sipping juice. From the entryway to the gap between the sink and medicine cabinet, we were surrounded by Guru. He was always watching me. He was always, always present.

My parents, striving to be obedient disciples, settled into their separate routines that Guru assigned them. Their schedules seemed to overlap only occasionally, and most often in their efforts to raise my brother and me to be model disciples. My father created board games such as Disciple Chutes and Ladders, where we dreaded landing on squares like "Did Not Meditate Soulfully—Go back ten spaces." He also told us favorite stories such as the day Guru achieved God-Realization at age eleven, when he saw the Supreme in the clouds, and how when Guru was fourteen, just like Lord Krishna, he outwitted an evil force that appeared in the form of his own guru, Sri Aurobindo, and destroyed the demon, and teaching tales of how Guru's third eye allows him to know the past, present, and future simultaneously. So when I wouldn't eat my bowl of spiced dal, my mother gently reminded me that Guru was watching and not at all pleased with my behavior, which made me look around and quickly shovel the lentils into my mouth.

My parents worked diligently for Guru, especially on Mondays—the night Guru came to our house to hold meditations. Preparations began a few days before with each parent taking on specific tasks. It seemed that they always had separate projects that kept them in different rooms of the house. I never saw them together tidying up the meditation room or raking leaves. They moved, it seemed, in opposite directions, with my mother entering a room just as my father had shut the door on his way outside. As my mother cleaned rooms, picked flowers, and bought groceries, my father arranged chairs, lit incense, and swept the path from the driveway to the side door. While all of the setup took place, Ketan and I were told to stay out of the way.

Monday afternoons, I sat on the kitchen counter while my mother cooked some of Guru's favorite foods. Guru was a vegetarian, and made vegetarianism mandatory for all of us. I had never even tasted meat; and I didn't want to, since Guru said that meat contained restless animal-consciousness, and anything that he declared could lower my consciousness was to be avoided at all costs. But Guru enjoyed food and was a voracious eater. Since he took great pleasure in eating, his weight would perpetually fluctuate, to his great dismay. He often complained about the large number of calories in ice cream and samosas, after devouring a heaping plateful of both. I knew that Guru could use his spiritual powers to do anything, and sometimes I wondered why he didn't touch his own stomach and make it go away. But then I also knew that Guru was teaching us some sort of lesson that one day I would understand. Often at meditations, Guru, in a teasing voice, asked us why our master was so fat, and when we told him that he was thin, he would shake his feet, then say that he was not as thin as Lord Krishna or Christ, and not nearly as handsome, but when we told him again and again that he was much more beautiful than any other avatar, he would lean back in his chair and smile sweetly. Then I could tell he was happy.

As Guru preferred foods from his native Bengal, my mother tried hard to learn classic Indian recipes such as aloo chop, saag paneer, and jalabis. Having lost her mother at age eleven, my mother grew up in the scotch-soaked stink of a Chicago apartment with her permanently drunk father and her neurotic older sister, becoming a surrogate mother to both. Nightly she fished change out of her father's coat pockets in order to provide dinner. Even as a child, my mother dreamt of family dinners and cozy memories, and so having Guru and the disciples come to her kitchen was like hosting Thanksgiving dinner weekly, and she strove to prepare an array of elaborate dishes, trying to anticipate Guru's whims. Just in case he might be in the mood for an okra curry, vegetable pakora, or tamarind chutney, wearing her Guru-blue cotton sari and red bindi, she scoured the local grocery stores until she found ingredients she could piece together into a Mogul feast. Often, after days of preparation, Guru wouldn't touch a thing, asking instead for pizza. That only made her try harder to please him, and the next week, she was at it again, mincing garlic and rolling chapatis.

Although the meditation was supposed to start at seventhirty, Guru was normally at least an hour late. My brother and I were not allowed downstairs inside the meditation hall unless Guru called for us, which meant my mother stayed upstairs while my father attended the meeting. Since the walls were thin and the floors were squeaky, it was mandated that we remain as quiet as possible so as not to disturb the meditation below us. Even for the golden child, this wasn't easy to do, especially with Ketan's ideas for having somersault contests or dare-jumps off the top bunk. Numerous spiritual seekers stormed upstairs urging us to shut up. When we tried to play quiet games, such as Guru and Disciple—one of Ketan's favorites, which involved the Guru sitting on his throne and barking a list of commands for the disciple, none of which would be done to his satisfaction—we still ended up being too loud.

"Good girl," Ketan said, sitting on his bed. "Go get me orange juice."

"Yes, Guru," I answered.

Ketan always played the Guru, making me the disciple.

I came back with a mug, spilling orange juice all over the floor.

"You didn't put ice cubes in it. You are a bad disciple. You are unspiritual. Now, pick up my stufties. Soulfully," he said, between sips of juice. "Stufties" was what we called our stuffed animals.

"Yes, Guru," I answered, scooping his stufties off the floor and arranging them on his bed like guardians.

"You did not do that soulfully. I am very displeased with you. Now let me keep Fluffity Bunny," he said, with a cheeky smile.

Fluffity Bunny? She was my favorite stuftie. He had crossed the line.

"MOOOOOMMM!" I screamed as loud as possible. "Ketan's a mean guru again!"

As my parents kept receiving menacing threats from women with folded hands when our thumps and banging proved too distracting for the culmination of peace, light, and bliss in our basement, my parents sought a desperate solution. For weeks, my parents had secret arguments spelled aloud for us not to understand, but we knew they were looking for a way to keep us quiet.

"It's H-A-R-M-L-E-S-S," my mother spelled, folding her sari.

"It's a B-A-D I-N-F-L-U-E-N-C-E," my father replied.

"T-O—U-G-H," my mother said, shutting the door behind her.

The next Monday, my father asked Guru if Ketan and I

could watch television in an attempt to keep us quiet. After careful research, my mother discovered that Monday night aired a double feature of *The Muppet Show* and *Little House on the Prairie*—both shows, just barely, were not too corrupting. Guru told his disciples that watching TV was like ingesting garbage. Most disciples did not even own a TV, and those who did were seen as suspect. My mother had a small ten-inch black-and-white TV that Ketan and I were forbidden to watch. When we asked my mother why she had a TV when it was so bad, she said she had a secret assignment from Guru, and that we shouldn't mention it to the other disciples. She hid the TV in her room, on a high shelf, out of reach. Guru had given my parents strict instructions about keeping us away from TV; while an entire generation of American youth was being raised by *The Love Boat, Charlie's Angels,* and *The Dukes of Hazzard,* we were memorizing Guru's aphorisms and using our *mala* beads to say our prayers. Some nights, however, from outside our parents' door, when my mother was inside alone, we heard the faint sounds of a canned laugh track leaking out into the night, and we understood that she was working on her top-secret assignment. Ketan plotted and waited for a time that eventually both Mom and Dad would go away long enough for him to scale the shelf and watch what Guru had declared as forbidden garbage.

Guru, tired of hearing the continuous complaints about the noise level, finally agreed that he would allow us to watch both shows. This was ecstasy. Monday nights became the hands-down greatest night. Not only would my guru come and bless us, but we could also watch TV. Ketan and I became instant addicts. Ketan imitated Gonzo and Kermit, and I laughed, prancing around the room like I was Miss

Piggy. We then gathered up extra pillows to sit upon as we watched the Ingalls family and their world. It was my first glimpse at how another family interacted. What? No guru? I asked my father why there was no guru on the show. He told me that there really was a guru that the family meditated with, but that was kept for special episodes that our TV antenna couldn't pick up. It made sense to me. All of his explanations and insertions of Guru were gospel. At our bedtime, in those few cherished minutes that my father spent with us, he read aloud from the small collection of outside books that he considered neutral enough not to corrupt us. However, he added his own editorial corrections that made the books more spiritual. He inserted sections, ensuring us that before the Hobbits went to bed, they meditated on Guru, and before Lucy went into the closet in search of Narnia, she asked Guru's permission. I never inquired about the Muppets' guru. I assumed that the two old men in the balcony were their avatars.

Long after the TV was turned off, inevitably, we were summoned downstairs for the showing of what the disciples called the Golden Child and her brother. Public speaking and stage fright have never been a problem for me. When Guru first called me to the stage, I was too little to walk, and so my mother or father carried me up for Guru's public blessing. By the time I could walk on my own, I needed to earn my blessing. Usually, I was asked to sing. Guru loved music, and in the ashram where he was raised, *bhajans,* devotional songs, were taught and sung as part of the meditation and played a large role in the spiritual practice of the disciples. Like many other aspects of his teachings, Guru imported this practice when he came to America, no longer in the role as a disciple but as a guru. Although Guru spoke English fluently, most of the songs that he composed were in Bengali, his native language. With simple melodies, Guru taught hundreds and hundreds of songs on his harmonium, a small keyboard that needed to be air-pumped for the notes to escape.

Guru sat on his Guru-blue throne at the front of the hall, dressed in a yellow dhoti, which reflected the golden hue of his skin. Wisps of gray hair, cropped close to the curve of his scalp, hinted at what was once a full head of hair. Guru placed his hands together in front of his forehead, creating a deep bow. He held this position, as we all matched his stance, bowing low to him. Slowly, Guru unfolded and straightened, dropping his hands into his lap; his dark eyes scanned the room from left to right before closing into his "lion's pose"— the eyelids halfway shut and his eyeballs flickering, his pupils lost in a span of white. This movement of the eyes was a manifestation of a state of consciousness that, according to Guru, only extremely highly evolved souls could achieve. But that certainly didn't stop a lot of disciples from trying, including me.

"Jayanti, good girl. You sing two songs."

That was my cue. I was on. I stood up, adjusted my sari, folded my hands, and marched up the aisle. I bowed to Guru, stood beside his throne, then turned to face the audience. On the floor beside his throne were arrangements of flowers, offerings from different disciples, some for special occasions, birthdays, or the anniversary of their coming to the Center, some just for an opportunity to have a bouquet near Guru, with a note that reminded Guru of their existence. Flowers always surrounded Guru, and each time I was near Guru I breathed in the sweet tropical scent.

I checked in with the important figures in the room: my mom mouthed the first few words of the song that we had rehearsed the entire day; my father was asleep, and his folded hands crashed into his lap, then his head rebounded awake; Ketan, from the back of the hall, kept his hands folded but poked his tongue hard from his right cheek to his left cheek in a concentrated effort to jinx me. I then scanned the rest of the audience—the men's side and women's side—Guru made them always sit on separate sides. I looked around for the favorite meditators whom Ketan and I secretly imitated: Anjana, a dramatic blond woman who kept her arms straight out in front, with her folded hands looking like the top of a pyramid; Prana, a frizzy-haired woman who consistently wore white and who stretched her neck, heaven bound, so we could see up her nostrils; Vivek, a short bald man, who brought his own folding chair, and spastically shook both feet. They were all there. I smiled, ready to go.

"Phule phule, dhule dhule, moranachi, khule khule, kotahathe eshe koto jabo . . ."

"Bah, Bah. Good girl," Guru said with a slight tilt of his head and sweet smile. "One more. Bah."

Number two.

"Ananda bola nirvana dola, tunga ala . . ."

"Excellent."

Guru was pleased. I had passed. I turned back to Guru and gave a deep bow, then I turned to the audience and gave them a deep bow. I had no idea what I had just sung.

When Guru taught songs, he rarely translated them. Music, he said, was the language of the soul, and it communicated perfectly; therefore it was unnecessary to translate. While I had hundreds of Bengali songs memorized, they could have been in Urdu, pig Latin, or Klingon, for all I knew. It didn't much matter anyway. What mattered was the consciousness with which they were sung.

"Most soulful, good girl. Most soulful."

Yes. I had done it again. I had pleased him. "Soulful" was what I aimed for. I was done. I could go back upstairs.

WITH KETAN AS the leader, I eagerly agreed to his plots, curious to see how far we could push our boundaries. No longer satisfied with just our TV triumph, Ketan began scheming for our latest, and most dire, rule manipulation: Operation Get-a-Pet. Guru forbade disciples from owning pets, and so Ketan wisely decided that on such a critical matter, the way to go was to exploit my Chosen One status to the fullest. The assault would have to come from me. Even the idea of having an animal made me shiver with glee. Ketan and I talked constantly in front of our parents about owning a pet, but we realized that we were wasting our efforts. The way things worked in my family was that my parents did not make any decisions.

"Ask Guru," they would say when it was a matter of anything from our bedtime to having a rope swing.

Though I knew Guru prohibited pets, my desire for a small, fluffy friend seemed to outweigh my desire for spiritual progress. We decided that if I asked for an animal that Guru hadn't mentioned by name during his talks about not having pets, then maybe it would be all right. Dogs and cats were officially on his bad list, but we had never heard his policy on rabbits.

After weeks of plotting, we chose one Monday in April as

the critical night. We had been extra quiet during the meditation, staying glued in our beds with the volume completely off during both *The Muppet Show* and *Little House on the Prairie,* and we had said extra prayers in the morning. And now it was time. Ketan nudged me forward.

With my hair in raggedy braids, wearing my best sari, I approached Guru after the meditation, as he lounged on his sacred throne that we were not allowed to touch.

"Jayanti, bah, good girl. All right?" Guru asked, holding a glass of mango lassi.

"Yes, Guru." I answered with folded hands.

Folded hands and properly addressing Guru was second nature. I could not have imagined it any other way. I could keep my hands folded and sit with a straight back, knees tucked in—feet could never be pointed at Guru for it was a sign of disrespect—without squirming for hours; I'd had lots and lots of practice.

"Next week, you come and sing two songs. Two songs, good girl. You sing next week."

"Yes, Guru." I said, inching closer to his chair.

Guru sipped his drink once more.

"Your mother made most delicious lassi. You tell her, most delicious."

"Yes, Guru." I nodded my head, making note of his exact words to relay his message properly back into the kitchen.

I sat there waiting with my hands folded. Guru put the drink on his table and shut his eyes. Often, without notice, Guru would slip off into a deep meditative state. During those periods, everyone would meditate. Sometimes it lasted for only a few seconds; other times hours could pass. No one disturbed him. Guru told us when he appeared to the outer, ordinary eye to be napping, he was doing very important work in the inner worlds. Guru repeatedly told us that to him, the inner worlds were more real and more important than the outer world. For Guru, the inner worlds were vivid planes of consciousness where he solved both disciples' problems and national and international crises. According to Guru, without his inner intervention, America would have had a nuclear attack by the Soviet Union. Luckily, he used his arsenal of occult power to avert an all-out nuclear holocaust. These were the types of activities that Guru managed when his eyes were closed and his feet jiggled. Who was I to interrupt? But my problem was more serious, more pressing than the obliteration of the human race: I wanted a bunny.

I sat and sat. I wanted a bunny. I waited and sat. I wanted a bunny. My feet fell asleep. I wanted a bunny. I still sat. I shifted position, holding my hands tightly folded. And I waited. And I still wanted a bunny. Out of the corner of my eye, I saw Ketan yawn. He stood against the wall, holding Big Teddy, his favorite ragged brown stuftie. His eyes drooped; he looked ready to give up. I wasn't. I wanted a bunny.

I continued to wait. I aimed my meditative powers at Guru, coaxing him to open his eyes and answer my question. I concentrated harder, half-shutting my own eyes to aid my effort, and pressed my folded hands against my chest. In my head, I spoke loudly to Guru. I knew he would hear me: *Give Me a Bunny.*

This went on for what felt like hours. My feet, after being reshifted, began the prickly phase of returning from dead sleep; I moved my legs under my rear. I was wearing down.

Suddenly, Guru opened his eyes and announced, full of vigor, "Bah, good girl. All right? Let us go."

His selected chauffeur for the night took off, rattling his keys. I was missing my chance.

"Guru?" I softly asked.

He didn't hear me and was putting his bare feet back into his white open sandals. He slowly started to push to the edge of the chair.

"Guru?" I asked again.

"Oi. You? A question? Ask, Jayanti."

"Guru, I wanted to know if I could, if I could get a bunny?"

I had done it. I asked the great question. I felt Ketan spring to attention.

"What?" Guru looked to my father, who had come back into the room, holding Guru's wool coat.

"She wants to know if she can have a rabbit." My father attempted to decipher my question.

"An animal?" Guru asked my father.

"A little bunny. Guru, can I please have a little bunny? I promise to teach it to meditate. It will be a very good disciple." I inched forward, led by my folded hands.

What could Guru do? That would be a tough request to deny for anyone. He was cornered by cuteness. He caved.

"Yes. You tell your parents you can have bunny. And you bring bunny to me for a spiritual name."

I was overwhelmed. I had received a special exception to the law, and the bunny would have a spiritual name. Life was good. Really good.

The next day, my mother drove my brother and me out to a small farm with a sign announcing free rabbits. After much debate, we selected a black-and-white dwarf bunny and brought it home. It was a girl. The next Monday, with the rabbit clutched against my chest, I managed to hold on to her with only half my stomach scratched up while Guru gave her the name Munu, meaning "Little Darling" in Bengali. I was ecstatic. I even tried once to teach Munu to meditate, forcing her paws together in front of a picture of Guru, but when she bit me, I gave up.

I WAS CONVINCED that with these new special TV and pet privileges, I would live happily ever after. Until the day my father, for the first time in my entire life, shopped. My father, a man who had once longed to become a *sanyassi* and renounce all material possessions, was known as the cheapest kid in Bismarck, North Dakota. Even as a teen, he never spent money. He enjoyed the challenge of seeing how long he could go without spending a single cent. His pride in his thriftiness only increased as an adult. He gloated that he had never shopped for a single piece of clothing or food, which left my mother the task of purchasing all the basics—clothes, food, toiletries—smuggling them into the house, and placing them in their presumed spots with all price tags removed, to make it appear as if they had just always been there. The fact that renunciation of material objects was part of the tradition that led to oneness with God pleased my father enormously. He enjoyed retelling the sacred tale of Prince Siddhartha stepping over the warm sleeping bodies of his wife and son and walking away from the gold-drenched excesses of his palatial dwelling in order to find God. When my mother interjected that our cramped house could hardly be considered palatial, my father accused her of being too bound by materialism.

When our ancient Chevy station wagon died, it forced my

father to scour the *Bargain News,* reluctantly open his tattered wallet, and buy a beat-up tan Dodge Dart for two hundred dollars. The car came without a muffler, speedometer, or heat.

"It's perfect," my father said, jiggling the keys.

Therefore it was a true surprise when my father brought home an expensive purchase, a roughly chiseled bust with abstract carvings for the facial features, pitted pockets for eyes, and a wide slab for lips. The head, seemingly decapitated, perched on a square base. When my father unpacked it, I was terrified.

"What is it?" I asked.

"It's Guru, of course," my father said.

"What happened to his body? And why does he look like that?"

"It's an interpretation of his highest *samadhi* consciousness," my father said.

"Do we have to keep it?"

My father shot me a disappointed look, and I faked a smile, like I had made a joke.

My father built a small stone shrine in our backyard to house it, and I took great pains to avoid it. During the day, I looped around the backwoods to evade its vacant stare. But the daytime was not my real concern; I suspected that during the day, with my family around, I was relatively safe; the real threat, I feared, came at night.

After Ketan was asleep in the top bunk, and the rest of the house was hushed into darkness, I imagined that the Guru bust hunted me, sprouting arms, tentacle-like appendages that expanded from its base. They slowly snaked down the stones, across the grass, up the shingles, through the window, into my room, extending, writhing to my pillow, and strangling me, airless and smothered. I lay awake, terrified, listening for its rustle across the grass or the creaking of the window screen lifting. My parents in the next room were millions of miles away. Even Ketan, directly above me, could not save me. It was patient and relentless. It would get me in the end. It was only a matter of time, but my family was utterly oblivious. No one could see the dangers of this supposedly holy figure but me.

ONE MONDAY NIGHT in late September, Guru instructed my parents to set up the meditation outside in the field beside our house. All afternoon dark rain clouds filled the sky as the wind whipped through the trees. When my father told Guru that a storm seemed likely, Guru pointed to his own third eye and said he was the guru and did not want or need suggestions. My father quickly bowed in understanding of Guru's wise teaching moment, then ran to the basement to carry Guru's throne outside.

Our field quickly filled with disciples. As soon as Guru began meditating, lightning flashed and thunder banged. Guru said he would give a special meditation to stop the rain, and he raised his folded hands. For ten minutes, the sky quieted. I smiled. My guru could do anything, even banish the rain without effort. But when fat raindrops landed in my lap, making my sari stick to my legs, I wondered what had happened. Guru scanned both the men's and ladies' sides and, in a voice coated with disappointment, revealed that some of the very same disciples who sat before him had inwardly expressed doubt at Guru's capacities. Because of this poisonous doubt, he had held off the rain for only a limited time, and now, to teach a true lesson, the rest of the meditation would be cloaked in rain. I looked around me, suspiciously, wondering who the doubters were. Who were the culprits who dared to disbelieve Guru? I was furious that these same people had the audacity to sit, attempting to blend in with the true disciples.

But by the end of the night, I had lost interest in whoever caused the downpour. I was drenched and restless. I whispered to my mother that I needed to use the bathroom. When I found Ketan stomping in huge puddles at the back, we decided to sneak off. We ran into the side woods, crouched inside the brambles, and watched the remainder of the function from our hiding place. Usually I was in the front or on the stage during functions. This was the very first time that I observed the disciples without being a part of them: row upon row of men and women seated on opposite sides, all facing one direction—toward Guru. They seemed prepared to sit lotus style in muddy puddles forever or until Guru said to stop. I suddenly felt inspired to move; I didn't want to sit in the mud. I sprang up like a can of soda after a violent shaking, then I crouched back down. Ketan covered his mouth to mask his giggles. I did it again and again. I too started to laugh. I was air bound, wild and untethered. I spun around and around, propelling myself in circles with my arms as oars, giggling, until my head rocked with dizziness, and then I stopped, steadying my feet.

Suddenly, I worried that I might have missed something. Guru might have called for me, and I was not there. I looked over the sea of sopping folded hands, eyes flickering with devoted bliss, for Guru, the grounding factor, the constant temperature gauge of my behavior, of my status. His reassuring smile, his wave of the hand, his affirmation that I was a good girl, echoed from his lips to my parents' ears, and to the disciples, which composed the totality of my world. But that night, when I caught sight of him in his chair, he was in profile, as my father stood motionless soaked from the downpour, with his long white pants and shirt plastered to his skin, holding an umbrella to keep Guru perfectly dry. The silhouette of Guru's head was suddenly transformed into the terrifying bust in my backyard that haunted me at night. I saw the same effigy that pretended to be benign, accepting flowers and folded hands, but then in absolute secrecy snaked its tentacles around me, muffling my movements, my thoughts, my breath. I rubbed my eyes, blaming the rain, but as I focused a second time, Guru's blanket, which covered his entire body up to his neck, revealed the same bodiless head that disappeared into a base in my backyard. I shivered, imagining the arms sprouting, then slithering their way to me and me alone. A minute later, Guru stood up, waved, then left.

That night I could not sleep at all. I was confused by what I had seen, and I was still terrified of the Guru doppelgänger, only yards away, plotting to get me. If I were a really good disciple, I would never have seen Guru as anything other than the Supreme. How could I imagine Guru—my beloved Guru, the same one who brought my soul to earth—as a serpentine monster?

My punishment came the next day. There was no stopping karma. And it went right for what I loved the most—my beloved Munu, my hard-won fluffy bunny.

Ketan discovered it first; a pack of wild dogs had torn through the wire on Munu's outdoor cage and mangled her black-and-white body, leaving a scattering of fur and blood across the backyard. By the time I was informed, my father had already left for meditation in Queens, leaving my mom to bury what she had scraped off the grass of our beloved bunny and comfort us. It was a rare night for us to be home, but this night was full of grief, as my loss was inconsolable. She was no ordinary rabbit—she was Guru's disciple, and she had a spiritual name. I shrieked and wailed, crying until my nightgown was damp with tears and snot. I climbed into bed, and for the first time in my life, I didn't say my prayers or even look at my shrine. If Guru controlled everything, which I knew he did, why didn't he prevent Munu's death? I pulled my blanket over my head, creating a tent to prevent my sobs from escaping. Suddenly, I understood. I was much worse than the doubters who sat before Guru but didn't believe in his occult powers. Because, according to Guru and karmic law, all wrong actions had to be punished; therefore I, the Golden Child, had killed my bunny. I was bad and evil. Guru knew it. He also knew that I dreaded his double that lived in my backyard, scheming to capture me each and every night. He knew it, and had given me fair warning.

2

Because Guru Says So, That's Why

FOR MY FIRST DAY OF KINDERGARTEN, I PICKED OUT MY favorite Guru-blue sari to wear. When my mother gently suggested that I dress in corduroys instead, I looked at her in shock. Out of everyone, she should have understood that this momentous occasion, like all others, required my best sari.

Upon entering the classroom, I introduced myself to Mrs. Wright, bowing my head with folded hands and explaining that my guru gave me the name Jayanti and it meant the Highest Victory of the Supreme in Sanskrit.

"Well, well," she said, writing an extensive note in her spiral notebook.

Mrs. Wright instructed the class to form a circle on the floor. I sat lotus style, tucking my sari underneath me, and folded my hands, assuming class would start with a meditation, but when Mrs. Wright began talking instead, welcoming all the students and the few scattered parents who remained fastened to their crying kids, I was deeply concerned. I scanned the room at the mixture of unknown boys and girls, none of whom seemed bothered by the lack of meditation. Aside from the few disciple kids whom we saw at functions, Ketan and I never interacted with children, especially outsiders. Those were Guru's strict orders. Guru didn't want us going to school at all, but since he didn't know home-schooling was an option, to avoid legal troubles, he reluctantly agreed that we could venture to the outside world to avoid breaking the law.

"Wowie. I like your dress," Betty said, skipping over to me after snack.

"It's a sari. Don't you wear saris to meditate with your guru?"

Betty nodded and tugged at her ringlet.

As far as I was concerned, the whole world had gurus. This was startling news. When I invited Betty to meet Guru, she cheered wildly. My first day and I already had found a new disciple. I was very pleased with myself.

"Can I touch it?" Betty asked, clutching the *pallu,* the decorative portion of the sari that hangs off the left shoulder.

"Betty," Mrs. Wright said, staring at my sari. "Do not make fun of others for being different. Be respectful of people and their ethnic diversity," Mrs. Wright ordered, fingering her gold crucifix against her gray turtleneck.

Later in the week, for show-and-tell, while the other kids carted in seashells from the Florida Keys, cookie tins filled with buttons, and Jellybean, Betty's one-eyed gerbil, I volunteered to sing Guru's Bengali devotional songs.

"Phule phule, dhule dhule, moranachi, khule, khule . . ." I bellowed out my tune and triumphantly bowed.

The kids cheered and clapped, flapping their hands up and down in excitement.

"And you made that up yourself?" Mrs. Wright asked, tightly crossing her legs.

"No, no. My guru did. He writes lots and lots of songs," I answered, giving full credit where credit was due. "I know hundreds of them. Do you want to hear more?" I offered.

I was a hit. I promised all my classmates that I would teach them, but they had to sing soulfully.

"That's more than enough for now," Mrs. Wright replied, walking back to her desk to make yet another notation in her book. I began to have doubts about Mrs. Wright. I didn't think that she would make a very good disciple. Unlike my classmates, she didn't seem receptive to Guru's light. As I skipped off to join the rest of the class, I understood that Mrs. Wright, like so many unfortunate outsiders, was not spiritually aware. I sighed, feeling sorry for her, knowing that she was missing out on so much, but I was not discouraged. There were plenty of classmates, faculty, and staff at the school with whom I could share Guru's special mission. I figured I'd have to take it slowly with Mrs. Wright, and that maybe, eventually, she would have an inner awakening.

However, by the end of the school year, I was seriously rethinking my academic career.

The lessons that were urgent to memorize at school—the names of Christopher Columbus's ships and the lyrics to "Yankee Doodle Dandy," among others, seemed utterly irrelevant to Guru and the Center. At no meditation had Guru ever even mentioned Christopher Columbus, let alone his ships. And though Guru sang hundreds of songs, he never once requested "Yankee Doodle Dandy." The complete lack of Guru in the curriculum troubled me. When I asked my parents

why the school didn't teach about Guru, they explained that
other children weren't as lucky as I was to study at Guru's
inner school. I felt sorry that the entire student body was
being deprived of a real education, and it solidified my worries that what filled my days in class and what filled my
nights in meditations had nothing in common. School's
pencil-and-paste busywork clearly squandered my precious
Guru time. For other kindergartners, learning to spell their
families' names might have been a significant goal, but for
me it was only a distraction from my one and only goal—
God-Realization.

Long before I could say "applesauce" or "shoelace," God-
Realization was part of my earliest repertoire. It was something that Guru guaranteed his disciples, and since I was,
after all, the Chosen One, I figured not only did I have a right
to it but I should get it before anyone else. Guru said he was
the only God-realized person currently alive; he was the
sole authority on the subject. Since Guru never went into
details to describe what God-Realization was, I tried to figure it out on my own. I imagined that it entailed gaining
superpowers—seeing through walls, talking to animals, skipping sleep forever—and that when it came, everything before it would be irrelevant. Guru convinced us his realization
meant that he was fully united with the Supreme, giving him
the ultimate authority to speak, act, and command all disciples on the Supreme's behalf, erasing any distinctions between Guru and God.

According to Guru, in his past lives he was also God-
realized, but when a person is reincarnated, even avatars
have to start their spiritual search over again in order to re-

gain their oneness with God. The way Guru spoke about his God-Realization made it sound as though it was as easy as locating something temporarily misplaced. In this lifetime, Guru said, he realized God when he was eleven years old. Even though I was nearly six years old, eleven seemed pretty young to have figured out everything. To catch up to Guru, I had only six years. That was stressful enough, but to make things worse, meditation was the only guarantee of God-Realization.

I didn't know how to meditate.

Every night, except Mondays, my parents dutifully brought Ketan and me to the meetings in Jamaica, Queens, where Guru had us sit for periods of silent meditation, lasting anywhere from ten minutes to twenty-four hours. I never knew what to do. Of course I knew I was supposed to sit still with folded hands, and I also knew that I was supposed to enter my heart chakra, leaving my mind behind, but that was where it became foggy. I imagined the heart chakra as a shiny red house, shaped like a heart made from red metal like the slide at the playground. I would pretend to walk up to the house and knock on the big door; it would make a loud, echoing noise and that would be it. I never got anywhere.

I then tried songs—Guru's, of course. When that failed, I moved on to lists; if I was at a meditation, I counted the flowers on the stage, sorting them by shapes. I checked the color of the women's saris: how many blue, how many green, how many white. Then I utilized my fingers to tally the number of stuffies that Ketan and I had at home. After that, I scanned the disciples around me, counting how many were asleep, their heads bobbing up and down, then snapping back to attention when their folded hands fell into their laps or their chins landed on their chests. My father was almost always asleep when I looked over at him.

I never asked my parents what they did during meditation or what I was supposed to do. I was sure that my question was inappropriate. They must have assumed I was a born "meditator." I was a special soul, and meditation should have just come naturally. I tried to convince myself that whatever I was doing to fill up the time was most probably the correct technique. It seemed to be working. Guru was proud of me, and when Guru was proud of me, the world was right.

Once, I gathered my nerve to ask not just anyone but my idol, Prema, about meditation. Guru had two personal assistants, Prema and Isha. From driving him, to washing his clothes, to typing his correspondence, these women were his closest disciples. Guru let them sit in the front row in the first and second place before his throne, and they arrived and left with him. The female disciples treated Prema and Isha with fawning flattery or wild jealousy. They were Center celebrities, carefully admired and ceaselessly scrutinized. To me, Prema represented pure bliss. Not only was she Guru's special disciple but she was dazzlingly beautiful. Although she didn't like children, she did think it was cute that I admired her, and she, knowing full well my special status, made a slight effort to acknowledge me. Guru assigned seats, and he bestowed on my mother and me the highly sought after seats directly behind Prema and Isha—seat one and two in row two. As a consequence of spending literally hundreds of hours in supposed meditation, sitting directly behind Prema, I studied her as though she were my own private experiment. I noticed how she secured her fine blond hair with narrow plastic barrettes worn behind her ears in shades carefully co-ordinated to match her sari, her burst of lily of the valley fragrance that greeted me every time she swept by my row and assumed her seat in front of me, and her precise and motionless stance that she maintained for hours, never shifting even the slightest during meditation.

One evening, during a break, while Guru was in his private chamber adjacent to the altar, Prema was joking with the other women in the second row. I wanted to ask about her meditation secret, but I had to do it subtly. I couldn't let her know that I was really trying to figure out how to meditate, so I asked her how she was able to meditate so well. How come she never moved, coughed, shifted, or even made a hard swallow during meditation? She laughed at my question, causing the rest of the women to laugh too.

"Do you want to know my secret?" she asked, teasing me with her large brown eyes.

"Yes, yes!"

"Well, I take a stick of special meditation gum." She reached into her white crochet bag and pulled out a pack of Trident cinnamon gum and unwrapped a piece. "I never chew it. I just keep it in my mouth beside my cheek. Here," she said, giving me a piece. "Now you have my secret."

I was thrilled. Now I knew. I asked my mom to support my meditations by keeping me sufficiently stocked with Trident, and I toted it with me at all times.

I HAD A lot of work to do to reach Guru's level, and Silvermine Elementary School seemed like an awful waste of time. I really needed to be stapled to the floor before my shrine with Trident gum. However, my schoolteachers were not at all sympathetic to my plight.

Mrs. Wright kept me after school one afternoon for a talk about my obsession with Voodoo and sent me to the guidance counselor's office. The guidance counselor drilled me with questions about my home life, asking if my parents provided me with food and shelter and if they regularly beat me. I found it hard to pay attention; I was too distracted by her coffee mug with a picture of a cow on it. I flashed a big missing-tooth smile as I proudly pointed to the mug, explaining that Guru said both my mother and I were not just regular cows but sacred Indian cows—fancy white ones—in our past animal incarnations. My father, I patiently continued, had been a giraffe, and my brother was a dog. As I left the guidance counselor's office, it was clearer than ever that being in school was an irrelevant distraction.

Ketan, on the other hand, was not at all fazed over how to manage school and God-Realization. In fact, I never heard him mention anything about God-Realization, or even God at all; his one and only concern was the theater. Ketan's Broadway genes came from my mother. As a child she learned the melodies and plots to all the classic musicals. Even though music other than Guru's was officially banned, my mother kept a secret stash of LPs of old favorites that she couldn't bear to part with such as *Hello, Dolly, The Music Man,* and *West Side Story.* Ketan, as if on instinct, found the contraband and claimed the treasures as his own. Instead of punishing him, my mother privately encouraged his forbidden vice and even intervened on his behalf when my father complained about his low consciousness. With the green light from my mother, Ketan quickly transformed our bottom bunk into a stage, hung a sheet over the front as a curtain, cast roles for our entire collection of stufties—Big Teddy as Tony, Fluffity Bunny as Maria—and designed Playbills.

Because Ketan's theatrical spectacles clearly were not part of Guru's sacred teachings, and would have been viewed as dubious, at best, by Guru's inner circle, my mother deliberately hid Ketan's passions for twirling around our Kermit puppet to the beat of "The Surrey with the Fringe on Top" from other disciples. Her safeguarding of Ketan's theatrical vices was but one of many ongoing issues and major disagreements between my mother and father. When they argued, I slipped away until I couldn't hear them. My mother had the last word when it came to us, because my father was never around long enough to enforce his own opinions. With all the work he was doing for Guru and the Center, he had limited time for us. It gave me great pride that he was busy with matters far more important than our family. I found it heroic and admirable. I, too, longed to be of greater service to Guru's mission.

Guru wanted his own lawyer and, per Guru's orders, my father dropped studying philosophy to complete law school. He passed the bar exam and was now officially Rudra Tamm, Attorney at Law. Guru blessed him by placing a white gardenia against his third eye, then instructed him to get to work. And he did. My father recounted to us that Guru told him that his first official lawyer duty was to obtain all of the rights and privileges afforded to other religious groups and register the Sri Chinmoy Center as a nonprofit, tax-free church. When he had carefully explained to Guru that in order to hold this status, like other churches, there would need to be a board of directors, elections, and transparency of all finances, after listening to my father, Guru closed his eyes and drifted off into meditation.

Guru finally opened his eyes and said, "The Supreme acts in and through me. You do not question what I do or tell you to do on my behalf. All commands are coming from the Highest Supreme. I *only* take advice from the Supreme."

My father told us he immediately understood the absurd inappropriateness of a brand-new lawyer carping to a messiah about petty and mundane regulations. He bowed his head, recognizing his error, understanding that his years of law school had not prepared him for this unique lawyer-client relationship. My father used this as a teaching story for us, a reminder not to question Guru. I solemnly swore that, no matter what happened, I would never doubt or disobey Guru.

Instead of my father working for a large law firm and having to socialize and network with clients, Guru instructed him to open his own firm. This suited my father fine, for he had always been antisocial, preferring to sit cross-legged reading a book on the Upanishads than chat with house guests. Harking back to his barefoot days at Yale, my father still relished the notion of stark discipline and rigid asceticism. He watched his caloric intake to avoid gluttony, set his internal alarm clock to 4:45 for morning meditation. Working for himself was ideal, for it seemed doubtful that he would have thrived in a corporate, partnered law firm dressed in his thrift-store polyester suit, Guru-blue tie, and sandals.

After searching for inexpensive rental space, my father found a room on the second floor of a brick row house in Darien, Connecticut. The other tenant, Bill, another independent lawyer, needed someone to split the space and the rent.

When Guru came to bless the office, he called for my family to gather for a photograph.

"Samarpana," Guru addressed my mother. "Your role is to serve Rudra. You become his secretary," Guru said, then quickly turned away from her.

We stood near Guru, with folded hands and our new positions. My father, freshly accredited, had all of Guru's permission to set forth and build a clientele, to study and argue cases, to interact and have a legitimate and worldly career. He was ready to embark on his split life between days filled defending clients in real estate deals and researching tax breaks, and his evenings reciting mantras on humility, purity, and surrender.

For the photo, my father glowed, dressed in a white dhoti and kurta to mark the special occasion. He seemed unaware of the photographer and on bent knees received Guru's blessings.

My mother, as always, was never called separately but summoned only when Guru sought the full family. She stood slightly behind my father, a fitting spot. Repeatedly Guru had told my mother that Rudra was the genuine spiritual seeker, and her duty was to tend to his needs and desires. Perhaps it was her newly official role of being my father's assistant that seemed to confirm what I sensed she had always felt, that she was a person of nonimportance whose task was to prop and support other people, people who mattered. She took Guru's sudden and public pronouncement of her designated job as a secretary as part of her spiritual *sadhana,* like the ancient tradition of seekers who, to find inner peace, take vows of silence for years or refuse to eat solid foods, denying themselves in order to arrive at enlightenment. Her official duty as my father's support staff lent credibility to her habit since childhood of blending into the background. And as my mother stood in the photo, with her hands folded and her eyes searching for Guru, she was present but hardly noticed, as she was obscured by the shadow of my father.

Ketan, always trying to be in the forefront, begging for star status, wedged his way opposite my father. With a wide, toothy smile right at the camera, Ketan beamed for the shot.

Tightly posed together with Guru and my family, I felt invincible. I had everything that I wanted within inches from me. It was perfect.

"Namo, namo, namo, shakti pujari . . ." Guru started singing, then nodded his head for us all to join him.

We stood with folded hands singing soulfully, while my father remained on his knees in a trancelike state with Guru's palm on his third eye. When Bill, who shared the communal office space, opened the door, he froze, momentarily taking in the scene, then quickly exited with an overpolite series of hand waves.

"BROTHERS AND SISTERS. May I have your attention?"

It was a Thursday night, and we were in Guru's new church, purchased by the disciples, located in a quiet working-class neighborhood in Bayside, Queens. The acquisition of the church had occurred suddenly, but that was how everything seemed to happen. Now, every night except Monday when Guru still came to our house, my family battled commuter traffic on Interstate 95 from Norwalk, Connecticut, to Bayside, New York. Sometimes it took us one and a half hours to get there, sometimes more. With such a large portion of our life spent in a hajj to Queens, it would seem logical for us to have a safe, comfortable car, but that wasn't the case. My father felt that part of his *sadhana* was to be in discomfort, denying himself the very basics of food and warmth, and he attempted to make it ours too.

As long as the car could get us to Queens—and many cars didn't, having to abandon them along the way—that was all that mattered. We loaded in and, before departing, meditated for protection on the large photo of Guru glued to the dashboard. The rest of the car ride to see my spiritual master consisted of dining à la carte from a brown bag and silently fighting with Ketan. My parents never said much to each other. It was my father's rule. He felt we should ride in silence, beginning our meditation the moment we left our house. When my mother spoke to my father about mundane matters such as money for bills and groceries, he answered in slight nods, as if to remind her she was breaking a rule.

We learned every bump and turn. With my eyes closed, I could tell if we had reached New Rochelle simply by the buzz of the worn roadway, or if we had passed Co-Op City by the sound of the tires rolling over the metal plates in the drawbridge. Over the years, we marveled as the landscape around us turned into suburbia, as the toll fares increased, as lanes closed and reopened for paving and repaving, and as on-ramps and off-ramps sprouted endlessly while malls and condos appeared, replacing woody lots. We knew all the side roads—if there was an accident on I-95, we found the twisty streets that released us onto the Merritt Parkway. With the aid of the car's static radio used only for the purpose of receiving traffic updates, we triumphantly navigated our way for Guru's blessings each night and safely back home again.

"Brothers and Sisters."

Girish, a tall man with puffy bags beneath his eyes like half doughnuts, stood with his back to Guru's altar, facing the disciples at the front of the church. A writer and scholar on world religions, Girish belonged to one of America's wealthiest families.

"As you know, lately, at every meditation, Guru makes alterations to our so-called spiritual practice."

This was highly unusual. Normally, before Guru arrived at the church we were meant to be silent, attempting to raise our consciousness to be more receptive to Guru's presence. Announcements were made at the end of the night. I had a feeling this was not meant to be happening. I sat on the orange shag carpet beside my mother, pleating the end of my sari as a fabric fan to create a breeze.

"Many times Guru claimed he was not leading a religion but a 'spiritual path.' But this church that we now occupy is an apt symbol of what the Aum Center has become." Girish paused, scanning the pews. As usual, the church was hot and crowded.

When I checked my parents' reactions, both were absolutely still.

"The meditation group that now only some of you original members recall has been corrupted into an organization with its own iconography, rituals, rules, and holy books."

At this, rumbles occurred from the back of the church. Sounds of people shifting and getting up whisked to the front.

"With the expanding list of controlling rules, such as his ban on all marriages"—Girish looked back and forth between the men and women, instigating a response—"avoiding any non-Guru–related social interaction with the opposite sex, restricting socializing solely to other disciples—this includes giving up connections to family members who are not disciples—are now enforced laws. Mandatory attendance at meetings, required daily meditations, songs, and chants." At the last one, he added extra emphasis and shrugged his shoulders. "Didn't we join this group as an alternative to the formal dogma of religion?"

"Sit down!" A shout came from the far back of the women's side.

I turned but couldn't see who it was that had decided enough was enough. It started an avalanche.

"Girish, be quiet!"

"We won't hear you anymore!"

"Someone, get him out of here!"

With new energy, he spoke louder.

"I ask you, Brothers and Sisters, is true spirituality bound by dogma? Doesn't the true spiritual search require self-guidance?"

Three male disciples surrounded him and nudged him toward the aisle in an effort to remove him.

As he passed by me and headed to the back, with a bellowing voice he said, "The Buddha said to question everything the Master says is truth and find your own tru . . ."

And he was gone.

My father, in his official capacity as Guru's attorney, followed him out. The entire church throbbed with outrage. Nothing like this had ever occurred before. If disciples had concerns, they kept them to themselves; Guru was never questioned, certainly not in public. My mother put her arm around me, pulling me into her and rubbing my neck with her thumb. Confrontation in general scared me, let alone a shouting spectacle at a meditation. The sacred space felt altered, and its shock hit me suddenly. The changes Girish had raged about had no meaning to me. What did I care or understand if Guru enacted radical policy reversals from arranging "divine marriages," as he did for my mother and father, to a permanent ban on marriage? So what if seekers either married before joining or remained forever single? No one, and certainly not my parents, explained to me its permanent impact, that it meant my future destiny was to be a nun. I suppose, even if they had, at the time, I would have found it a wonderfully exciting adventure, a way to remain forever attached only to Guru.

Looking back, however, Girish was right. By the midseventies, everything had changed, even the name of our group. Originally called the Aum Center, Guru renamed it the Sri Chinmoy Center, the first of many programs, objects, places, and awards he named in his own honor. The fact that we no longer met for official meditations in Guru's house, and now went to the church, was another enormous change that happened overnight.

Only days earlier, in the long car ride home from Bayside, when my parents assumed Ketan and I were sleeping, I overheard my father break his own law of maintaining meditative silence in the car to discuss the events that had led to the sudden move to the church. The New York meditations used to be held inside Guru's home, and Guru's neighbors, from their front stoops, gawked at the smiling throng who filed into the blue house each night. My father spoke about one neighbor in particular, a petite married woman a few years older than Guru, who lived directly across the street. Curious about the Indian man, the woman began having neighborly chats with Guru. Charmed by Guru's attention, she decided to attend meditations and soon became a regular fixture at Guru's house. Her husband, a no-nonsense laborer unimpressed by the flocks of what he considered young hippies crowding into the house across the street, began questioning his wife as to what she was doing at a black man's house. When other neighbors confided to him that they had spotted his wife, alone, tiptoeing in and out of the Indian's house in the middle of the night, rumors of an affair seemed confirmed. The husband had had enough.

My mother had turned around, to ensure that we were both sleeping, before my father continued. I squeezed my eyes shut and leaned against Ketan's snoring body. My parents had already lost me. We all went to Guru's house. What was the problem?

A call was received by the Queens Building Department, my father continued, that the house was being utilized as a church in a neighborhood not zoned for religious buildings. Building inspectors arrived unexpectedly late one afternoon and, seeing the rows of chairs in the living room, issued a stern warning. Guru would not be able to hold meditations inside his house anymore. The disgruntled husband was ready to go public with allegations of the affair. Guru was furious. He gathered a few disciples, explaining that the Supreme, at times, commands that instead of using compassion, he should use justice.

Sure enough, the Supreme had bestowed his benevolent justice and the police were called the next day because the neighbor's house had been pelted by stones in the middle of the night. When my father described the shattered glass that littered the sidewalks, I felt disturbed. Stones were dangerous, and the fact that stones were thrown right across the street from Guru's home, made me scared that Guru could have gotten hurt. I wanted to interrupt my father and ask how we could always protect Guru, but then I remembered that I wasn't supposed to have heard any of what he was saying.

Shortly afterward, the neighbor's house went up for sale, the church was bought, and Guru created the Guards, a group of close male disciples chosen to serve as personal bodyguards for Guru. This news gave me great relief.

These guards—the same ones who had ushered Girish from the church—now escorted Guru to and from events, standing on patrol near his throne, preventing anyone from approaching Guru without being personally summoned. To make their duties official, Guru had them wear uniforms— white pants with a Guru-blue stripe down the side, a white shirt, Guru-blue tie, and a numbered badge. They were given a ranking and their badges were a reflection of their order. Guru was a strong believer in rank and order. His insistence on rating people seemed to be a throwback to the traditional caste system of his native India. Many times Guru proudly proclaimed that his own family was Kshatriya, the warrior caste, an esteemed rank, which naturally elevated him over those unfortunate enough to be born into lower castes. By assigning rank and order and creating his own caste system within the Center, Guru fostered a competitive struggle between disciples. Close watch was kept on disciples' rankings, which provided built-in incentives for those eagerly aspiring to improve their status, and provided Guru with plenty of leverage to demote or promote disciples at his pleasure.

My father, always in the forefront, was given the rank of guard number three, a position of considerable honor. Ketan decided that when he was old enough, he hoped he, too, could wear the proud uniform and stand on patrol.

Hours later, Guru finally arrived at the church after having been filled in by the head guard about the evening's events. As Guru entered through his private side door in a green dhoti, he walked with a slight limp, as though the earlier episode had already lodged within him as a physical attack.

"Though many of you are here, very few are true disciples," Guru said.

Tension filled the hall. Disciples from both the men's and women's sides shifted.

"Dear ones," Guru said. "True disciples never doubt their guru."

Some folded their hands tighter, while others searched for a notebook and pencil to write down every precious word.

"To make the fastest progress, you need one hundred percent faith in your guru. I am giving you messages from the Highest Supreme," Guru said with closed eyes. "True disciples do not doubt their guru. Doubt is poison. It leads to the destruction of your spiritual life. Faith, unconditional faith, must be present to be a true disciple. Anyone who doubts is not a real disciple."

Not only his words but the energy driving the words seemed tired, as though the disciples' failures caused a leak inside him. He was lagging, flat, disappointed in a physical manner.

I wanted to run to the stage and climb his throne, shouting that I was sorry. I would try harder. I should have tackled Girish and made him stop. No one could hurt or doubt Guru. I then thought of my own secret fear of the Guru-bust, and I swore I would be better and worship it, too. I would make alterations to my spiritual life. I would amend my errors. Then my progress would make Guru happy. I had noticed that Guru was happy when we did what he asked us to do. I'd listen, I promised. I'd do anything.

After a long meditation and the *prasad,* an item of blessed food distributed by Guru that traditionally followed a session of meditation, in an instant, Guru lifted the sorrowful air, and magically transformed himself into a storyteller.

With a gleam in his eye, Guru coyly teased, "Now, I have barked at you all. Is anyone interested in hearing some rubbish tales? Absolute rubbish tales?"

"Yes, Guru," we shouted back, with my voice the loudest.

Of course we were interested, how could we not be? These were stories about Guru's childhood—the fact that he even had a childhood gave me hope. His past seemed remote and vague, except for the rare occasions when he re-created it for us.

Instantly, Guru's posture changed. Slouching his shoulders, he tucked one leg upon his throne, and rested his arm on his knee. His voice cleared of the low and often raspy tone that accompanied his first words after a prolonged period of silence. He now spoke quickly as his sentences finished with exclamation marks.

Guru's childhood was a realm of adventure and innocence. In Guru's remembrances, he was usually involved in some type of trouble or mischief, and then, just as easily, slipped out of it without a scratch. From stealing sweets meant for the family shrine to climbing the mango tree to gorge himself on its fruit, Guru was intent on exploring options and testing limits. Guru's status as a young troublemaker was lovingly accepted and sanctioned. Though his birth name was Chinmoy, his nickname was Madal, which meant "noisemaker," and that was the name that he carried until he arrived in America. Then he took the special honorarium reserved for holy men and women and renamed himself Sri Chinmoy. It was Sri Chinmoy whom I had known my whole life, but it was Madal whom I was most curious about. The idea that Guru had a prior life—involving siblings, parents, scoldings, and trouble—was fascinating.

Tonight, as always when Guru recounted his tales, time evaporated. In the middle of one story, he veered off toward another anecdote and then another until an hour later, as though finally noticing that he somehow had taken an alternate route, he stopped, asking how he had gotten there. I did not mind, sitting enraptured, as his stories blurred from one episode into the next. Guru often repeated stories, and I recognized his favorites, which quickly became my favorites, too: Guru's survival from the overcrowded commuter ferry that sank; Guru's face-to-face encounter with a tiger in the dark forests of Bengal; Guru's near rescue by his family servant, after standing too close behind an imam's machete poised to sacrifice a goat. As Guru spun his childhood reminiscences, he was relaxed and happy, as if he wished to be back in a time before he was responsible for the salvation of souls and his only responsibility was keeping monkeys from snatching away the fruit he would carry home to his mother.

What we knew about Guru's family we learned from his stories. Guru's father worked as a train inspector for a railway line that ran from Chittagong to Assam and later founded a bank. Guru's mother stayed home to raise their seven children. Even though he was an orphan when he was only twelve years old—his father passed away when Guru was only eleven, and his mother died the following year—their loss seemed raw, as if their absence still left a hollow space inside a holy man filled with God.

"Oi," Guru finally said, as if waking from his own sweet spell. "Oi. I have talked too much. Let us go, dear ones," and with that the meditation was over. The book of his childhood was tightly closed, and, as always, I greedily wished he had shared more.

After the meditation, a select group of disciples was usually invited to Guru's house. Although the official meditations were relocated to the church, Guru continued his practice of hosting unofficial gatherings that spilled from his living room onto his porch. These invitations to Guru's house became a prized honor, evoking jealousy and envy for those who were regulars on the special list. My family was almost always invited, which meant that already late nights became even later.

Now, Guru appeared to have returned to his earlier weary and stern state. He sat quietly on his couch with his palm over his forehead. Finally, in a raspy whisper, he said, "You are all dear to me, very dear. The Beloved Supreme has a special task. Write, write very strong letters to Girish for speaking against me. Very, very strong, you write. Insulting him. Be merciless. Use all of your special American language to insult and scold him. You know his worst qualities, you know his weaknesses. You tell, tell all of this to him in letters that you send. Letting him know he is not a third-class disciple, not a fifth-class disciple, but the lowest of low class of disciple. You people, serve the Supreme by using all kinds of language to insult him."

I watched as heads nodded in agreement.

Yes, Guru. Of course, Guru.

He is so bad, Guru. His massive ego has poisoned him, Guru.

He has lowered our consciousness, and he insulted us by insulting you, Guru.

Right away, Guru, of course, Guru.

I silently wondered, how could Girish be so bad?

The car ride home was quiet. I immediately began composing my own letter of insults, but since I had never written that kind of letter before, I realized I would need my mother's help; I wanted to ask her if we could start this morning, skipping what few hours of sleep still existed before I had to go to school, but my mother stared out the window. Ketan was asleep, gently snoring. My father drove, with both hands tightly clutching the wheel, as if trying extra hard to steer us in the right direction, though everything seemed to be pulling the opposite way.

3

The Divine Cage

"ALO DEVI IS A FAKE," KETAN SAID.

"I'm telling," I threatened, retreating to my standard response to most everything Ketan said or did.

"Go right ahead," Ketan smirked, keenly aware that he had just bombarded me with the most shocking and sensational blow of my childhood.

He played it off calmly, casually buttoning his prized jean jacket. Since Guru did not approve of denim, Ketan was never able to wear it to meditations, hiding it in the car when we neared Queens, but all other times, even in the summer, he wore it constantly with matching blue jeans, and a plastic comb in his back pocket to fluff up his blond pompadour.

We sat across from each other in our hot kitchen. My father was at work, and my mother had dashed to the grocery store for vegetables to cook a curry for the evening's meditation. Ketan rocked his chair, resting his feet on one of the four mismatched seats cramped around our square table.

Often when Ketan claimed he had hot gossip, I'd just sigh or shrug my shoulders, feigning disinterest, in an effort to lessen Ketan's gloating. I squinted at him skeptically.

"You seem surprised." Ketan mocked.

With news this explosive, Ketan could not bear to hold it in for a second longer.

"Alo's not a God-realized soul. Not at all. She's a big problem for Guru. Guru feels sorry for her, so he doesn't cut her off totally. We're all supposed to pretend that she's just like Guru. But we shouldn't meditate on her or anything like that. Just when she's around we need to fake that we like her and fake that she has powers. But that's it. You know how we have pictures of her on our shrines? Well, most disciples don't. They removed them all."

I had been punched in the gut.

For all of my eleven years, I had worshipped before Guru and Alo. Alo Devi was Guru's Canadian-born companion who met Guru when he was a simple disciple at the Sri Aurobindo Ashram in India, where she had arrived alone to immerse herself in the yogic philosophies of the ancient East. After Guru befriended her, she helped Guru leave India, get a green card, and settle in New York City to build his own mission. Given the role of Divine Mother, a spiritual consort, Alo added familiar Western traditions and culture to Guru's path. To me, she was part grandmother and part saint. It was Alo who wrote my name in calligraphy on the day I was born; she blessed me, meditated on me, and had given me countless presents.

Ketan relished my openmouthed shock.

"You know how Alo's not really around that much anymore? That's done on purpose," he said.

It was true that Alo spent little time in New York, and when she was in town, various disciples, including my family, were asked by Guru to take Alo on long outings, purposely causing her to miss Guru's day appointments and evening functions. Most of the time, however, Alo wasn't in New York at all. She was in Puerto Rico, a second home for her, or she was on visits back to Canada, or working on her biggest project—arranging the Christmas trip. What began as a one-week visit to Florida, the Christmas trip had become an annual monthlong end-of-year spiritual retreat for Guru and a group of disciples to locations from South America and the Pacific Islands and beyond. Since children were not allowed to go, I loathed the event that left me at the airport, in tears, waving good-bye to Guru, all my disciple friends, and worst of all, my mother. Sometimes my father went, and a few times, they both went, leaving us to stay at the house of a disciple who had no clue as to what to do with two children. On one of those occasions I ended up in an emergency room for a tetanus shot after a horse chomped my behind when my appointed caregiver had dropped me off at a farm to explore.

"That's right," Ketan said, as if reading my thoughts. "Guru keeps her away on purpose. She nags him and is really jealous. She wants everything to be about her, too. But, really, how could it be? Seekers wouldn't understand. They'd see two thrones up on stage and think they're married. People don't get the fact that Guru and Alo aren't like that. And even about Alo and Guru living together. People would think that they're, you know, *together.* It's crazy. Alo is on the third floor and Guru is on the second. But still, people think *that* way."

What way? Although I didn't understand, I needed him to continue.

According to Ketan's unnamed sources, Alo resented the fact that Guru was getting so much press and had many new disciples all over the world. As Guru's position and status grew, Alo found her own position diminished. In order for Guru to avoid dispensing to the public the complicated answer to the question of who Alo was, Alo was strategically tucked away. When Guru gave public lectures, Alo now sat in the audience. Alo's shrinking role had become enforced in private, too. Even at the church, on the shrine area originally fitted for two, now Guru's throne alone dominated the stage, and for the occasions that Alo came back to town, a small white wicker chair was placed near the dais's edge, and then mysteriously vanished when she was sent off again.

But, according to Ketan, what made Alo the most outraged was the influx of *gopis,* female disciples, who were always at her and Guru's house. In particular, it was my idol, Prema, and her counterpart, Isha, whose constant presence and elevated status irritated Alo the most. Though they were not related, nor friends, Prema and Isha, two women in their early thirties, like it or not were linked together. Guru had made them his two favorite disciples. Although Guru tried to keep their rank equal—he hadn't made a specific order for them—it was clear to all of us, and Alo, too, that they were his number one and number two devotees. Precisely because Guru never formally solidified their order, Prema and Isha were always battling to claim the title of Guru's number one. At times, they conducted their power struggle publicly. An ongoing competition was who would receive prasad first. When Guru called for prasad, both women slowly rose, straightened out the *pallu,* draped it across their backs like a shawl, then languidly moved toward Guru with folded hands. A few times they bumped into each other in the process, which caused a great fuss; neither one apologized, but one needed to back down, allowing the other to go forward. Most days Isha made sure to beat out Prema's soulful steps and reach Guru first with a concentrated expression of soulful bliss, yet when it was Prema's turn to receive the blessingful fruit, she paused, extending the moment when her eyes locked with Guru's just enough to reassure us that though she was not always first, her devotions were purer. Different in every way, from looks to personality, when it came to marking their position, Prema and Isha were strikingly similar.

Though I adored Prema, and was constantly in awe of her motionless meditation and snappy dress, I also loved Isha. Short and thin, Isha was all angles. She had concave cheekbones, a narrow nose, and small vibrant green eyes with thinly plucked matching eyebrows. Her long red hair swung like a pendulum when she marched up to Guru. Her lack of outgoing friendliness was understood as part of her spiritual advancement. Every once in a while, she noted my sari or complimented my singing, and I beamed proudly.

Both Isha and Prema, Ketan confided, were Alo's sworn enemies. Alo resented the two young women who had taken over her house and her relationship with Guru. Though they had apartments of their own, only blocks away, they were Guru's cooks, drivers, secretaries, maids, caretakers, and confidantes and were always at his side. Alo insisted Guru banish both Isha and Prema, but for Guru, this was not up for negotiation. He would not hear of it.

Believing that the arrival of the young, pretty female duo was the cause of her fallen status, Alo felt constantly under assault, even in her own home. According to the rumors, Alo was aware that her decline in status was eerily synchronized to her decline in youth and Guru's financial ascent. Alo was used to having Guru all to herself, being his main woman, his spiritual consort when he was just a barefoot young man in ragged clothes. Guru attempted to soothe her by assigning her two devoted followers of her own—Roshan, a bulky male ex-marine, and Heera, a young woman originally from Germany, with a thick accent and a dimpled smile. Both Roshan and Heera were assigned to travel with Alo, assisting her to create the Christmas trips and with any other projects Alo wanted that were safely far outside the tri-state area.

Ketan also told me he had heard that Alo had begun to develop unusual traits, one of which was that she worried incessantly about the CIA. She was convinced that she was being followed. She knew that tollbooth collectors and hotel concierges were only fronts for CIA agents to track her down. Since Alo was always on the lookout for someone coming up behind her, she developed the capacity of sleeping only for short periods of time. She took naps. Lots of them. Every time she sat down at meditation, her eyes closed and her head bobbed, until her chin rested on her chest, as her back, already hunched, seemed to curl like a possum's.

I looked away from the table, down our narrow hall.

One of the last times a meditation was held at our house, Alo had arrived separately from Guru, since Guru traveled with Prema and Isha. I had been in my bedroom, and when I opened the door to the hallway, I saw Alo standing before the oval mirror that hung on the door to the bathroom. Only inches from the mirror, she stared, talking to herself. The conversation, apparently, was so engaging that she was illustrating her points with her arms. I watched, utterly still, hoping that I wouldn't disturb her. Her words were mumbles, but her eyes never faltered from her own gaze. Eventually, Roshan entered through the kitchen door and politely announced that he had the car all warmed up. For a second, she looked at him as though she could not recognize the strange man in white pants and matching white shirt who said it was time to go home, and then she dropped her shoulders and nodded, obediently following him out the door.

Ketan continued to chat, as the sun shifted through various windows, until it finally slid from view altogether. I needed some time to sort all this out. Information was coming too quickly. Across from where I sat, above our telephone with the tangled cord, hung a black-and-white photograph of Alo and myself in which I was just learning to walk, attempting to balance on my pudgy legs, as she stood behind me, clutching on to my raised arms, lending me support.

THAT NIGHT, WHEN I questioned my mother, she urged me to remain loving and kind to Alo, and not to worry about the rest.

I suspected she was lying. It couldn't be that simple.

And it wasn't.

I soon discovered that there were two distinct groups in the Center—those who knew that Alo was not God-realized, and those who didn't. The people in the know about Alo were mostly Guru's close disciples in the New York area. Few of the visiting disciples from around the country, and even fewer from the increasing number of meditation groups in Europe, knew Alo was a fraud. I quickly realized that knowing put me into the elite category. These were the disciples who, when Alo was away, made fun of her, laughing at everything about her from the way she warbled when she sang to how she always tried to move her chair to be closer to Guru.

I, too, joined in. It was fun. I imitated her bad posture and protruding chin. When Alo was in town, like the rest of those who knew, I overacted with full devotion, bowing lavishly to her after receiving prasad, and applauding loudly for her shrill singing. This was doing what Guru wanted, pleasing the Master unconditionally, which made him happy, and to make him happy, after all, was the only reason I even existed. I wrote her thick, fake letters of gratitude, praising her spiritual heights, and attributing to her all of the many eye-opening lessons I was learning in my spiritual life.

DURING THIS TIME, Guru was perpetually on tour throughout the United States and Canada, giving free concerts and lectures in a frenzied effort to expand his mission, and so were we. Weekends, therefore, meant bus trips.

In the bus, Guru reserved the first row for himself, and then positioned Prema and Isha on the seat across from him. The rest of the bus was by invitation only and getting onto Guru's bus was a prized privilege. Other buses trailed behind, with sad disciples who sat facing their windows with folded hands, just in case they might pass Guru's bus in traffic, and they could have a few seconds of a highway blessing via Guru's window. My family always got invited onto Guru's bus, which meant that in addition to being entertained by Guru spontaneously singing, telling stories, and passing out prasad, we received special perks like keeping count of the drawings that he did on everything from place mats to napkins. The buses we traveled on were not luxury models, but low-budget rejects, like retired school buses without heat. Inevitably, on each trip, we had mechanical problems.

One freezing and sleet-drenched night, on our way back home from Guru's public concert, the bus's engine began smoking, and we quickly pulled off the nearest exit. A few of the guards, including my father—who also rotated as one of the official drivers—bundled up and headed outside to fiddle with the engine.

Alo had been at the concert, but she had driven down from Canada with Roshan and Heera. I had watched Alo in the auditorium. She was in the row in front of me, and for the entire concert, her head drooped asleep, like a wilted tulip. In her defense, even a short concert for Guru was at least three hours long.

His concerts always started late. He began with a silent meditation, then improvised on many musical instruments, none of which he knew how to play. As usual, before Guru entered the stage, the hall was full. Disciples responsible for producing the event wanted to give Guru a packed house, and so for months they soaked the city with posters, gluing everything from bulletin boards to phone booths, and blitzing neighborhoods with leaflets. The more people in attendance, the more pleased Guru was with the event. Numbers mattered. If Guru was going to transform humanity, it was advantageous for him to appear before big crowds.

The biggest audiences came when the famed guitarist Carlos Santana, whom Guru named Devadip, became a disciple. After receiving initiation, Guru instructed Santana to marry his girlfriend, Deborah. Although they lived in California, they often came to New York to bask in Guru's divinity and have Guru as their muse. As a great honor and privilege for Santana, Guru invited him to perform during Guru's concerts. Inevitably, however, though the house may have been packed at the beginning of the night, after Santana finished playing, bowing both to the audience and to Guru, then left the stage, most of the audience fled. Those who did stay to see Guru's follow-up act exited shortly after as Guru scraped a bow across his cello while singing Bengali songs. For nine years as Devadip, Santana devoted himself to Guru's path, receiving special attention from Guru with every visit, until suddenly he was gone. I remember Guru sitting on his porch, chastising Santana and his wife, blaming their broken spiritual lives on their disobedient desire to start a family. Santana instantly became an ex-disciple. Guru told us Santana would drown in the "ignorance-sea," and immediately all of his relationships with the Center were formally and permanently severed.

I was used to this by now. When a disciple left, Guru forbade any contact. It did not matter how fond one was of the person—that ex-disciple had to be discarded. So many disciples came and left that cutting off a person from my life, even someone I had known from when I was learning to crawl, now felt normal. One couldn't, or shouldn't, get too attached. I'd learned how to scab over quickly, until I couldn't feel anything anymore, and an ex-disciple was just another name added onto the rapidly expanding blacklist.

Santana's break with Guru, however, did have a profound effect on concert attendance. With Guru as the headliner and only act, the less than full houses had early, mass evacuations. Although I understood that the concerts were hours and hours long and the music was unbearable, the people who left, I concluded, were simply unenlightened and didn't understand the larger purpose. I felt sorry for them. Here they were given an opportunity by the Supreme himself to become a disciple of the highest avatar, and they blew it. It really was their loss.

At three in the morning, shivering, I huddled against my mother in the broken-down bus. Due to chronic mechanical trouble, the bus's engine stalled. From my seat beside the window, frigid winds seeped through the glass. Besides the distant beads of lights from the highway, everything outside was dark. I sighed with the realization that if the bus was repaired within the next hour or so, I might still make it home in time for school. Not only would I not have had any sleep but my language arts report, like the majority of my homework, had not even been started. When I asked my mom if she thought I'd make it to school on time, she told me not to worry, that she would happily call in sick for me. With all of my absences, I was the sickest kid enrolled, the local hypochondriac. I didn't mind since I always felt absent at school even when I was present.

Long after I had stopped dressing in saris and decorating my cubby with photos of Guru in *nirvakalpi samadhi,* an elevated state of consciousness, the kids at Silvermine Elementary School still remembered. Tommy Frangelo, a boy who lived down the road from my house, told a legion of kids that he saw my family sacrificing a monkey and then drinking its blood. Because one of the ancient Hindu sacred signs is a swastika, it became standard knowledge that on top of everything else, the Tamms were Nazis, too.

In school, on the rare occasions I had received an invitation to a big event like Susie Thompson's birthday party at McDonald's, I was not allowed to attend. Guru had clear rules that socializing with outsiders was forbidden. Even when I begged my father to go, he seemed baffled as to why anyone would even want to go to a birthday party. Social events, for my father, were worse than searching for files at the town clerk's office. My request to attend the class year-end roller skating party caused him to stare at me for a long time, as if unsure that this strange little person was somehow the special soul that Guru had selected. Then he'd ask if I had meditated that day.

Since every night and every weekend we were in Queens or somewhere else spreading Guru's message, instead of chatting about play dates and birthday parties, I'd attempt to share news with my classmates about the many special events that occurred during our two sacred holidays: April, in honor of Guru's arrival in America, and August, in honor of Guru's birthday. During those times disciples from all over the world congregated in New York for nonstop festivities that included our own parades, Olympics, and circus. But the girls at Silvermine School weren't impressed. Soon even the rare birthday party invitation ceased. Sitting in the cafeteria by myself, it dawned on me one day that I was labeled the weird kid not only by my classmates but by the teachers as well.

When I failed the poetry presentation in Mrs. Sanders's class, I stayed after school for clarification. I had done the assignment, a rarity, having chosen a poet—Guru, of course—I memorized the poem, recited it before the class, and made a posterboard illustration to accompany it. I didn't know where I had gone wrong. Granted, all the other students chose Robert Frost and Shel Silverstein, but it was unclear to me what the problem was, until Mrs. Sanders accused me of making up the poet.

Although at this time Guru had already written more than five hundred books and was cranking out a book or two a week of short spiritual aphorisms, I kept quiet. More and more, defending Guru didn't seem to be worth it. Leaving Guru out of school altogether felt like a wiser choice. I figured that it wouldn't insult Guru. My academic career was never something that he emphasized, or even mentioned. When I did receive a surprisingly good grade, Guru was quiet. Education was not what he wanted from me, and he made that clear. What he wanted and expected was my unconditional obedience and undying love, and for that, I suppose, it didn't matter if I ever returned to school. I might as well just have sat on his tour bus forever.

Guru woke up.

"Oi. Are you people still alive?" Guru asked, tapping on the microphone of the bus's broken PA system. "Or are you all in the sleep-world?"

Toward the front of the bus, a few muffled murmurs responded from beneath mouths wrapped with scarves.

"I am in such pain. Excruciating pain," Guru said.

I knew Guru hurt. His slight limp at the beginning of the concert became a definitive wobble that caused him to move extra slowly, pausing between steps onto the bus. Seeing Guru in such obvious discomfort pierced me with guilt. The blame was mine, as well as all the other disciples who were constantly failing him with our selfish needs. My complaints about the freezing bus, the lack of sleep and food, I knew were ungrateful and uninspired, which resulted in desires and longings for myself rather than Guru. And the price was paid by Guru, yet again. I slunk into my seat, wishing I could reverse all the damage that I had done.

"You cannot and will never know what this Guru has to carry. So much dead elephant weight. I suffer from carrying your problems. Vital problems, which are emotional problems. Mental problems. But my suffering does not end there. So merciless does Alo torture me. Endless are her attacks on me. Her fierce jealousy and her demands create such problems. You people will never know what type of problems she makes for me in the inner and outer world. She is determined to make me suffer and to make the Supreme's will suffer. The pain you see I have in the outer world is so insignificant to what, at every moment, I have in the inner world. Most excruciating. Most excruciating. Alo is responsible for wanting to ruin me and the will of the Supreme."

I had never heard Guru speak about Alo in such a blunt and negative way. From the disciples I had learned that joking about Alo in her absence and worshipping Alo in her presence were politically advantageous. Beyond that, I overheard comments Prema and Isha tossed over their shoulders at meditation, forewarning that the witch was returning to town, but I had not realized the severity of Alo's effect on Guru and the suffering she caused for him. I knew my own ignorance and lack of spiritual aspiration created his pain. He had given me proof in a written statement proclaiming my worst quality.

Three years earlier, at a fund-raiser, for twenty-five dollars, disciples could stand before Guru as he wrote their worst quality. My parents thought this was a great idea. For a special gift, they signed me up. After my turn was over, I needed help from my mom to explain what it meant: "Deliberate disobedience on the lower-vital plane." I did not understand. My mother informed me that the lower-vital plane was the part of the being that harbored impure thoughts, emotions, and desires. At nine, my impure thoughts had been that Ketan could be a jerk, and my dad wore the same stinky, sweaty T-shirt that he had run in and then dried off on the radiator for the remainder of the day. Guru had officially confirmed the depths of my disobedience, my grave sins.

To witness Guru speaking about Alo with such pain in his voice was new and surprising. The problem of Alo, obviously, was dire. But, as with everything else, I had been too selfish and unaware to notice. What was wrong with me? My own intuition was nonexistent. I loved Alo. And secretly—even though it was bad—I still loved her. This probably caused Guru extra suffering.

"Guru?" a woman asked.

"Oi?" Guru replied. "A question?"

It was dark, and in my seat I couldn't see into the rows behind.

"Is there something that we can do to help you with Alo?" she questioned.

I was glad that she asked this. I really wanted to know.

"Could you not kill her?" Guru said.

The world paused. Stuck in a moment, frozen. Only the wind moved, bleeding through the glass onto me, giving me chills. I did not want to hear any more. I felt afraid of Guru and what he wanted. It all felt wrong. I turned away, toward the window that offered an illusion of the world outside with no lights and only deep darkness. Somewhere, I remembered the snaky arms of the Guru-bust in the backyard, curling and lapping their way toward my bedroom, awaiting my eventual return.

Half an hour later, the bus was fixed and merrily on its way, when Guru told the driver to pull over to a Howard John-son's rest stop. As the sleepy disciples stretched and stumbled off the bus, confusion churned in my head. Nothing made sense. I must have misunderstood Guru. Language had different meanings for moments, and words slipped between meanings quickly, as when crossing between rooms. What I heard Guru say felt wrong, yet I knew that was impossible. He could never be wrong. Unsettled and with my stomach throbbing with discomfort, I turned toward my mother, who stood in the aisle zipping up her coat. There was a line to disembark as disciples packed tightly in front and behind her. I wanted to confess my distress to my mother, but I knew I couldn't. In my family, as in the Center, we did not speak openly. Guru's standard policy was that disciples who questioned him were problematic and needed to be turned in for punishment. Criticisms, concerns, and suggestions about the Center were evidence of one's spiritual corruption. Rather than expose my own weaknesses, and risk being reported, it was much safer to keep my concerns to myself. As the Chosen One, I had a lot to lose.

"Mom?" I asked in a low voice.

She looked at me with deeply tired, apologetic eyes.

"I had a good meditation tonight," I said.

THE REST STOP was populated with truck drivers smoking and chatting up the waitresses, who jiggled while refilling coffee cups. All heads turned as we entered. We looked like we suffered from severe personality disorders—our top halves resembling skiers, bundled in earmuffs, scarves, and parkas, and our bottom halves meditators from which flowed our matching Guru-blue saris, the color selected by Guru as our standard uniform for all public concerts and events. The finishing touch below our saris, the outer symbol of our contemplative lives, was our footwear—various sizes and colors of running shoes, which demonstrated our shared enthusiasm for Guru's latest obsession with running. The male disciples all matched one another, wearing white pants, white shirts, and running shoes. We loaded in, filling the restaurant to capacity.

Umed, a male disciple, carried Guru's portable chair, blanket, area rug, and tray. As always, Umed was prepared to set up a mini-shrine wherever Guru went. Vanita, who, along with her sisters, Sarisha and Upala, owned an Indian vegetarian restaurant in Guru's neighborhood, stood by armed with multiple thermoses filled with juice, water, ginger ale, and teas for Guru as well as bags with snacks, just in case Guru was hungry or thirsty. No matter the location, from meditations at the church to gas stations, one of the three women was permanently on call with sacred snacks and beverages for Guru. With these standard procedures, any area—public or private—was transformed within minutes into a meditation hall. Disciples always cleared a respectful circle around Guru, never daring to come too close, and always careful to leave the best area for Guru to occupy, as they stood gazing lovingly with folded hands, positioning themselves to have a clear view of Guru and for Guru to have an even clearer view of them. This was not always easy, since the standard seating chart seemed to apply no matter where we went. Guru's strict seating order remained and if a disciple simply forgot, there were others to remind the person by standing or sitting directly in front of them. A first-row seat in the church meant a first-row seat, or area to stand, anywhere.

The waitresses' mouths sagged in surprise at our arrival. I

was used to it. We created a scene wherever we went. At the Pan Am terminal in Kennedy Airport, before a trip back to India, Guru held a meditation followed by prasad at the departure area gate. Having three hundred people converge with folded hands in such a small area had alarmed airport security. My father had to use all of his negotiating skills to talk down airport officials from calling in SWAT teams, assuring them that we were not staging a threat but were merely waving good-bye to our church leader. Gawks, whispers, hoots, leers, and having the authorities question us were everyday occurrences.

"It's those Moonies," a truck driver in a red-and-black-plaid jacket announced with authority. "They sell crap in airports."

The waitress nodded and told the short-order cook she was going to need some backup.

I turned to the man and, with my hand on my hip, I sighed extra loud and rolled my eyes in deliberate exaggeration, to let him know how absurdly ignorant he was. Even if I was having a crisis in faith, I wasn't going to let a man with bacon caught in his beard insult my guru. Though we were frequently mislabled Moonies, Hare Krishnas, and the Kool-Aid group of Jim Jones, we found it a personal affront, swearing that those oddballs had nothing in common with us; we were a "spiritual path," and those others, according to Guru, were just crazy cults.

"Oi, Jayanti." Guru nodded toward me.

He sat upon the HoJo orange stool, leaning both elbows on the counter in a pose that seemed far too casual for an avatar. I hesitantly approached him with folded hands. There was no doubt that Guru's occult powers had sensed my fears.

"Yes, Guru," I answered sheepishly, pressing my hands upon my heart.

"Jayanti," Guru said through closed eyes, in a low voice.

Beloved Guru I love you and nobody else. Beloved Guru I love you and nobody else. . . . I tried all of my devotions to repair the inner damage I might have caused myself. Trembling, I braced myself and leaned to gather up his disappointment.

"I have a very important job for you," Guru said.

My stomach collapsed. I felt sick. Was I supposed to kill Alo? As the Chosen One, of course, I was the obvious candidate, and why shouldn't I be? Guru selected my soul in order to serve him and him alone. His mission was my only purpose. Besides, I had just passed the deadline of God-Realization by age eleven, and both Guru and I knew that I was not even close to it. Here was a way to expedite my progress and solidify my seat at his divine feet, and I was doubting Guru. No matter what Guru asked, now or in the future, I needed to carry it out, swiftly and obediently. I needed to be a divine soldier—fearless.

"Yes, Guru," I vowed, steadying myself for my order.

"Buy hot chocolate for everyone. You need to count. Bus people. Car people. All. You get special hot chocolate prasad," Guru said, handing me a crisp hundred-dollar bill.

I must have looked stunned.

"Oi. All right?"

I was confused and needed clarification.

"When you were talking about Alo, earlier, in the bus . . ."

"Good girl, my sweet Jayanti. Of course your guru meant inwardly. All inwardly, Jayanti, divine." Guru smiled lovingly, adjusting his voice with a slight cough.

Though I was still shaking, I bowed, feeling relieved for his words and shame for ever doubting him.

Setting off on my task, my brain couldn't hold the numbers together, nothing followed, nothing stuck. After my third attempt at a recount, I asked Vanita if I could borrow a pen and paper.

Later, when the order was complete, and I was handing each Styrofoam cup to Guru so he could offer it to the freezing and overjoyed disciples who beamed at the opportunity to approach him, delighting in the fact that he was noticing, one by one, who had made the journey with him and who had not, I saw firsthand the rapture on everyone's faces. I still felt queasy. A massive circle packed tightly around Guru and me. Hundreds of eyes gazed toward him, craving even the slightest return glance. The disciples' distance from where I stood next to Guru seemed endless. Although I was closest to him, I felt the farthest away.

Guru's fingers accidentally brushed mine with the presentation of each cup like a formal ceremony from an ancient king's court. My position beside Guru was where his disciples, young and old, male and female, all desired to be. I knew this because they told me, constantly, scribbled on birthday cards, confessed through stalls in the bathroom, murmured through faraway stares.

"I wish I were you."

"How did you ever get to be so blessed?"

"You are the luckiest person in the whole world."

Their loving adoration felt both flattering and baffling. I could not take any credit for it. I had not achieved anything. None of this was my doing at all, but I did not remind them of that; I smiled and blushed, my cheeks always giving away my secret discomfort by flaring pink. The disciples' imaginings of my blessed existence did not include the garish reality of my flawed and crooked self—a fake who did not know how to meditate, who was not anywhere near God-Realization and was bothered less and less by that pressing matter, and, worst of all, who at times dangerously doubted Guru. Of course Guru was not asking for someone to really kill Alo. Guru wasn't at fault—I was, for misunderstanding his wisdom. Tears soaked my eyes. I saw the streak of a camera's flash preserving yet another blessingful moment of me with Guru. I rubbed my eyes with the back of my hand, and inwardly begged forgiveness for being so undeserving to be the luckiest person in the whole world.

To show his infinite compassion, Guru called the disciples who were not invited on his bus to receive prasad first. An excited push came from the crowd that wove into a single-file line. There were always many, many disciples who were not included in special groups and gatherings. From new disciples who had recently joined to disciples who had been in the Center for years, there was a mass—many who appeared nameless and faceless—simply filling in the empty seats at the back of the hall and driving their cars throughout the night in the hopes of being seen by the Master. Among that group was Chahna's family.

A hardworking couple from Bayonne, New Jersey, Chahna's parents came to the Center soon after she was born. Chahna was five years younger than me, and as far as Center rankings went, her family was definitely not invited on Guru's bus. With an eccentric father who inserted wacky jokes into every conversation and a mother who collected *Star Trek* memorabilia, Chahna's family seemed happier to be toting along at their pace in their own vehicle. Chahna smiled, her round face flecked with freckles lighting up, when she saw me looking toward the back of the line. She waved, her two long dark braids tossing wildly, and then got embarrassed for doing so on such a soulful occasion. In her ugly yellow hat with a pompom on top and her brown corduroy coat misbuttoned, Chahna was my own special friend. The first time I spotted Chahna, she shyly hid behind her mother's legs as her mother tried to walk her up to the stage with the rest of the child disciples; I loved her instantly. I had grabbed her hand and told her to come with me. In that moment, Chahna dropped her mother's grip, blinked up at me with grateful relief, and accompanied me to Guru. I knew then that I had gained a permanent and loyal sister.

As others watched me standing next to Guru, and as Guru extended his hand toward me, awaiting the cups I'd place in the grip of his delicate hand, I knew everyone longed to be in my position next to Guru. Chahna, I knew, just longed to be my friend, for me, and for me alone. Having friends was always difficult. Guru banned any friendships with people outside the Center, and friendships in the Center were complicated. Guru often created my friendships, advising me to stay away from certain disciples because they were undivine and steering me toward others because he said they were spiritually worthy. It always felt strange to hear Guru veer me away from certain disciples and nudge me closer to others. A few times, he reversed his pairing and had me befriend someone who originally had been on the banned list. Though I found it confusing and secretive, I obeyed, knowing that it pleased Guru. To him, controlling friendships was an important way to monitor another aspect of his disciple's lives. However, Chahna was a friendship I created on my own. She was mine, and Guru remained silent, never officially sanctioning or denying our relationship.

Seeing Chahna approach Guru for prasad, for the first time in what seemed like years I smiled. She stood before Guru, her serious gray eyes blinking rapidly, and though Guru did not even smile or pause, let alone say a word to her, when he handed her the cup, her entire face beamed with joy as if she had been given a magical gift. She bowed low, and nearly skipped her way to the back, vanishing among the crowds.

THAT SUMMER GURU gave me a job. With long hours and no pay, I was the envy of all the disciples. Daily, my mother would drive me to Guru's house in the early morning. I quietly waited by the side door that led directly to Guru's basement, the site of the Madal Zoo. No one was allowed to ring the bell or knock. The policy was to wait patiently until someone on the inside noticed you and allowed you to enter.

Though Guru generally enforced a no-pet rule for his disciples, he began buying pets for himself. His disciples, through their strong oneness with him, could then share the joys of having pets without the burdens of emotional attachment. It started with Sona, a white Maltese puppy, and rapidly expanded. After Sona came a large parrot, followed by a pair of monkeys. Soon the word was out that Guru sought new and exotic pets. Like all of Guru's sudden interests, this became the disciples' sudden interest, too, and disciples from Guru's ever-expanding meditation groups, which had spread to South America, Australia, eastern and western Europe,

Asia, and even Africa, rushed to provide Guru with unusual and spiritual pets.

Many of the disciples took the opportunity to bring these offerings with them when they came to New York. Because these animals were for Guru, and anything done for Guru was really done for the Supreme, meant that it not only had the highest priority but also was exempt from any mundane and low-consciousness rule and regulation set by the government. As soon as disciples declared they were on a project for Guru, they felt entitled, even obligated, to get it done the quickest way—regardless of the consequences. Laws were merely man-made manifestations of ignorance that could impede Guru's mission and therefore were of no consequence. If Guru wanted exotic birds and animals—especially ones that reminded him of his Indian childhood—then disciples went to the black market to smuggle them. Of course, keeping exotic birds and animals in a private residence in New York City was illegal, but that certainly did not deter anyone. In fact, having to perform illegal actions for Guru made the disciples feel more devoted, more committed.

Soon new pets were arriving all the time, although some didn't make it. Gathered at Guru's house, we heard disciples' stories of both successes and failures in attempts to expand the Madal Zoo. Aarpit, a Center leader from Australia, had driven days into the Australian outback and paid a toothless sun-scorched man hundreds of dollars for a rare cockatoo. Upon arriving at the airport to leave for New York, Aarpit crammed the bird inside an empty tennis ball container and hid it inside his zippered carry-on. Just as he was about to board the plane, his nylon bag began squawking incessantly.

Having to choose between getting barred from the plane and miss seeing Guru or keeping the bird, Aarpit ducked into the nearest men's room and, in a split-second decision, dumped the tennis ball can in the garbage. Other disciples admitted similar difficulties, and tips were shared, including how to sedate the animals for a guaranteed quiet flight. Often, after a long flight, the animals having been given the wrong doses of sedatives remained quiet, never to move or speak again.

Our family had our own exotic wildlife adventure. When Whiteitty, the wild cat that we tried to adopt, left us a stunned and shaken baby chipmunk, we nursed it back to health in a shoe box and then presented the chipmunk to Guru for his zoo. When we brought it to Guru's house, Prema vehemently shook her head in protest, and Guru decided that this chipmunk was best for our family to keep with his blessings. Even I, who still longed for a companion, realized that a chipmunk was a crappy pet, and we opened the box and let our rejected spiritual pet go.

To house all of the animals that were accepted into the zoo, Guru had the guards redesign and excavate his property. Deep beneath the basement, a series of rooms were dug to house the animals. Late at night, thick cement walls were erected to muffle the hoots, squawks, and chirps. This was a clandestine operation that eluded both the neighbors and Queens authorities. The success of this mission we attributed to Guru's inner powers rather than sophisticated engineering. Ownership of endangered birds and animals was illegal and highly unsanitary. Along with the drums of feed and sacks of seed came an influx of unwanted creatures, namely cockroaches and mice. The roaches, in particular, felt welcomed into such a bounty of animal mess, and soon they marched their way from the chambers belowground into Guru's upper living quarters.

Besides the two monkeys that lived in a special cage on the front porch, and the dogs—now there were two—the rest of the creatures that comprised the Madal Zoo, as Guru named it, dwelled deep belowground. Since they were so far below the main floor where Guru spent his days, Guru eventually stopped visiting or keeping track of them.

The Madal Zoo was the one area where Prema, Isha, and Alo all agreed—wishing it never happened. Noises, messes, and stenches were not looked on with great delight from any of them. Alo, a person who never had an affinity for animals, was appalled from Guru's initial purchase of Sona, his first pet, and warned Guru to stop all the nonsense with the creatures. But Guru always knew how to charm Alo. One day when I was at Guru's house, Alo stormed downstairs, furious to find her best sari torn by Sona, shouting that the dog must go immediately. Guru artfully diverted her attention by gossiping about a disciple who was causing him trouble. In an instant, she quickly forgot her original gripe about the illegal zoo, and hunched over, listening intently, hoping Guru would ask for her advice.

Since Prema and Isha were nearly full-time inhabitants, they made it clear to Guru that his divine plan of having them be the official caretakers of the zoo was not acceptable. Guru's vision of keeping both Prema—in charge of small mammals—and Isha—caretaker to the birds—quickly backfired, and they quit.

The basement crammed with Amazon creatures then became a highly coveted space—not for any more birds or animals—but for disciples eager to work for Guru inside his holy residence. Beneath Prema's and Isha's unchecked top-notch status were endless tiers of disciples who served Guru via Prema or Isha. Each had her own clan of followers who, through their allegiance to Prema or Isha, found a shortcut to Guru, and since there were now openings at the zoo, these were the ones summoned for this special blessing, just as I was.

One Saturday morning in July, after my mother dropped me off at Guru's house, I stood beside the side door patiently waiting for someone to remember to unlock it for me. We were told to avoid the front door, so as not to disturb Guru if he chose to lounge on the porch, his usual spot during hot days. Exhausted, as was my normal preteen state, I leaned against the Guru-blue shingles. Through the exterior, I smelled the rank cloud of stale rot, oozing from below. The thick humidity and lack of clouds meant it would be another endless sweaty Queens summer day. I closed my eyes, trying to remember if I got any sleep from when the meditation ended the night before to when I was awoken by my father at 5 a.m. in order to pray for Guru's Nobel Peace Prize victory. While the normal time to rise for morning meditations was 6 a.m., I was invited into a special club, created by Guru specifically for the purpose of praying each morning for the Nobel Peace Prize committee to award Guru their highest honor. These prayer sessions were highly coordinated global events. Groups from Bonn to Buenos Aires actively used prayer power to convince the Oslo officials that Guru deserved the prize. In addition, selected disciples, like my father, wrote letters to esteemed Nobel laureates and world leaders with the great news that they could nominate Guru for the Nobel Prize.

After years of either no replies or curt notes requesting my father to remove their names from his mailing list, Guru reassessed his chances of winning, deciding that for all his contributions to humanity, his best chance to win was through his pivotal role at the United Nations.

In 1971, Deepal, a waiflike Argentinean native who worked at the United Nations, became Guru's disciple. When Guru learned about her profession, Deepal quickly received her spiritual name and entrée into Guru's inner circle. Guru had always wanted to be connected to the world's most powerful international organization, and he asked Deepal to discover a way to introduce him into its folds. As it turned out, the United Nations had a collegial atmosphere, offering its employees many clubs and activities in an effort to foster a close-knit community from the myriad foreign nationals. Two signatures of full-time employees was all it took to form a club, and so Deepal and one of her friends created the Sri Chinmoy Peace Meditation at the United Nations club. Guru was official.

Twice a week, Prema or Isha chauffeured Guru to the circular entrance of the Secretariat Building, where he was escorted past the ambassadors and dignitaries into a small room for a meditation for any interested members of the UN and greater diplomatic community, which usually consisted only of disciples. Wanting his presence at the UN to grow, Guru decided his mission needed to be better represented at the world body, and he instructed anyone who wanted to be a "good disciple" to obtain a job at the UN. To please their master, scores of disciples applied, obtaining positions as low-level clerks or secretaries. What was important was that they were in, and so was Guru. For maximum exposure, Guru instructed all his women disciples to wear saris to work at the UN. While there were many international employees who were garbed in their native dress, it was more unusual for tall, blond women to show up at their office in saris and sneakers. After Guru's connection was firmly rooted, he promoted his UN position at every opportunity, announcing that he had been invited by dignitaries of the global community to be the official meditation leader and Peace Ambassador of the United Nations.

Chandika, my father's sister, who had followed her big brother's lead and become a disciple, obeyed Guru's mandate, landing a job as a secretary at UNICEF, to her great delight. Soon more than one hundred and fifty disciples had infiltrated the hallowed halls, and they began to make an impression. The Secretary-General at the time was the Burmese statesman U Thant. As a dignified and devout Buddhist, U Thant was well versed in the ancient traditions of Eastern philosophies, and he was far from objecting to the presence of non-Western faiths in the pantheon of beliefs represented at the world's leading diplomatic epicenter. In a show of his commitment to a broad definition of international faiths, he received an invitation from Guru to attend a special gathering in his honor. When Guru heard that U Thant's secretary had confirmed his acceptance, Guru was elated. He quickly phoned India to brag to his sisters and brothers. Guru knew that since his siblings were still residents of the Sri Aurobindo Ashram, his impressive news was guaranteed to spread quickly and eventually reach his old critics. Within a large portion of the ashram, his pursuit of a career as a guru in New York City had been viewed skeptically, as proof of his unholy ambitions. Guru wanted his doubters silenced. To

Guru, U Thant's visit signified his acceptance not only at the UN but on the world stage. Not every Bangladeshi immigrant was invited to the UN to become its Peace Ambassador and host the Secretary-General. Guru was ecstatic, and so were we.

The preparations for U Thant's visit lasted for weeks. The event was to be held on an old rambling estate, complete with a running brook, windmill, and large fields just outside the city. Guru micromanaged all the extensive arrangements, but when the greatly anticipated day finally arrived, rain poured on the festivities.

U Thant, the ultimate diplomat, sat stoically beneath an umbrella held by my father for the duration of the endless, soggy event. Through songs and poems and plays, Guru pulled out all of his charms to honor U Thant. I spent the hours huddled underneath a garbage bag fashioned into a poncho. Wet and cold, as the hours trudged past I concluded that I hated the UN and wished it would just go away so I could go home. Guru, on the other hand, was elated by the visit. Soon the photograph of Guru and U Thant bowing with folded hands to each other was being publicly distributed along with typed comments excerpted from U Thant's kind words.

Guru used the photos and comments so much that U Thant's office was notified by some high-level officials who had been keeping close watch. Several top executives viewed Guru as a charlatan who claimed his role at the UN was of an official capacity, and urged the Secretary-General's office to keep their distance. Thus began the long-standing game that sometimes felt like Risk and sometimes like dodgeball between the Secretary-General's office and Guru. Certainly no Secretary-General after U Thant ever spent hours sitting in a wet field with Guru again. They had learned their lesson. But nonetheless, with the ongoing efforts of his disciples, Guru became a permanent fixture as he continued to expand his role and presence at the UN.

The side door finally unlocked. I opened my eyes. I napped so often now, I wasn't even aware when it happened. All of my Nobel Prize prayer sessions inevitably ended in my jerking awake and peering at a clock that registered that hours had passed. This happened in meditations with Guru as well; I felt as though I had caught the contagious disease that caused many disciples to conk out at a second's notice.

Gitali stood with an extra large smile on her sweaty face. Her frizzy black hair was tightly pulled into a bun, and she wore a sari and yellow latex gloves. I must have been standing outside for at least an hour, waiting for her to open the door, but she didn't acknowledge that fact, as she handed me a stack of garbage bags, informing me that I would be cleaning the birdcages today.

I knew Gitali adored the zoo; with it she had a purpose and need—a way to belong to Guru's coveted domestic space. Gitali, like the majority of Guru's disciples in the New York area who did not work for disciple-owned businesses, or "divine-enterprises" as Guru called them, was employed at one of the UN branches. Even with permanent contracts, high pay, great benefits, and the ability to meditate with Guru twice a week on their lunch hour, most disciples, still longed to be with Guru, every day, all day, as full-time devotees. Gitali, a full-time UN worker and part-time Madal zookeeper, was no exception. She was in Guru's special close circle, assigned to Isha's friend pool. Since Gitali worked at UNICEF during the week, which she claimed as her spiritual *sadhana,* having to deal with outsiders for eight hours a day plus ride

the low-consciousness subway, her time at Guru's zoo cleaning bird droppings was her refuge.

I put on a pair of mammoth cleaning gloves that were
itchy from bleach. Even before opening the door to the bird
zone, the thick stench and their shrill squawks clawed through
the basement. Always a fan of soft, cuddly animals, I neither
understood nor liked birds. Their unblinking eyes and pointy
beaks, coupled with their reptilian talons, made me wary. I
didn't trust them. When I walked inside, I felt as though my
eardrums had been ripped out. Caws, shrieks, whines, and
whistles collided at a shattering pitch. Maybe because they
never saw sunlight, or were forced to live in cramped condi-
tions, all of the birds seemed extra neurotic, pacing in mad
circles in their own messes on the floor, or furiously pecking
at the cage bars.

"Nice birdie," I said, tentatively reaching my arm inside a
cage of black mynah birds that had been smuggled by a disciple from Indonesia. Some of the creatures stood their ground,
staring me down, as others flapped spastically on metal
perches.

"Okay. Nice birdie," I said, keeping an eye on the one that
seemed about to dart in my direction, at the same time pulling
out the newspaper sopped with white, green, and black puddles of creamy waste.

After wiping down the concrete floor and relining it, without ever losing sight of the black beasts, I safely removed my
arms and locked the cage again, with great relief.

When I first received word from Guru that I was allowed
to join my older sisters and be their assistant in the zoo, I
was thrilled. I loved going to Guru's house, and anytime Guru
included me with the grown-ups, I was especially proud. I

smugly enjoyed being the only kid invited into such exclusive society. I imagined that helping with the animals would involve sitting in a comfortable place petting a furry cute friend.

"There is a dead finch in the finch cage," Gitali had said on one of my first days in the bird zone, coming up from behind, scaring me. She had to repeat herself three times, until I could hear her over the deafening squawks.

"So?" I shouted.

"There are little Baggies up near the washing machines. You can use one of those." She smiled and continued on.

I soon realized that my special blessing of being with the grown-ups in Guru's zoo was not what I had imagined. Far from being a perk, this felt like purgatory.

I moved on to Raj's cage. Raj was the scariest of all. A massive parrot that looked like it belonged perched on a tattered pirate's shoulder, it seemed to wait for me, daring me to even unlatch the lock, before lunging at me with his broad beak that ended in two points like the ends of a protractor.

"Hey there, Raj. You like me, right? Sure you do. Nice Raj." As soon as I unfastened the lock, he puffed out his feathers as a warning.

It was now late afternoon in the bird dungeon. I imagined way aboveground, the bright sun shone on people on earth. I looked at my sari, soaked and stained with various bird body liquids. I peeled some damp feathers off my arms. By now I could not even hear the desperate calls of the birds, and the stench, too, seemed normal. On my knees, I sighed, imploring Raj just to give me a break. He was my last cage.

As soon as I reached in, he flapped his wings, lifting them back, prepared to strike. I tried to rip the paper up, but it was stuck to the floor. With a yelp, Raj swooped down, latching onto my pinky finger.

"Motherfucker!" I screamed.

My free hand grabbed my dust broom, and I whacked Raj.

"You fucker! Let go of my fuckin' finger!"

I smacked Raj over and over until he loosened his clamp and hobbled away to a corner of the cage. I stared down at my bluish finger and wondered if it could still bend.

"Are we finished yet?" Gitali asked, appearing out of nowhere carrying a bucket of bird seed and wearing a smile.

I looked up, holding my finger. Suddenly I hated her.

"You know, in a few years, when you finish having to go to yucky school, you will be the luckiest person in the world because you will be blessed by Guru to have the opportunity to become his full-time bird keeper. How wonderful." Gitali smiled, looking wistful. "For your whole life, every day, all day, you will get to be in Guru's blessed world and work only for Guru alone. You will never ever have to enter the outside world."

She sighed and patted my shoulder.

"You really are the luckiest person," Gitali said and walked past me toward the cockatoos.

I sat on the concrete floor, nursing my finger, as a tidal flood of fear and doom filled me. This was what my future was? A lifetime of this—feathers and shit. I knew I shouldn't be feeling this way; being at Guru's house and cleaning the cages was an incredible honor. But I didn't want it. To me, the idea was horrifying. Even if Guru had me on the fast track to God-Realization and was preparing me to succeed Prema and Isha, it still felt like torture. I didn't care if working in this basement was my sacred destiny. Every squawk and scoop felt filthy and stifling. I panicked, and my heart thumped until it hurt. I thought of Chahna. She was probably in her sunny backyard or in her bedroom playing. I wished I could be with her instead of being in this hub of blessings, but I knew I couldn't tell that to anyone, even her. She had been so excited for me when I had bragged to her about tending Guru's animals. Chahna, who had never been invited to visit the animals, made me promise I'd describe all I saw and did with exact details. Knowing how happy Chahna was for me made me feel terrible. Why couldn't I be happy? I looked around and tried to fake a smile, but it felt impossible. Instead, I scrunched my knees into my chest, forming a tight cocoon, while cockroaches scuttled past. I decided then, for the first of many times, that being the luckiest person was for the birds.

4

The Supreme Is Your Boyfriend

OST PEOPLE SETTLE IN GREENWICH, CONNECTICUT, an oasis of French boutiques, polo clubs, and waterfront rambling estates, as the culmination of a lifelong dream to enter the gated community of New England's elite. Not us. For my family, Greenwich was a disappointing substitute for Jamaica, Queens. As most disciples moved to Queens, and others just faded away, the once illustrious Connecticut Center no longer served as a holy temple and returned to being a leaky basement. My parents pleaded with Guru to allow them to flee Connecticut altogether, but Guru refused, explaining that he wanted to maintain a presence in the state. My father decided that the way to obey Guru by still living in Connecticut was to move to Greenwich, located only steps away from the New York border.

In a tiny corner of Greenwich that brushed against Port Chester, New York, the depressed town housing the many illegal Hispanics who served as maids, chauffeurs, masons, and landscapers to the mansions of Greenwich, we bought an old pea-green, three-story house. With two floors to rent to tenants to aid with the mortgage, we occupied half of the first floor and made the other half my father's office in an effort to save money. Shortly after establishing his practice, my father had aligned himself with a clan of real estate developers and gradually became involved in their schemes, spending the majority of his business hours flipping properties rather than defending cases in court. Everything about my father's dealings and finances was a mystery to us. Even though he worked as a Greenwich lawyer, my father proudly professed that he never had money. He didn't feel comfortable billing his few clients, and instead of regular payments, he'd work out deals that gave him a cut of the property, which did little to assist with the immediate basic needs to cover our household expenses. The money that my mother did unearth from my father's coffers all went to Guru. As a result, I was the poorest kid I knew who lived in Greenwich with an attorney for a father.

The opportunity to slip out of Norwalk and shed my reputation as a kooky and possibly dangerous outcast was a welcome relief to me. I was in junior high school, and I was quietly eager to gain a fresh start. My game plan was not to cause any waves with Guru or at school, although I felt moody and anxious about both. Guru's lack of awareness over my concerns regarding my future and my rapidly waning interest in God-Realization reinforced my doubts that his inner powers were working as well as they used to, at least on me. Guru seemed somehow oblivious to the fact that I was attempting to conceal my involvement with him from the outside world. He also didn't seem to notice that I felt increasingly irritated with his strict limitations on all aspects of my daily life—from telling me what sport to play to how to wear my hair. Rather than burst into my new junior high as one of Guru's public ambassadors, I planned to conceal all traceable evidence of my discipleship, making myself as anonymous as possible, until I was finished with school altogether.

"What are you doing?" I asked my mom one morning, as she sat at the kitchen table with a long list of phone numbers to call.

She was breathless, flushed at her news.

"Can you believe it? Guru is coming here, to our house, to lift an elephant!" she shrieked, with the phone draped over her shoulder. "I'm calling all the local newspapers and TV!"

So much for being anonymous.

When Guru's knees made sprinting and long distance running, his former passions, unendurable, he began a new craze of weight lifting. But as with all of Guru's hobbies, he did not follow traditional standards. Bored with dumbbells, Guru assigned his guards to build him apparatuses so he could lift objects. They engineered a contraption that resembled a calf-raise machine with a platform that was used to hoist gigantic pumpkins, people, and motorcycles; this way, Guru found, in addition to receiving exercise, he received press, and lots of it. Eager to expand his fame, Guru was bemused to add "sports nut" and "weight-lifting champion" to a résumé that included author, musician, UN peace ambassador, and spiritual teacher. The title of "heavy lifter" seemed to get Guru more coverage than the others, which intensified Guru's expanding quest to find new angles and objects to lift in order to arouse the media's interest.

Careful to conceal my hesitancy about the blessing of having Guru lift an elephant at my house, I dutifully helped my parents organize the event, blowing up balloons and stenciling arrows onto signs around the neighborhood to ensure the reporters found our house tucked into the back lot of the dead-end street.

Four houses away from me lived the Johansons, a Swedish family whose older daughter, Kristina, was a ninth grader at my school. Waiting for the bus in the morning, she had introduced herself while constantly brushing her blond feathered hair. Wanting to make a new friend, I took a new approach and casually failed to mention anything about Guru; instead I tossed endless questions to her, which she was only too pleased to answer, blabbing about herself while snapping her gum.

"Did you tell that sweet girl that rides the bus with you to school that she was welcome to come watch Guru lift the elephant?" my mother asked, folding press kits to distribute at the big event.

"Yeah," I mumbled.

I hadn't told Kristina about the impending elephant, and I hoped none of the Johansons, especially Kristina, would find out.

When I was sent out to hang a massive gold banner in letters proclaiming "Congratulations!!!!" across the shrubs in the front yard, I carefully peered down the street, checking if Kristina's family's station wagon was in its driveway before darting out with a baseball hat pushed down to conceal my face.

Later that afternoon, a massive truck with *Zack's Circus and Exotic Animals* airbrushed across the front cab idled in the middle of my street, clogging traffic as neighbors from every house in Greenwich, it seemed, stood around incredulous, watching an elephant lumber down a metal ramp into our tiny front yard while throngs of disciples sang and clapped.

The weight-lifting platform, because of its careful design, worked so that when Guru hunched beneath the padded shoulder stands and hoisted his thin bent legs straight, a lever lifted the platform area ever so slightly. Depending on where the person—or elephant—stood, some weight would be lifted and some wouldn't. The farther back the object was placed from Guru, the lighter the area became closest to Guru's lift. This allowed Guru to continue to lift bigger and more dramatic objects, from people to elephants.

The next day I cringed when I saw a front-page article in the local newspaper with a large photograph of Guru, the elephant, a few disciples, and me. With elaborate, breathless quotes from both my parents—described as "followers of the Guru"—I was outed to the entire town of Greenwich.

When Kristina asked me about the elephant while waiting for the school bus, I casually tried to play it off as just one of those weird things that parents like to do. But Kristina persisted in her questions about the Indian elephant-man.

I mumbled something about my parents being his sponsor and was relieved when the bus pulled into view. At school, when I was questioned about it by the gym teacher in front of the whole class, I denied having any knowledge of the event, politely suggesting he must have mistaken me for someone else.

Later that night, at the function, I could barely look at Guru, fearing my denial of the Supreme, the Avatar of the Era, my beloved guru, would be reflected across my third eye.

I had sunk to new lows, and what was worse was that I knew I was braced to go even lower. I was Judas, the traitor. Instead of silver coins, I was ready to send Guru down the river for the chance to feign normality or, at the very least, anonymity.

Guru called all the children up onto the stage. On average, there were always about twenty kids in the local area whose parents had become disciples at any given time. Some parents had sought a brief respite from the world, surrendering the steering wheel of life's decisions. Those parents were content to float without having to navigate; some were burned out; some were running away from tragic family lives or abusive relationships; some were unstable and found in Guru's alternative lifestyle a safe haven where societal outcasts came to unite; some were sincere seekers fed up with the scramble for possessions and wealth and aiming for a deeper meaning. Some experienced a hovering aura around Guru, and, as a result, they shed their former life, bringing along their unsuspecting children, who were suddenly draped in saris or matching white shirt and pants like year-round Halloween costumes.

That night, Guru had the children sit on the floor in front of him. Chahna settled beside me, careful not to crowd my space, but close enough so I could hear her cloggy nasal breaths as Guru began telling stories about his earliest days as a disciple in the Sri Aurobindo Ashram. It was the death of Guru's parents that caused Hridoy, the eldest of Guru's six siblings, to place the family in the care of the Sri Aurobindo Ashram in Pondicherry. That decision instantly transformed the orphans into *sanyassis,* casting their lives in the ancient Indian tradition of disciples bound to the wisdom and tutelage of a guru. At twelve years old, Guru was told he was now a renunciate, a celibate monk.

Out of all of Guru's siblings, only his sister Lily came once to visit. Since Lily enjoyed nature, my family invited her to Connecticut during her stay. Charmed by our hospitality, sitting in our back garden, she told us stories of Guru's past. She remembered the early burning ambition of her little brother, the way he observed the ashram elders seated in the front of the meditation hall, how they received prasad first and greeted visitors. He studied the hierarchy of the ashram, working out its complex system of favorites and favoritism. Wanting a promotion into the coveted clan, Guru aligned himself with Nolini, one of Sri Aurobindo's closest disciples. As an assistant to Aurobindo's assistant, Guru was positioned to make his mark, be noticed, and quickly ascend the ranks. Yet, according to Lily, Guru was not satisfied with usurping Nolini's position—Guru wanted to replace Aurobindo himself, becoming a guru with more disciples, more exposure, more power, and more prestige.

Guru had to start somewhere, and so, for a few years, he was Nolini's lackey, running errands. Guru's rewards were scraps of praise. Years later, when Guru's own discipleship grew and he started meeting celebrities and world figures, Guru always sought a strong quote—a positive endorsement— about himself. Nothing pleased Guru more than a glowing comment from a celebrity, which was repeated endlessly, printed and distributed and repeated again.

Lily told us that since Sri Aurobindo was considered an esteemed author of both poetry and prose, Guru decided that he, too, would take up writing. Wanting recognition for his talent, Guru typed up some of his own verse and gave them to Nolini to read, hoping Nolini would pass on his poetry to Sri Aurobindo. Guru's desire came true. Nolini gave Sri Aurobindo Guru's writings, and after scanning through some poems, Sri Aurobindo uttered words that Guru endlessly quoted: "He has promise. Tell him to continue." Guru was in his glory. Nothing could have been better. The comment was simultaneously vague and specific. Recognition of promise and an urge to go forward was perfect for young Madal. Coming from his guru, a God-Realized soul, an avatar who had achieved the fruits of liberation, these words were a confirmation of everything Madal wanted to do and become. *He has promise. Tell him to continue.*

Inside the clay and concrete walls of the ashram, Madal read about the broader world. The West, in particular America, intrigued him. He told us that he once imagined America as a large, eager child, waving and welcoming him to play, ready to share its toys and abundance with him. The sedentary life of the ashram was not his choice. He wanted to take on America.

He has promise. Tell him to continue. What was set in motion needed completion. In her soft voice and hesitant English, Lily had explained that Sri Aurobindo had never encouraged his disciples to be missionaries, even in India, let alone in America; Aurobindo believed that seekers who felt an inner calling would find his teachings, and he disapproved of swamis who actively recruited in order to claim large numbers of disciples. In fact, with his lack of contact with his ashramites, Sri Aurobindo seemed more inclined to be without disciples altogether and to be left alone for contemplation. Madal knew that he would neither be asked nor would receive permission to venture to America as a representative of Sri Aurobindo. There needed to be another way. *He has promise. Tell him to continue.*

SEATED BEFORE GURU onstage, I closed my eyes while Guru recounted his favorite tale about the ashram when he was fourteen and received a direct order from the Supreme to go to America. He had been strolling alone along the shore of the Bay of Bengal, the backyard of the ashram, a site where land dissolved into shimmering blue waters. It was dusk, and the beach was empty. As he looked across the vast horizon, suddenly the sky cracked and flashed, blinding him. In the clouds was the Supreme—a figure complete with a voice and a message for him alone. The Supreme "commanded" him to go to America and be of service to the aspiring souls who were searching for a spiritual guide. As he heard these words, he felt afraid and began to cry. The Supreme consoled him, bestowing upon him the confidence and the knowledge that he had the capacity to be "my instrument, my supremely chosen instrument." And as he longed for answers to questions of how and why, the figure in the clouds disappeared, leaving him alone, contemplating the daunting enormity of his mission.

For the first time, I realized that while he had been brought into the ashram by his family, he had left on his own, ending his life as a disciple and beginning his life as the Guru Sri Chinmoy. I wondered how difficult the decision to leave must have been and how it had changed his life forever. In departing the ashram, he had to give up everything he had known—his home, family, and Guru—for the daunting, vast outside world of the unknown.

A few times, years later, Guru suggested some of the opposition that he faced as he announced his intentions to leave the ashram and go off on his own. Nolini told Madal he no longer needed an assistant. His friends became distant. His brothers and sisters—his doting surrogate parents—wondered just who was this thin man in baggy khaki shorts and dusty callused feet who suddenly spoke of Manhattan? When had he arrived? And when had their Madal, the smiley, mischievous noisemaker departed?

I dared to imagine myself deciding and then preparing to leave behind Guru's ashram in search of a different world thousands of miles away. Instantly, I felt both terrified and thrilled.

"Jayanti, all right?" Guru asked. His stories were over, and the other children, even Chahna, stared at me.

I blinked hard, embarrassed to be caught thinking about leaving Guru. My cheeks flared pink.

"Bah. Now let us have a soulful-smile contest. All stand up and turn to the audience. Give your most soulful smile, and the audience will vote."

From the longest hair contest for the women to the best abdominal muscle contest for the men, Guru enjoyed competitions that set up disciples against one another. I was used to them but still wary. At a meditation I missed due to the chicken pox, Guru had held a contest for the ugliest girl. When I heard that Barbara, a relatively new disciple with a boil the size of a large gumball beside her nose, had won, I sighed with relief, grateful that my mother had kept me home that night.

We turned with our backs to Guru. In the shuffle, Chahna stood beside me. She smiled wide, the gap between her two front teeth on display. Across from me stood the boys, of various heights; some squirmed around, while others adapted a perfect pose. Ketan dazzled a dimpled smile.

I still did not understand what "soulful" meant, even though Guru used it constantly to describe everything as either being soulful or not. What I discovered was that when Guru interrupted midsong the various disciple singing groups who performed at every meditation because they were not soulful enough, when they resumed singing, the tempo had slowed down dramatically. Soulful, therefore, I had deduced meant slow. I worked my lips into a slow, upward-turned arch, hoping I'd faked soulfulness.

When the results were tallied up, I had won for the girls, and Puran, a small, quiet child three years younger than me, won for the boys. Chahna did not even place. I had done it again. I had successfully faked soulful, scamming the entire audience, Guru included. No one had yet figured out what I realized more and more—that I was rapidly becoming the least soulful of all.

THE NEXT DAY at the junior high school, as always, I was trying to keep a low profile, slinking into classes early to avoid the drama between periods when notes were passed urgently, gossip was exchanged, and the popular girls got their butts pinched by boys. Only once, while walking to social studies, I felt a quick squeeze on my behind. I had turned with great excitement. Attempting to play off an annoyed look, I saw a stunned Andre Banducci.

"Oh God," he stammered. "I thought you were some-one else."

Since then, I spent the five minutes between classes—an interminable length of time—hidden from view.

"Hey," a voice urged from the back of the empty room.

I decided not to look, assuming no one would be trying to get my attention.

"Hey, you with the long hair."

I looked back and saw Colin McLevy in the last seat in the corner. Colin was tall, lanky, and never without headphones and his tape player. Beneath an acid-washed denim jacket covered with buttons and patches, he wore a hooded sweat-shirt draped over his head like a monk's hood.

"Come here," he said. "I wanna ask you something."

Colin had never spoken to me before even though we had three classes together.

No boys talked to me. In fact hardly any girls talked to me either. This must be an accident.

"What?" I said, making the walk toward him as slow as possible, struggling to portray disinterest.

"Sit down. Pull up a desk." He leaned over and closed the carefully created gap between the rows, by dragging the desk and parking it right beside his.

I remained standing until he hit his right hand against the back of the neighboring chair, his silver rings—one for every finger, including the thumb—clanking upon the metal.

As I sat beside him, I surmised he had an agenda: he needed to copy last night's homework. He had assumed in-correctly that I had done the homework. Of course I hadn't. I never did. By the time I got home in the early hours of the morning from the meditation and our special invitation to Guru's house, homework was the last thing on my mind.

"I didn't do the homework," I quickly said, to spare him from any more efforts.

"So?" Colin said, squinting through the dark brown bangs that hung in front of his blue eyes.

I looked down at my hands, naked of any jewelry—Guru forbade it—and nail polish—also forbidden. My chewed-up cuticles, some with tiny scabs mixed in with rips of skin and lopsided nails, were ugly. I balled my hands into tight fists away from Colin's view.

"Skip sixth-period study hall with me," Colin said.

With his headphones still on, the faint residue of synthesizers and drums seeped into the air.

Mrs. Catonia burst into the room, her heels snapping against the floor, followed by the rest of the class, talking loudly, recapping the latest hallway scandals.

I nodded.

For a few minutes I worried about breaking Guru's rule against mixing with boys. But since no disciple went to my school—Ketan was already in high school—I figured Guru would never find out. Besides, maybe Colin was really a spiritual seeker and wanted to talk about Guru. In that case, I justified that I was doing the right thing by agreeing to help him in his inner search. Satisfied with my reasoning, I straightened the barrettes in my long, straight, Guru-approved hair, and set off for Colin's spiritual intervention.

During sixth-period study hall, I knew right where to find him. Behind the brick wall of the building where boys played handball was an area reserved for the rebels who skipped classes. Although teachers regularly patrolled this delinquent domain, since it also served as an extra parking lot for faculty, there were always cars to duck behind and avoid detection.

When I had skipped class before, I had hidden inside the bathroom to avoid a test or project that I had not completed. I had never dared to venture to the official skipping zone. That would have been ridiculous. One needed an invite. Besides, mostly boys hung out there, and the only time I spoke to boys in school had been when I was assigned to be their group partners in class.

Colin sat on the pavement, leaning against the brick wall, still listening to his music. As I approached him, I hoped he would remember that he had asked me to come and prepared an escape route in case he didn't.

"Hey," he nodded. "You like Depeche Mode?"

"Sure," I said, not knowing what he was talking about. Besides my mother's old Broadway show tunes, I wasn't allowed to listen to any music that wasn't Guru's. According to Guru, it strengthened the lower-vital and slowed spiritual progress.

"Here." He popped out one earphone from the plastic holder and handed it to me, while he kept the other one shielding his ear.

Because the wire was so short, I had to sit right next to him, close enough to smell the orange gum he was chewing. I scanned the surrounding area, double-checking that no disciples lurked behind the cars.

When I'm with you baby I go outta my head ... I just can't get enough ... I just can't get enough ...

The synthesizer, the cold pavement, the brush of denim—

Colin didn't want to discuss Guru, and I suddenly didn't care. Guru who?

I nodded my head, pretending I knew the whole song. When it ended, he rewound it and started again. I waited patiently, staring at the cracks in the pavement, wishing study hall would never end.

After rewinding it a fourth time, Colin turned his head and looked right at me.

"Hey," he said.

I slowly turned to find him only inches from my face.

"You know how to kiss," he said, without a hint of a question.

Before I had time to back away or stall for time, Colin leaned in and smashed his lips onto mine. Within a second, he had pried my mouth open, and his tongue was flicking in and out.

Stunned, with wet slobber oozing from my lips, I followed his lead, my tongue darting into his mouth, attempting to mimic his moves.

The bell rang.

"Oh shit. I got a math test," Colin said, jumping up and scurrying inside.

THAT SAME AFTERNOON, dazed with reckless passion, I composed my first love letter—pledging Colin my eternal love, praising his hazy blue eyes, brown hair, and exquisite taste in music.

What I hadn't accounted for was that Ketan would find it first.

Ketan, always keenly aware of what would give him the upper hand in his ongoing battle to wipe out the Chosen One, had discovered a draft of the letter and delivered it straight to the source—Guru.

I spent the entire meditation that evening playing, rewinding, and replaying my kiss. Though I knew I had committed a grave act of disobedience to Guru, I couldn't stop myself from relishing my wild passion. I was a woman in love.

After prasad, Guru summoned me to his throne, pushing the microphone away for privacy.

Uh-oh.

"Oi. I am very, very disappointed in you and your spiritual life."

Oh no.

"Such a special soul, I brought down especially from the highest heaven to serve the Supreme in me. Such disappointment. Such news. Your lower-vital life is breaking my heart. Boys are poison, poison to your inner life, your spiritual life."

Guru had his eyes closed, as though he could not bring himself to look at me.

"Your disobedience is causing your guru and your own soul great pain. This behavior will not be allowed. The Supreme is your eternity's boyfriend. The Supreme is your eternity's boyfriend."

I slunk down from the stage feeling fully exposed and utterly mortified. I had fallen and failed. Ready to renounce my entire spiritual life so recklessly for a boy. Some Chosen One I was. What was wrong with me to cause me to deliberately displease Guru? Tears filled my eyes, and I silently vowed to Guru that I would change my life and end my world of darkness. If only Guru would forgive me, then I could settle in and enjoy my real boyfriend, the Supreme. Since, as Guru explained, the Supreme was my boyfriend, why would I ever even want or need another, especially if, as I hoped, he was utterly devoted to me and me alone, and, more important, if he was cute?

THE NEXT DAY at school, prepared to break the tragic news to Colin McLevy that I could not be with him, although I loved him, because I was promised for eternity to another, I noticed whispers and giggles as I walked through the halls.

"Ribbit. Ribbit," Jesse Doran said to me when I passed him on the way to my locker.

Taped to my locker was a Magic Marker drawing of a green frog with a long black tongue sticking out. My name was written across the tongue.

Gigi, who had the locker next to mine and regularly smelled of bananas, came for her books.

Even though I knew that Gigi was about as likely as I was to be in the loop of gossip, I was desperate for answers. When I asked her what was going on, at first she pretended she was too busy looking for her science workbook to respond.

"Colin McLevy has been telling boys and girls that you—you—you . . ." She stared into her locker, embarrassed by what she was about to say.

"You kiss like a frog." She dropped her head and looked away.

I ripped the paper off my locker and ducked into the bathroom, where I found the stall farthest from the doorway and converted it into my home for the rest of the school day. It was while seated upon the bathroom floor, inside the locked stall, that I recommitted myself to my real purpose—that of being Guru's number one disciple—and reconfirmed the uselessness of the outer world and, in particular, of boys, especially Colin McLevy.

I NEEDED TO atone for my transgressions. Since Guru's scolding, I was trying extra hard to please him, but I had a new problem: I wasn't used to competition for Guru's attention, and the rare times when I sensed it, I didn't like it. Of course there were always Prema and Isha, Guru's number one and number two personal assistants, but they didn't count. They were older. They had their place, and I had mine. But, like me, Pallavi was fifteen. She lived in Avignon, France, with her parents, who were the head of the Avignon Center. When she came to New York, it was always with her family, and she was merely another European disciple, one of the hundreds who flooded Queens twice a year. But this time she came alone, and everything was different.

"Pallavi, divine," Guru said, scanning for her from his throne on stage. Pallavi stood up at the far back of the meditation hall, the area designated for disciples who had not yet earned from Guru an assigned seat on the floor. When Guru located her, he invited her forward. Just as she was about to step onto the raised platform of the Guru-blue-carpeted stage, Guru stopped her.

"Good girl, you stay with Oditi, no?"

"Yes, Guru," Pallavi answered, pausing right beside me.

"Then you get a promotion. You come sit beside Oditi." Guru smiled.

I heard Oditi, a lanky Englishwoman who always festooned herself in gold and silver saris complete with matching pumps and handbags, clap with glee and giggle with delight at hearing Guru announce her name.

Pallavi bowed her head in gratitude at her seat upgrade.

"Your flute? Divine, bring your flute," Guru said to Pallavi.

Pallavi looked at her empty hands, turned, and sprinted to the back. At this Guru shook his legs and smiled, and the entire hall shared a moment of amusement. Guru's intoxicating presence made it so easy to slip into his playful world and forget about everything else.

I turned to watch Pallavi's return up the aisle. Her sari was all white, and she wore a white turtleneck underneath it. Her round face was pale. Her straight blond hair reminded me of the corn broom my mother used to sweep the floor.

Guru told her to play two songs on her flute. While she played, her cheeks turned bright pink. By her last squeaky note, she seemed to be gasping for breath. Guru clapped with both hands held above his head. Following Guru's lead, everyone joined in a hearty ovation.

"She's such a sweet girl, and that was so soulful," my mother said as she genuinely applauded.

"No, it wasn't," I said, politely tapping my palms together, eager to show my mother, Guru, Pallavi, and everyone else in the hall what soulful really was. I wondered if Guru would ask me to either sing or recite a poem. I was equally prepared for both.

"Bah! I'm very, very proud of you, Pallavi. Very, very pleased with you. You come." Guru reached down beside his throne and pulled out a thick Banaras red silk sari with an ornate gold filigree border and a matching blouse. The fabric gleamed from the stage, and the women murmured in admiration. Asutosh, the official photographer, was already up on stage to capture the moment when Guru handed it to Pallavi.

As Guru gave her the sari, he whispered to her for a minute, and her head nodded. When she turned to the audience, she had the sari cradled in both arms with the flute beneath it.

I offered up a smile to her, but she seemed to be in a far-off land, nearly floating off the stage to land in her new seat. By the end of the meditation, I was still waiting for my turn to ascend the stage and display my soulful skills, but it never came.

Often in lectures, Guru told us that all of his disciples were dispensable, that no one was indispensable. He warned us that even if all of his current disciples left him, he would replace us with an army of new seekers, more devoted, more dedicated. These talks always made my stomach knot. The idea that I could be swapped with someone was incredibly threatening, keeping me always looking over my shoulder to see if someone was getting just a little too close for comfort.

That night when I arrived at Guru's house where only the specially invited disciples gathered for extra blessings, Pallavi was already there, sitting beside Gitali with the sari draped across her lap.

I went into the basement to find Ketan. I needed answers as to what exactly was going on. Ketan, always a control tower for any gossip floating across the Center airwaves, was my source for all news. At seventeen, the day after graduating from high school, when he permanently moved to Queens to share an apartment with six key members of Guru's personal bodyguards, our relationship changed. He didn't have time for me now. He was far too important. He was a full-timer, and I was just a commuter herding back and forth to Queens each night with our lame parents. Nowadays, in order to get gossip updates, I had to corner him at meditations. Knowing which disciples were on spiritual probation from reports about undivine crimes such as singing without folding their hands or conversing with a member of the opposite sex gave Ketan a distinct and powerful advantage, and he relished it.

When I asked Ketan why Pallavi was suddenly in New York without her parents, Ketan shrugged his shoulders, but he couldn't keep his lips from arching into a smirk. Just like years ago when I wanted Ketan to give me something, he always had a price, whether it was the handover of a beloved stuftie or the act of making me tie his sneakers into double knots. Tonight, he faked a cough and remarked how utterly thirsty he was. When I promised I'd treat him later to a coffee—the only beverage he now drank—he let loose. According to Ketan, Pallavi had discovered her father had been criticizing Guru's public displays of weight lifting, claiming they were undignified. Pallavi's father felt the weight lifting presented an undignified public image for the Avignon Meditation Center, which he promoted as a sanctuary to study ancient Vedic philosophical traditions. As a result of Pallavi's report to Guru, both her parents were stripped of their status as Center Leaders and temporarily kicked out of the Center. She was then flown to New York as a reward.

Ketan noticed that the collar on his white button-down

shirt had flopped down, and he flipped it up so its pointed tips extended like antennae.

"Wouldn't it be great to catch Mom or Dad doing something bad?" he said. "You live with them," he remarked, as if to rub it in. "Have you spotted anything fishy? Any rule breaking?" His white-blond lashes blinked quickly over his blue eyes.

"You're stupid," I said. "It's Mom and Dad. They don't break any rules. They're just annoying," I said.

But Ketan was right. If Pallavi's meteoric rise resulted from reporting on her father, I hoped I, too, could find out something about my parents to report. I instantly rewound the last few days to see if anything out of the ordinary had occurred, but I couldn't think of anything. My parents were hardly my main focus. I had my own concerns.

"Ready to be jealous?" Ketan asked. "Guru just made me an official guard. Eat your heart out," he said, and turned to leave before I could respond. "Hey, don't forget to watch Mom and Dad. And if you find anything, tell me right away. I'm a guard. I'll do the reporting," he said, walking upstairs.

As a fifteen-year-old, what was clear to me was that reporting on my parents was not only the spiritually correct thing to do but also held the promise of immediate payback in the form of attention from Guru. Ever since Guru's scolding over the Colin McLevy fiasco, I understood that my position as Guru's number one was no longer guaranteed, and I sought ways to please Guru and steal his pride and approval. If it meant turning in my parents, so be it.

At the time that I pondered my parents' imagined reportable crimes, unknown to me until twenty years later, my mother drove three towns away to avoid bumping into any Connecticut disciples as she nervously bought a pregnancy test. It had been years since she had been pregnant with me, and the signs and symptoms she had experienced then seemed to have occurred to an entirely different person—but she needed to be sure. She was two months late, and the simplistic plus or minus sign was now only seconds away. The distance from the bathroom floor where she sat to the sink where the results awaited seemed an impossible journey.

When I got home from school, I found my mother pacing the kitchen, opening cupboards to stare inside as if looking for something, then quickly closing them. When she reached one end of the kitchen, she crossed over to the other side and worked her way through the cupboards above and below the sink. By her third lap, I looked up with an exaggerated display of irritation. I was attempting to compose my list of "expressions" for Guru. She seemed oblivious to the utter importance of my labors, even though I'd made it very obvious by setting up my office in the kitchen with notecards, pencils, highlighters, and books straddled open with paper clips across the kitchen table.

"Would you cut it out?" I shouted, then crunched my teeth into a perfectly sharpened number two pencil.

Just last Wednesday, when Sajani announced to me that I was officially accepted as part of the select group who submitted "expressions" to Guru, I took this as a significant step toward reaffirming Guru's confidence in me. Under Sajani's management, each week a core group was blessed with the unique opportunity to aid Guru in his hyperprolific outpouring of poetry by submitting phrases and images that would inspire his verse. After completing his *Ten Thousand Flower-Flames,* a series of aphorisms totaling ten thousand, Guru didn't waste any time. How to top ten thousand? Twenty-seven-thousand, of course. In accordance with his philosophy of self-transcendence, which I translated as "more is better," Guru quickly launched his next project, *Twenty-Seven Thousand Aspiration-Plants.* In order to generate this high volume of poetic output, Guru bestowed upon a chosen few the blessing of aiding him. Often at meditations, even during singing, I'd see disciples hunched over books on topics from self-help to seventeenth-century French literature, scanning for metaphors or lines to lift up and off the page to be divinely transformed by Guru. The few disciples selected for this task were the same ones who edited the final manuscripts before they were sent to Guru's own printing press for publication. Though Guru openly disapproved of intellectuals and academic pursuits, this group was as close to a sanctioned band of academic elite as there was in the Center, and I had wanted entry in the worst way. Now that I was inside Guru's poetic team, I needed to prove myself by compiling expressions that would not only generate aspiration-plant poems but would give Guru another concrete reason to retain his love for me. The very next day, I cut all classes and remained in the school library scouring the shelves for books that were ripe for metaphor plucking.

All I needed was a sanctuary where the urgency of my work would not be disturbed.

My mother opened the refrigerator door and leaned inside. It buzzed.

"God! Can't you see the importance of what I'm doing here! Guru's waiting right now for my expressions. I'm on deadline," I yelled to her half-disappeared form. "So get out. NOW." I flipped a page as forcefully as possible.

Slowly, she stepped back from the refrigerator door and stared at me. For a few seconds she held her pose, then parted her lips ever so slightly as if she were about to whisper a secret.

"What's with you?" I huffed.

There was nothing to say; there was nothing she could say—frank discussions were not permitted in the Center or in our family. We plodded along separately, isolated by our devotion to Guru. Doubts, fears, and shortcomings were to be reported directly to Guru for immediate disciplinary action.

As if suddenly woken up, my mother looked at me, closed her lips, and left the room.

"What's Mom's problem?" I asked my father later when he crossed through the kitchen.

"Isn't she home?" My father, as usual, answered a question with a tangentially related question.

"Sort of," I said, rolling my eyes, while dragging a fat yellow highlighter across my two latest proud and glorious expressions: *glittering wings of gleeful glee* and *sipping slowly from serenity's saucer.*

My mother went into her room and closed the door. She had to write to Guru. Years ago, when the unexpected surprise of my entry into the family occurred, she and my father, newlyweds politely adjusting to life in a relationship neither one had sought or desired, together had informed Guru in our living room. Though Guru had expressed initial frustration because he had already enacted a policy of no sex and no kids, they had talked it through with Guru late into the night in a way that suggested that, as their personal guru, he was the compassionate father who, no matter what the children did wrong, in the end could not help but lovingly and patiently accept and aid them. The result was, of course, me. And so, as my mother wrote to Guru that another baby was on its way, part of her dared to imagine that again, Guru would transform her error into his own miracle.

Unlike the last time, my mother did not mention the pregnancy to my father. She felt that even if he knew, he would not have cared. Although he may have had to answer to Guru about breaking the celibacy rule, with all of his legal work for Guru and the Center, my father had stored up vast amounts of spiritual credit, and often Guru decided the punishment for major and minor offenses based on a disciple's service, power, and influence. It seemed the more active a close disciple was in serving Guru, the more leeway was given when Guru's rules were broken. Of course, Guru had the final say as to whether the disciple's error would be overlooked or not, which always gave Guru the final upper hand. Still, my mother believed this matter, or any matter concerning her, was out of my father's realm of concern. My father knew shortly after their "divine marriage" ceremony was that they had nothing in common besides Guru, and he had settled into an irrevocable and unhappily accepted state of cohabitation. While my mother clutched on to motherhood as a way of fulfilling the gap of not having a real marriage, for my father, if the matter at hand didn't have to do with real estate development, tennis, or Guru, he wasn't interested. Besides, like everything else with our family, my father knew Guru made all the decisions and had the final word. Period.

"Let's go!" I banged on her door. It was already six-thirty, and if we were to make it to Queens by Guru's new strict cut-off door policy of seven-thirty, we had to leave now or face being turned away by the guards who smugly blocked all late entry.

A plain white envelope clutched in my mother's hand, we barreled off to Queens to meet our Master—all four of us, in my secretly expanding family. Since Guru's mission continued to boom, we had permanently outgrown the Bayside church. The new headquarters was a large second-floor rental space above a tire store and auto-repair shop on the corner of Hillside Avenue, a main thoroughfare crowded with used-car dealerships and fast-food restaurants near the Van Wyck Expressway. "Progress-Promise," as Guru named it, housed our functions. With a large area up front for seating on the cold linoleum floor, and homemade benches that increased in height toward the back, the venue held a few hundred disciples. Guru had a private entrance with a staircase leading into his own chambers.

My mother was assigned by Guru to be the official caretaker of Progress-Promise. Maybe Guru thought that since she had prior experience from looking after the Connecticut Center, she was the most qualified for the job, or maybe it was because no one else really wanted it; in any case, my Greenwich mother was now an official janitor. With cheerful determination, my mother shopped for giant supplies of bleach, ammonia, lemon-scented suds, mops and brooms, spending most weekends and evenings following the meditations scouring the sacred floors, while I mopped behind her. Picking up the remnants of Dunkin' Donuts prasad left on the benches and in the bathrooms of disciples too full of bliss to walk past a garbage can was not my idea of fun. My mother had the diligent, hardworking, sacrificial personality that kept her going interminably with little or no recognition for her efforts, but I didn't have that at all. Even when I did the slightest task, like moving all the cardigans and windbreakers left in the coat area into a box of lost-and-found, I sought appreciation, in particular from Guru; I wanted him to know how hard I was working for him.

The one perk my mother had from her janitorial job was that she got to tidy Guru's separate staircase and private rooms. This was the only part that I found interesting, having access to the zone where no one, unless summoned, could go. I'd offer to help her dust Guru's room, or even vacuum, while carefully scanning for any special gifts or objects. While my mother scrubbed his bathroom toilet and shower on her knees with a special cleaning product and brushes used only for Guru's area, I'd poke around in his large Guru-blue sitting room, enjoying my special access.

To ensure utter privacy, her urgent appeal could not join the rest of the disciples' written correspondence dropped inside Guru's letter box by his throne. Before each meditation, disciples tried to nonchalantly place in the container their communications to Guru about their lives, from critical health problems to reporting on a fellow disciple seen outside a movie theater. My mother knew that the box, gathered at the end of each evening by either Isha or Prema, depending on who got there first—yet another challenge in their ongoing battle for top status—was often left carelessly upon the porch at Guru's house where the piles of letters accumulated. On days when Guru felt uninspired to read the letters himself, he chose one of the women to read the private letters aloud to him.

This needed an immediate answer, and my mother was not going to risk the chance of anyone else serving as translator or intermediary. After pacing through his private sitting room, she decided it was still too public, and she propped the envelope in his bathroom, right beside the sink.

The meditation that night was long, with Guru teaching a few new songs and selling another volume of *Twenty-Seven Thousand Aspiration-Plants*. I handed Sajani my expressions that I had encased inside a Guru-blue folder decorated with glittery stars, spelling out my name across the front. All night, while I squirmed in anticipation of how my expressions would be received, my mother sat beside me waiting for Guru to go to his bathroom.

Near the end of the night, Guru left the stage and went into his room. When he returned, he proceeded to sell a photograph of himself cuddling his beloved dogs, Sona and Kanu, on his lap, for ten dollars. Prema and Isha strode to their money-collecting positions: Isha to the men's side and Prema to the women's side. Normally, when Guru sold anything, my mother insisted that either Ketan or I, or both of us, reap the blessings of having the opportunity to stand before Guru to purchase the sacred object.

That night my mother never took her eyes off Guru. Her face was drained of color, and her forehead was slick with sweat. She pulled ten dollars from her purse and cut in line. When it was her turn to stand before Guru, her critical moment, Guru dispensed the picture while leaning over to grab a handful of cashews. She paused for his counsel, or even a brief sign, but the woman who was behind her and wasn't about to wait, sidestepped my mother and extended her folded hands to receive her photo. When my mother returned to her seat beside me, she was shaking.

"Are you sick?" I asked, looking at her for the first time all day.

She didn't answer.

When Guru's picture sold out, it was time for him to leave. As he slowly stood and slipped his white-socked feet inside his sandals, my mother leapt and darted toward the back. I thought she was going to throw up.

She shot straight into Guru's bathroom. The letter was out of the envelope and littered across the sink. Not knowing if he would again return to his room, she waited for him in the shadowed hallway where his room and his private side staircase merged.

He whistled as he approached.

My mother didn't wait for him to acknowledge her.

"Oh, Guru!" my mother whispered in desperate panic. "What should I do?"

In four words she condensed all of the hope, shame, faith, and wonderment of her six-page letter. He was our avatar, the direct representative of our insignificant selves to the infinite pantheon of divinity. He was both father and God, the sustenance of our lives. My mother folded her hands tightly against her heart, the heart that held her full commitment to Guru, while sharing it with her family, that impossible balancing act that never lay equal. In Guru's world, my mother's love for her family was a weakness, an attachment, binding and dangerous. She knew this, and readily accepted the fact that this weakness reduced her in the eyes of all of those whom she loved: Guru, my father, my brother, and me.

Guru didn't stop walking. He never even broke his stride or slowed his pace.

Without a brief pause or bothering to look in her direction, he flatly stated, "Do the abortion," as he descended the stairs.

5

Miracles of Faith

"DIANA ROSS ALWAYS BLOCKS THE ENTIRE PARKING LOT," Claire Milani said. "That's so fucked up."

Idling in her white, convertible Rolls-Royce, Diana Ross, wearing oversized white sunglasses, her loose hair a bushel of glamorous curls, waited to pick up her daughter from school.

"She just wants attention," Claire said. "Oh, that's my ride. Later."

With a swish of her blond, shiny hair, a chauffeur opened the back door of a black Jaguar and whisked her away.

Heiress to a multimillion-dollar luxury shoe empire, Claire was considered an ordinary student at Greenwich Academy, an all-girls' college preparatory day school founded in 1827. With a serene, rolling campus, complete with a mansion serving as the official welcome parlor, Greenwich Academy was the prime choice of society's debutante elite and the daughters of world leaders, national politicians, Hollywood celebrities, and New England's aristocratic families. It was also the prime choice of Guru for keeping his Chosen One boy free.

Guru mandated that I transfer to the all-girls' prep school

not long after Dom Cappeli, a fellow sophomore who lived two streets away, rang my doorbell, asking to hang out. He was greeted by my father, who slowly and carefully explained that I was not allowed to talk to any boys because of our spiritual vows. I was once again in trouble. I had a hunch that if my mother had answered the door, she would have invited Dom inside. I had noticed that my mother, who had always publicly stood behind the rest of the family whom she selflessly served, had become strangely quiet and reserved about Guru and the Center. Though she never once made any comment or hint about a lessening of her drive toward Guru's latest commands and programs, I silently suspected she had faded, removing herself from the constant race toward Guru's favor, but I never dared to ask, and she never risked revealing anything. As long as my father, whom Guru acknowledged as the head of our family, was unswerving in his devotion to Guru, she remained quiet, concealing her own concerns and doubts about the Center.

As I kneeled before Guru awaiting my punishment, Guru quizzed Harish on the number of cities already committed to declaring his birthday, August 27, Sri Chinmoy Day. In honor of his age, Guru wanted fifty-five. Not one less. As Harish frantically flipped through scribbled papers to offer a total count, Guru simultaneously inquired after cities he considered especially worthy. It was clear that Guru had an abundance of projects much more important than me. Besides, I was now a repeat offender. When Guru finally finished with Harish and he remembered I was next to him, he was rushed and preoccupied. He succinctly stated I was no longer trusted to be in the same institution as boys. Then he motioned for the next person waiting in line to approach.

My parents swiftly carried out Guru's order, scrounging enough money to cover tuition at the all-girls' school Greenwich Academy, my own private nunnery. I had been ushered through into a new closed society, another group. As I was fitted for the school's uniform—a kilt in a hunter-green tartan with a solid color blouse—I sighed in resignation. This wouldn't be all that different. Every night at meditation, the sari was my uniform, and the girls were separate from the boys, so this felt vaguely familiar, only with kilts.

When the school year began, I discovered that I had nothing in common with my classmates. Eventually, tired of being silent and alone, I extracted select parts of my life to share with them. Since turning fourteen, I was allowed to journey with Guru on international concert and lecture tours, and also on the annual Christmas trip, which, in a continued effort to keep Alo Devi out of Guru's way by having her spend months planning and preparing the travel arrangements half a world away from Queens, had become expanded journeys to exotic lands. When the Greenwich Academy girls spoke of holidays in the Hamptons or yachting trips to Monte Carlo, I casually mentioned having taken jungle treks in Sri Lanka or camel rides in Egypt. With Guru, I had been to every continent except Antarctica, and though we stayed in hotels that didn't qualify as anything other than perhaps two stars, tops, and during most of our visits Guru sat in the hotel meeting room teaching songs, exercising with weights, and getting massaged, my new classmates didn't need to know all of that.

I also kept pace by name-dropping. As my classmates gossiped that they had spotted Martina Navratilova on the ski slopes in Aspen, I would yawn, mentioning how little sleep I had had since I was hanging out with Carl Lewis until early in the morning. I just didn't specify that the eight-time gold medal–winning Olympian Carl Lewis had become a disciple and that besides standing alongside twenty other disciples serenading him with the songs Guru wrote in his honor, I rarely spoke to Carl directly. Carl Lewis was first introduced to Guru by Narada Michael Walden, an old-time Connecticut Center disciple who had left the Center to go out to California and eventually struck celebrity as a record producer for such artists as Whitney Houston and Aretha Franklin and then returned to the Center as a big shot. Carl became a regular, receiving his spiritual name, Sudhahota, and even bringing his mom, sister, and coach. But Carl Lewis was by no means the only celebrity Guru hosted. Since Guru's success with the United Nations Secretary-General U Thant, a major portion of Guru's energies went to successfully procuring a steady influx of high-profile people from all walks of life. Casually mentioning to my classmates my weekend visit to Leonard Bernstein's Manhattan apartment was never a lie, nor was dining with Muhammad Ali or hosting New York City mayor Ed Koch. Though I was not part of Guru's official Manifestation Committee—a group charged with promoting Guru's mission around the world and bringing celebrities to meet with Guru—Ketan was. Ketan loved it; he was schmoozing with celebrities while scoring spiritual benefits. He was thrilled, and so was Guru.

A photograph and a zealous quote from a public figure opened doors, not only to other public figures but to media interests. The Manifestation Committee produced an array of glossy public relations materials that chronicled Guru's encounters with famous people from all walks of life. From

Pablo Casals to Pia Zadora, for celebrities a meeting with "the Sri" was a dollop new age and a dash exotic, a curious encounter that, if nothing else, could produce a zany anecdote. Guru, well taught from his early ashram days as Nolini's apprentice, understood that accolades produced the most favorable results. The celebrities never suspected that their invitations to meet with Guru were for anything other than an occasion for Sri Chinmoy to honor them for all of their accomplishments and countless ways in which they contributed to humanity. To formalize all of this, Guru developed awards such as the Heart of Peace Award, and the weight-lifting invention of Lifting Up the World with a Oneness-Heart Award—a small medal on a rainbow ribbon to be placed around the neck of the world leader or pop star after he or she had climbed up a rickety ladder to stand on a platform, clutching at a thin metal pole as Guru stood beneath the platform where a U-shaped cradle supported a bar that he heaved up, which raised the rocky platform and then dropped it down quickly. Congratulations! Guru leaned close to the guest while the cameras flashed. A song composed in the person's honor was sung and the adoring throngs in the rows of benches cheered. The celebrity left with gifts, flowers, medals, feeling daring, bold, and brave while mystically moved by the holy man in the tight undershirt and thin nylon short-shorts.

While I name-dropped with my classmates, I eyed with suspicion the parade of movie stars, politicians, and dignitaries that arrived at meditations. For the celebrities' one-hour pit stop to Guru's world, they blitzed in like tourists who had never read a guidebook, let alone a single article on their destination, and just commanded a driver to drop them off long enough to say they'd been there, before moving on. It didn't seem fair that they received such lavish praise and attention from Guru without having to put in any of the grunt work. Unlike the core disciples, these "honored guests" weren't required to endure the true hardships of disciple life, such as weekly weigh-ins where being a single pound above Guru's assigned body weight meant suspension or not converting enough new disciples to fulfill Guru's target number of aspiring souls meant expulsion. I suspected that the celebrities didn't know about any of that.

The more attention I paid to the workings of the disciples who labored over importing celebrities to Guru, the more I saw firsthand that the background information they were giving about Guru included little more than a brochure of posed pictures of Guru at the United Nations and snapshots of Guru meeting other celebrities. All of the specifics about disciplehood and the real workings of the Center were eliminated from their promotional materials. From what they saw, Guru's Center looked like an exclusive new age VIP club. As long as celebrities saw that other celebrities had been to Guru Land, they figured it was a safe place to visit.

When the one person I did care about, the legendary German tennis player Steffi Graf, came to meet Guru at his private tennis court, I was nervous with excitement. Because Guru had been interested in tennis, my father had picked up the game that he had once played back in high school, and soon taught me. Smacking a ball as hard as I could was strangely therapeutic, and tennis soon became my favorite sport. Guru's enthusiasm for tennis led to the disciples' buying a few acres of land in Queens that became his own private tennis court and the new ashram where all the meditations were held. When Guru put out the order to "bring big-name tennis players," disciples began staking out the players' entrance at the U.S. Open in Flushing Meadows, offering invites to Guru's court. Soon some of the greats of the game—Mats Wilander, Monica Seles, Gabriela Sabatini—were Guru's latest guests. When I learned that Steffi Graf was coming, fresh after yet another one of her many Grand Slam victories, I counted down the days. Decked out in my favorite sari, I made myself readily visible to Guru prior to Steffi's arrival, certain he would give me a special task of sitting in the honored seats beside her or having me give her flowers upon her arrival, but it had no impact. Throughout the entire visit, I was crammed into the bleachers with the other insignificant masses. After Guru lifted Steffi overhead on his contraption, he invited her across the street to watch videos of his myriad accomplishments in the comfort of the disciple-owned Indian restaurant. Afraid of losing my chance to at least say hello, I darted over to Steffi, nearly tripping on my sari pleats to shake her hand and ask her to sign my lucky tennis ball. As I was one step away, I looked up at Isha, who knew nothing about tennis but was blabbing to Steffi about Guru's athletic prowess, and she gave me the indignant look reserved for a vagrant trying to squeegee windows at a stoplight with an old newspaper. She shook her head with an emphatic no, signaling me to back off. My cheeks turned the same color as my fuchsia sari, and when Steffi turned to see what Isha was doing, I hid my lucky ball beneath my sari. Not knowing what to say or do, I bolted down the gravel driveway to hide.

I knew my relationship with Guru and, by association, with his inner pack, was strained after my exile from coeducation landed me in Greenwich Academy. Guru's attentions or lack thereof were scrupulously monitored and measured by both regulars to Guru's house and those waiting to get on the invite list. Though I was still invited to Guru's house, my extra helpings of attention had been visibly absent. This made me edgy. As the Chosen One, I felt I was still owed all of the perks that I once had, without question. But I was less and less inspired to put in the effort to pursue them. More and more, it was not only a challenge but an increasing burden to dazzlingly live up to my reputation, and my new school didn't seem to help.

"Five more hours," Ramona Edwards said, lacing up her sneakers for the field hockey game. "And I'm gonna get so fuckin' wasted."

Minutes after Monday morning's swapped tales of who passed out where and who puked how many times over the weekend, the official countdown launched toward Friday night's binge. By Friday afternoon's round of field hockey games, madrigal practice, and modern-dance club, the countdown was in its last throes, and my classmates quivered with anticipation. The details spread rapidly for the weekend festivities—whose parents were abroad was the only key piece of information; everything else fell into place.

"Sounds great," I said, watching Ramona apply lip gloss before cramming her plastic mouth guard into her mouth.

Far from getting wasted, my weekend was slated for more mornings that stretched into afternoons that blurred into evenings stuck to the benches of the tennis court as Guru heaved weights and fiddled with new weight-lifting contraptions.

"You going to be around this weekend? Party's gonna be at the Whitmans'," Ramona said, grabbing the keys to her new convertible BMW, a gift for turning sweet sixteen.

I wished I could have gone to the party, but there was no chance. Every weekend, like every evening, was spent in Queens with Guru. Since Guru had directed my father to buy a house two blocks away from Guru's own in Queens, it was now my official, permanent home away from home.

"No, I've got that event—party—to go to," I said, trying to be cool. "Remember, I told you how I was hanging out with Steffi Graf last weekend? Well, you know Clarence Clemons? He plays saxophone in Bruce Springsteen's E Street Band? I'm going to be hanging out with him."

"That's so sick! I hate you!" Ramona shrieked. "Have a drink for me and tell him to tell Bruce I'm available anytime!" She winked and ran out of the junior lounge. I waited until everyone cleared out, then I walked down to the end of the gated entrance, outside the massive stone pillars, away from the chatty patrol of the other kilted girls and their glamorous moms who clumped together forming tennis dates. Since Guru refused to let me drive, I waited, far from anyone, for the unmistakable sound of my father's car chugging up the windy hill, sputtering and backfiring, clotting the air with burning smoke. I thought about Clarence Clemons and his upcoming visit to the tennis court and the ten songs written about him that I still had to learn. Clarence Clemons had become another disciple. Sort of. A "disciple," when it applied to celebrities, meant that they dropped in for a meditation a few times a year and received a spiritual name and tons of attention, cakes, songs, presents, awards, and photos. I was positive that Clemons, like Roberta Flack and others who came as new disciples, would not be told on for talking to a member of the opposite sex or listening to rock music on the radio. I, on the other hand, had just been scolded for having cut my Guru-mandated long hair to give myself some wispy bangs, and even though I securely bobby-pinned them off my face during meditations, my delinquency had not gone unnoticed with yet another message expressing disappointment from Guru.

"Drive," I commanded my father, urging a quick getaway, after heaving the dented door shut with both hands.

"Good day?" my father asked.

"Yeah right," I said, smearing sarcasm.

Lately, my mother and father were like two massive canker sores; even thinking about them made me irritable and edgy. I blamed them for my current status both at Greenwich Academy and in the Center.

"It stinks in here." I winced, covering my nose with my left hand from the collection of my father's stinky stained Sri Chinmoy T-shirts in the backseat.

"These stupid windows don't even open." I sighed with deep exasperation.

My father's explanation of having been tarring the roof of a new condominium project just made me more irritated. Other Greenwich Academy girls' dads didn't walk around in ripped tar-stained sweatpants and T-shirts, nor did they transport used roof shingles in their car in one of many regular runs to the dump. Though some of my classmates had parents in building development, it meant that they just owned or traded real estate. My father bought funky parcels of land, mostly with dilapidated houses, which he then sold or traded for yet another odd-shaped lot of land. It seemed he was always engrossed in at least two real estate projects, but nothing happened at our house nor did we ever see any profits roll back to us.

My mother and my father, I decided, were determined to be a constant source of humiliation for me. My mother seemed to be always poking around in my business, and since Guru had stopped talking to her, I decided that she wasn't one to pay much attention to. My father no longer crisscrossed the East Coast giving meditation classes or working on manifestation for Guru. Spending the majority of his time on his own projects, my father, however, was still a front-row occupier at meditations and Guru's trusted lawyer, which meant that he maintained his reputation as one of Guru's most important and close disciples. At that time, his opinion held clout with Guru, and he was often invited to Guru's house even on nights when I wasn't.

I felt constantly edgy. I needed something to jolt me toward inspiration. I needed a miracle.

THE MIRACLE WAS awaiting me when I arrived at the tennis court the next morning. The court was being frantically decorated with crepe paper garlands, tissue paper ornaments, and masses of flowers. Guru had done it. A miracle. He had lifted seven thousand pounds with one arm. An enormous blown-up photograph of the moment graced the middle of the court, surrounded by hundreds of flickering white tea candles. In the photo, the steel bar that held the plates stacked like a massive roll of LifeSavers was supported on each end by a U-shaped cradle that hung slightly above the height of Guru's shoulder. The design was created so that when Guru pushed on the bar, it braced against the side of its cradle and slid up the side, then when Guru released the weight, it clanged back into its base. Photos captured all of Guru's previous lifts, and as the weights got heavier, the angles of the photos changed. To make the feats clearer to the public, Guru instructed the photographers to shoot from a low angle, to provide the most dramatic shot.

In the photo, wearing a white singlet and tight shorts, Guru grimaced as his right arm strained against the monstrous weight.

I was stunned. When had all this happened? How had I missed out on this?

The guards, busy tidying up, and the assembly line of volunteers who were packing special bags of prasad to honor the occasion, worked excitedly to finish before Guru's arrival.

"Thanks a lot," I grunted to my mom, as though she had simply forgotten to fill me in on the events.

"Honey, this is all a surprise to me. You know I wasn't invited to Guru's house last night. Only your father was," she said, taking a seat in one of the side benches.

Even a gift of sour candy with a note filled with animal stickers from Chahna didn't help my rotten mood. I merely nodded an acknowledgment of her offering when I spotted her waving to me from her seat at the back. I knew Chahna would never consider her lack of awareness of Guru's latest news as a concern or drawback, and that fact, in addition to everything else, was an irritant to me. Her detachment from her low status in the Center never failed to amaze me. While I valued Chahna's loyalty and undying friendship, parts of her character seemed beyond my understanding. Everyone in the Center cared about status. What was the matter with her? I decided it must be a flaw, a lack of spiritual drive.

When the "good singers" were summoned to practice a congratulatory song for Guru when he walked through the gates, I joined them, pretending that I had known about the lift and even hinting that I had been present at the event.

Isha's car crunched up the gravel driveway and when the gate opened, Guru entered to our song. He folded his hands together and walked over to the gigantic picture and meditated before it as the photographers scrambled for a prime shot. Guru's throne was brought into the middle of the court, near the photo, where he then invited the disciples who had been at his house the previous night to share some of their experiences of the lift. One by one, weepy disciples stood before the microphone, gushing their gratitude at Guru's transcendent one-arm miracle lift. But my father remained silent.

I had known that my father was invited to Guru's house after the meditation, and by the time I went to bed, he hadn't returned. That morning, when I woke up, he was still out for his traditional long weekend run, so my mother and I left without him. I was jealous that he had witnessed the miracle firsthand while I had been asleep only blocks away. It was so unfair.

Guru then announced he was selling copies of the picture. Disciples raced down to line up with handfuls of cash to purchase the sacred relic. I nudged my mother to hand over the money and cut in line. When I stood before Guru, he held the photo with both hands and concentrated on me before stretching out to release the photo. I folded my hands tightly together, pressed upon my chest, and stared at Guru's golden face. Across his third eye, the morning sun dazzled its reflection, until his entire face was drenched in light. The arrangements of congratulatory flowers garnished the air with perfume, while the heat from the candle flames quivered low. The second I stood barefoot before Guru, I felt overwhelmed

by his humbling and beautiful presence. The waves of energy
that surrounded him enveloped me completely, erasing all
thoughts. This was what I loved about Guru. Being in his
presence created a tangible change in me; it made me holy,
better.

"My Jayanti," Guru said. "You see what your guru can do?
Through the Supreme's infinite compassion, anything can
be done."

He reached to his side table and gently lifted a pen to the
picture. Across the span of his white singlet, over his own
heart chakra, he wrote "Jayanti," and drew a series of curly, in-
terconnected birds that formed a tight protective circle around
my name. When he finished he tapped his finger against my
scripted name etched onto his heart.

"Jayanti, divine. My infinite love and infinite pride, my
own Jayanti," Guru said, extending the photograph to me.

I reached for it with both hands, gazing into Guru's vener-
able face. I never tired of looking at him. Guru's face had
been my focal point for my entire life, and it still offered an
endless series of surprises. When he joked, deliberated, or
scolded, his expressions were unrestrained, natural. Depending on the sun's position, Guru's skin shifted from shades of
saffron to amber to gold. I studied his eyes, watching them
silently broadcast blessings.

Flanked by his staging of flowers and incense, I longed to
sit on the ground before Guru's throne and never leave. With
a sweep of ancient devotion, all my outer strife and worries
seemed to utterly wash away. Rid of desires for wild freedoms, suddenly I wanted to spend my life inside his trance,
drinking in his light, his consciousness. The way he made me

feel when I stood near him, fixated on his presence, was a sense of completion—I was aligned, whole, and safe.

Mesmerized, I didn't put the photo down and carried it with both hands like it was a sacred tablet for the entire function. Seven thousand pounds was beyond a human or even superhuman feat. I felt awed, humbled, and instantly renewed. Guru's lion roar of determination and his arm raised in triumph over the mountains of dead ignorant matter realigned my skewed life and reaffirmed the real reason for my existence. It dwarfed all the absurd babble that was the everyday. Greenwich Academy's self-importance shrank to crumbs to be brushed away. Binge drinking and Polo shirts, debutante balls and make-out sessions—who cared? With my name emblazoned on the photo, Guru made me part of his miracle. I was practically an eyewitness. How many of the billions on earth could make such a claim? Who wouldn't want to be in on one of the greatest miracles, the parting of the Red Sea or the raising of Lazarus from the dead? And this was better, by far. Unlike those miracles confirmed only by hearsay and vague tales, we had empirical proof. We had eyewitnesses, photographs, and a video.

"Dad," I shouted, running to catch up with him after the function ended.

He continued walking.

"Dad!"

Still no reply.

"DAADDD!" I got beside him, panting, still displaying my photograph. "You need to tell me totally everything that you saw."

I waited for his story, rich and full of detail, the inside

scoop, the backstory for the miracle. I wanted nothing left out.

My father, never one to display a crack of emotion, didn't slow his pace.

"You'll have to see for yourself," my father finally said to me.

THOUGH I WAS renewed by Guru's weight-lifting miracle, I now found both of my parents to be mysteriously distant; my father dropped out of all manifestation committees and removed himself from most extracurricular Center activities. My mother continued propping me close to Guru, as she too drifted further away.

Although the Center was rapidly growing, especially in eastern Europe, where the end of the cold war brought hordes of seekers eager to experience new religions, the core of older disciples was in flux. In particular, many of the other disciple children, as they grew up, became less involved. When they did turn up at a meditation and Guru called the children to the stage, I noticed the girls wore eyeliner and the boys' hair was too long for acceptable disciple standards. Eventually all but a handful of the original members dropped away, and they were soon replaced by a whole new crop of kids, guided by eager parents who had recently joined Guru's path. I didn't pay much attention to the new disciples, nor did I really miss the ones who had left. For me, as long as Chahna was still a disciple, I was happy. Fiercely protective of her, I wanted to keep close guard on Chahna in order to protect her from committing some of my own mistakes.

⌇

TRUDGING THROUGH public school in Bayonne, New Jersey, Chahna now braced for high school with dread.

"You're lucky," Chahna said, tearing the skin off her prasad orange as we sat on the front stoop of the Queens house. "You're basically done with school forever."

With my high school graduation two weeks away, I was almost officially school free and apprehensive of what was next. Secretly I longed to be college bound like the rest of my class, but I knew Guru would never allow that. Any attempt to sway my parents away from Guru's decree would be hopeless; they always seemed to obey.

"I wish I were done," Chahna said.

"Yeah. Just be sure not to get caught up in any of the crazy college pressure," I said, adding a chipped giggle for believability. Not wanting to be a bad influence, I resisted telling Chahna how much I wanted to go to college.

"I'd never want to go to college," Chahna said earnestly. "I asked Guru if I could stay in Queens this summer to work in the health food store. I can't wait."

I had been dreading that Guru would assign me to work there for the summer and, even worse, as a full-time job when I graduated. With its lack of customers and spare shelves, the store was depressing.

Chahna's excitement over working at the disciple-owned health food store silenced me. I suddenly realized that instead of being the good big spiritual sister, I was actually the bad influence. Without receiving any outer attention from Guru, Chahna was fiercely devoted to him. On many occasions,

I overheard her begging her parents to bring her to meditations when her parents had just popped a mound of popcorn to settle in for a *Star Trek* marathon on TV. Chahna knew where she wanted to be, and she was diligent in her spiritual practice. Although I was careful to keep my past disobediences with boys private, once I had asked Chahna if she had ever liked any boys. When she responded simply, "What for?" I knew then my Chahna was spiritually pure and wholly committed. I didn't have anything to worry about for her, but I wasn't so sure about myself.

What would happen when I graduated from Greenwich Academy in two weeks was uncertain, to me at least. My classmates had their futures all figured out; the reason their families had selected the prestigious prep school was for its near guarantee of Ivy League acceptance. Most of my classmates had had private SAT tutors and essay coaches since freshman year, polishing and retooling their college applications. The rest was a waiting game with college visits and phone calls from their alumni parents to other high-powered alumni. All students had mandatory sessions with the college counselor, Mr. Holland, a red-haired man who always wore silk stripe ties and moccasin loafers.

My visits to Mr. Holland, where the colorful banners of the Ivy Leagues decorated his office like coats of arms, clearly left him baffled.

No, I hadn't thought about what my top choice colleges were. No, I hadn't visited any campuses. No, my parents didn't have a preference.

He stared at me like I was a severely disabled child who up until now had been forced to live this way because my

parents had not bothered to investigate a simple corrective
procedure.

"You do realize that this is the most important decision
you will ever make, don't you?" Mr. Holland asked, speaking
extra slowly, folding and unfolding his tortoiseshell glasses.

On his round table lay glossy brochures with blond pony-
tailed young women clutching books and striding beside a
blazered professor with a goatee, his hands in a wide gesture.
Around them students sat in multicultural clusters beneath
autumn trees, engaged in animated discussions. A neogothic
clock tower loomed in the background. The idyllic scene hyp-
notized me. I wanted to be there more than ever.

"You are taking this college process seriously, Ms. Tamm,
aren't you?" Mr. Holland's glasses clicked faster.

He slowly put his glasses back on, signaling serious
business.

"You give me no choice. I'm going to have to write a letter
to the Tamms, informing them of your lackadaisical attitude
about the college process. If this letter does not return to me,
with their signature, then I will be forced to invite Mr. Tamm
in for a conference to discuss this matter. You wouldn't want
me to have to bother Mr. Tamm from his busy schedule to
come in, would you?" Mr. Holland asked.

I wanted to explain how much I longed to go to college,
that I was not allowed, but I couldn't. It was too strangely
complicated. He would never understand.

Guru did not approve of college for his disciples. Never
having graduated high school, Guru made a clear distinc-
tion in his philosophy between the mind and the heart. The
mind was the source of doubt, of stubborn questioning and

intellectualism, whereas the heart was the apex of faith, of unconditional surrender. In Guru's aphorisms, he praised the childlike heart and chastised the obstinate mind. Repeatedly, in both formal lectures and front-porch chatter, Guru blasted institutions of higher learning. College, Guru felt, was a deterrent to the spiritual life. Fostering the mind was negating the heart. Unlike years ago when Guru had urged my father to pursue law school, the rules had changed. Now, disciples who joined the Center while attending college were quickly persuaded to drop their outer studies, if they were serious about pursuing their inner studies. Disciples who shunned college proudly felt superior to the unfortunate disciples who, in their dark pasts, had obtained degrees.

The remote vision of myself as a normal student inhabiting the world of the glossy autumnal college brochure, living in a dorm surrounded by friends and activities not focused on manifesting the Supreme, seemed magical. Never having given much thought to what I wanted to be when I grew up because I knew it was not going to be my decision, college, in my fantasy, had less to do with career goals than with the luxurious freedoms of a life away.

Since my father had an advanced degree, I thought he might understand the necessity of college for me and would argue this point to Guru, but he didn't seem concerned. Whenever I brought up college fairs or application dates, he remained quiet, sifting through stacks of tax forms.

"Write to Guru," my mother said, still her answer for everything, when I hinted at my desire to attend. She knew very well that decisions were not hers to make.

My official answer to the question of college came in a phone message from Romesh, Guru's official message carrier.

The owner of a vegetarian restaurant, Romesh was a heavy-set, balding man known for his overabundance of energy who bounced from foot to foot while talking in a big, yelpy voice.

"Guru said that your soul does not want you to go to college. When you graduate from school, Guru will confer with the Supreme as to what he wants you to do." Romesh panted with excitement.

I held the phone far from my ear, waiting for Romesh to finish the message I had expected. When I told my mother she seemed to have pinned a smile to her face. My father nodded in agreement as he laced up his tennis shoes for a quick match.

To avoid a spectacle, I had Mr. Holland send off transcripts to the college he felt would be the best fit for me, and kept my true plans to myself. As the year ended and the drama of receiving thin college letters versus thick envelopes nearly capsized the entire school, I mimicked my classmates' mood swings and debates about whether to live in an all-girls' dorm and whether or not to join a sorority the first year.

In my room, I stared at my framed photo of Guru triumphantly hoisting the seven thousand pounds. Why was I fretting? Guru was in control. He held me in his firm grasp, and, like the weight, I needed to surrender and allow myself to be moved, miraculously lifted by his grace. The day I received an acceptance letter from Bennington College, I didn't wait to show it to my parents. I took the wad of Bubble Yum I had in my mouth and pressed it between the folds.

6

Amore at the United Nations

"GURU WANTS TO SEE YOU NOW," PREMA SAID, POKING her head onto Guru's porch, where I sat waiting alone. "He's in the kitchen. In a pretty good mood," she added with a slight smile.

She knew what this was all about—the answer to my letter asking Guru what I should do with my life written on a piece of stationery with puffy clouds, rainbows, and a unicorn posed in the corner. I strained to return a smile. It was July. The rounds of congratulations that had followed the elaborate graduation from Greenwich Academy had quickly stopped. I had invited Guru to my graduations, but, of course, he did not go. When I invited Prema, she told me with a laugh that she hadn't attended her own graduation and wasn't about to go to one now. To be diplomatic, I invited Isha, and much to my surprise she accepted, turning up that day in a shiny homemade red and white satin dress. Where Isha went, so did her own assigned posse, who donned modest dresses that amply covered every part of their bodies like chadors. But my favorite invited guest, the one I was most happy to see, was Chahna, squinting in the June sun. She flung her arms around me in an oversized hug.

"I didn't realize I was coming to your wedding," Chahna's mother, Nitya, said to me.

True to tradition, all the seniors wore white formal gowns with white gloves and carried a bouquet of flowers down the aisle escorted by a flower girl while classical music tinkled in the background. It was, I realized, the closest I'd ever get to having a wedding.

With my family and few disciples garbed in what Guru considered "Western clothes"—not wearing saris and whites—which always made me think of cowboys wearing jeans, chaps, and boots, I felt like the ringleader of a group of impostors. From my elaborate white gown, bought after bargaining for hours from a raggedy Chinese factory on the Christmas trip in Singapore, to the listing of my name in the program with Bennington College as my choice for the fall, I couldn't have been more relieved to have the entire graduation and prep school experience over.

For a few weeks, I relished not having to get up for school or for anything. I split my time between Connecticut and Queens, hanging out at the tennis court with the group of disciples who turned up all day every day at the court, as though that was their full-time occupation. For Ketan and the rest of the tennis court guards, however, it was their official job, and Guru paid their salary. I was always welcomed, and Guru made a point to encourage me to play as much tennis as I wanted on his court. Tanned and fit, I floated along, letting whatever schedule Guru had serve as my only agenda.

"So what are you going to do with your life?" Mayar, one of the tennis court guards, suddenly asked me.

Out of all people, I was unnerved that Mayar, whose agenda consisted of whatever Guru ordered, from painting lines on the streets in the middle of the night to marking out a jogging course for Guru, to scouring shops across the tri-state area in search of the perfect samosa when Guru had a craving for a savory snack, he knew perfectly well that this was not a question that I could answer or even be allowed to answer.

I wanted to reply, *Be rich, successful, and happily married,* just to shock him, but I knew better than to joke like that. A comment of that nature could have wound up getting me reported to Guru.

The more I thought about my future, the more panicked I became. I looked around at the disciples who during the day ventured in and out of the tennis court. First there were the workers from the disciple-owned Indian restaurant. Notorious for hiring disciples, mostly from visiting centers, to slave for twenty dollars a week, they labored long hours, mopping floors and schlepping buckets of potatoes up and down from the basement to the slop sinks in boiling heat. They were allowed to duck into the court for prasad or a quick walking meditation, and I could always tell they were near because they smelled of reused frying oil. I shuddered at being told to join their ranks.

I observed the disciples who worked at the other "divine-enterprises," Guru's name for disciple-owned small businesses whose profits supported Guru. Because the owners of the stores were off doing other tasks for Guru, their employees ended up working from opening to closing and missing out on events, including Guru's many trips. Even when they had a rare day off, they were limited in their activities because as workers in divine-enterprises, they were paid only a few dollars a week, yet they were grateful. Without health care or a retirement fund, they happily worked in the stores, feeling fortunate to be sheltered in Guru's atmosphere rather than the outside world.

As far as the option of working directly at Guru's house, besides Prema and Isha, Apala and her handicapped brother, Mihir, were the only other full-timers. Over the years, as the menageries of the Madal Zoo had been dying out, Apala still cared for the tough surviving zoo inmates, while Mihir sat on the front porch in his wheelchair, dressed in *sanyassi* robes while sneakily listening to Howard Stern through his headphones. I didn't see any position open for me, and I was relieved.

When I had hinted to my parents that I was concerned about my future, they seemed aloof. My father told me I should start doing strength training, and my mother suggested that we make lunch.

"Jayanti, good girl." Guru sat in his kitchen on a white chair, his legs resting on a stool. A large plate of chickpea curry and a tall glass of red energy drink rested before him.

"You sit." Guru motioned to an empty chair beside his feet.

I had never been seated on a par with Guru in his own house. I was always on the floor while he was in a throne, chair, or couch.

"Your letter was most soulful," Guru said, spooning a heaping portion of chickpeas into his mouth.

I waited while Guru chewed.

"Your outer schooling is finished, finished. But your inner schooling is to continue, always continue. That is the real school. The only school. You are so obedient to me. Others have gone on to college and, oi, their inner lives destroyed. Such poison. Such mental poison."

I nodded, agreeing with Guru, agreeing how bad others were for going to college. I loved it when he confided to me his displeasure at the disciples. The more he complained about their undivine behavior, the more secure I felt. I sat up straighter, feeling suddenly confident with my position.

"I have meditated on your soul, good girl." Guru gathered up another mouthful of food and chewed with his mouth open.

I waited, paused for my set of directions, my life's instructions, as Guru munched. Then he drank. And ate some more. He spilled, a curry stain splattered onto his white tennis shirt, but he remained oblivious.

"To please the Supreme, the absolute Beloved and your own soul, you will work at the United Nations. So many of my disciples, like Gitali and Hemal, work there in order to serve me."

Guru's phone rang. Suddenly our heart-to-heart, the conference about my life's direction, was over. Guru was on to other tasks.

As Guru reached for the phone, he added that he had already instructed Hamsa to work on getting me into the UN. Then he lifted his hand to dismiss me and took his call.

When Hamsa tapped me on the shoulder that night at the function, handing me a manila folder with United Nations application forms, I wondered how much longer Hamsa had known about my future than I had. Having toiled her way up through the ranks of the UN, Hamsa now worked as a professional in human resources, which made her even more useful to Guru as he instructed flocks of disciples to become full-time UN employees.

"So how fast do you type? How fluent are you in dictation?" Hamsa asked, fixing the plastic comb straining to hold back her frizzy gray hair from overtaking her face.

When I explained that I couldn't do either, without dropping her smile Hamsa said the first step would be typing school.

Sitting at a cubicle with large padded headphones, typing letter patterns at a dated second-floor secretarial boot camp above a tuxedo rental shop, I removed my fingers from the typewriter's keys long enough to question my soul. This was what my soul had wanted? I looked around at the other typists furiously pecking at the keys. How did typing and filing become necessary qualities for spiritual seekers? Surely sages in India didn't have to go through all of this. Guru must have gotten something wrong, I decided, and I hoped he'd quickly realize his obvious error.

I failed my first typing test at the United Nations. Shuffled into a room with sixty desks, each with its own typewriter, the proctor of the general service test, a Malaysian woman with a microphone held too close to her lips, causing chaotic feedback, informed us speed and accuracy were what mattered. The hot room filled with nervous typers lacked oxygen. I stared at the keyboard to remind myself where my fingers needed to be. As soon as she yelled "Start!" and the microphone crackled, we were off. The clanking of the keys sounded like a horse race. Other typers were galloping, and their speed made me feel like I had to catch up. My fingers were flying off the keyboard and landing randomly on any key. I was trying to hang on, not lose total control of the reins, but it was too late. When the race was over I had done thirty-eight words per minute with twenty-two errors. All bets were off. I had lost.

Guru was sympathetic when I reported back my results, and he cheered me on to practice and try again. Weeks later, after I failed my second test with even worse results, Guru consulted Hamsa about a backup plan. In addition to the various UN departments located around the Secretariat Building, each member country of the UN had its own base of operations nearby. The United States Mission to the United Nations, directly across the street from the Secretariat Building, was where Kumud, a disciple for more than twenty years, worked. A tall southern woman, Kumud had told Hamsa about an opening for a secretary in her own department at the U.S. Mission. Being an official part of the State Department, the job didn't require passing any of the UN's general service tests. Instead it meant having a thorough background check by the FBI and obtaining a high-level security clearance.

When the FBI agent came to my house to interview me and my parents, I was sure I would never get the job. My background consisted of one thing: Guru. Allowing high-level security clearance to someone whose church leader publicly declared he had been a lion in his animal incarnation, and during his many human incarnations had been the Emperor Akbar and Thomas Jefferson, among others, seemed like a long shot. My references, all disciples, would be proof that I wasn't the optimal, stable candidate for high-level security clearance. But I was wrong. Perhaps the State Department was more open-minded than I thought, or their background investigations left a lot to be desired, but I was offered an entry-level position with high-level security clearance in the same division as Kumud. Kumud was the executive secretary, working directly for the head attaché. Her solid work ethic had gained her the respect of her colleagues, and they tried to overlook the other element that she brought with her to work every day—a mission to manifest Guru. Dressed in a sari, Kumud's desk was a homage to Guru, and twice a week when Guru visited the UN to give his peace meditations, Kumud dutifully traversed the office inviting the ranks from the ambassadors down to custodians to join her. They always declined, prepared with a variety pack of polite excuses.

Being brand-new and stationed on Kumud's floor, she hovered about me constantly. When the other secretaries, Maria and Lucy, in confidence, asked me how I knew Kumud, I casually explained that she was an old family friend. I was advised by Hamsa to keep my connection to Guru quiet. News had surfaced that an anti-Guru campaign was brewing at the UN, and a concerted effort was in place by the executive administrators not to hire any more of Guru's disciples. Guru decided that to ensure disciples were still hired, they would have to go in "undercover," dressed in "Western clothes" and even having to revive their original "prespiritual" names.

On my second day of work, Maria and Lucy entered my closet-sized office to gossip about every State Department officer who worked on the floor. They had just started to describe the new junior press officer, Todd, whom they thought would be a perfect match for me, when Kumud came into the room.

"It's twelve-fifteen," Kumud said. "We don't want to be late for the *meeting.*"

The secretaries eyed each other and skirted out the door.

Kumud could hardly wait to bring me to my first UN peace meditation as an official employee. Since having found the Chosen One a job, Kumud was suddenly on Guru's inside track, a place she had never been.

Guru's United Nations peace meditations were held inside an ordinary conference room. Though mostly filled with disciples, both those openly "out" and those still "in the closet," scattered through the room were a few nondisciples, colleagues brought to the event by their eager disciple coworkers. Guru entered the room late, stood up at the front, and meditated. He recited a few aphorisms on peace, and then asked for the prasad. To each attendant he handed a small chocolate wrapped elegantly in silver and blue foil with the UN crest embossed. When it was my turn, he smiled and held the chocolate lovingly in his hands for what seemed like minutes, before he blessed me. I knew then that Guru was pleased. I was where he wanted me to be.

One week later, when my first paycheck arrived, I signed the entire check directly over to Guru. It was the least I could do. Other disciples gave half, if not all, of their salary to Guru in regular donations he called "love offerings." Now that I finally had my own money, I, too, wanted to give Guru everything, just like he had given me.

After a few months, even though I knew Guru was proud of the routine he had orchestrated for me, the novelty of the outside working world quickly wore off, and I wondered if a post at Guru's house would have been better; at least it might have offered some variation to a nine-to-five routine. I was restless alphabetizing and filing documents. Stuffing envelopes and answering phones felt monotonous and disappointing. Nothing about the Center had prepared me for the slow-but-steady work ethic and compliance required for a low-level career in the State Department's bureaucracy. Guru advocated spontaneity, out-of-bounds thinking, and even rule-breaking, as ways to achieve rapid results, and since Guru rarely played by the rules, I didn't want to either.

One Thursday morning, I passed the security checkpoint and chatted hello. When I stepped onto the elevator to my floor, I nearly crashed into a man wearing jeans and a wrinkled T-shirt. He was reading a tattered paperback copy of Nabokov's *Lolita* that covered his face.

"You're new here," he confirmed, lowering his book and squinting at me. "I set up your office."

"You work here?" I asked, scanning his rumpled outfit.

"They keep us locked in the basement and call for us when they need the dirty work done. It's called 'Office Services,'" he said with a smirk. "You wouldn't have noticed us. We're the local untouchables."

I scrambled for a comeback.

"And so part of your job is reading while riding the elevator?" I asked.

"It's a great story. You should read it," he said as the doors snapped shut.

When I discovered later that afternoon that my desk chair just wouldn't adjust to the proper height I needed, I eagerly called up "Office Services" to ask for a replacement. Ben, a grumpy older man, huffed that he would send someone to fix it. I waited, making sure not to leave my office. Sure enough, Oscar, the elevator reader, made the call.

"I hear there is a chair issue," he said, leaning against my doorway.

He was of slight build, and his black hair, too long to hold its current cut, drooped into his dark eyes. He rolled in my new chair and told me that my office needed some type of personal ornaments—pictures, postcards, and plants—that reveal a person's private side.

"What's your deal?" He blew the hair off his forehead and sat down. "Why are you here?"

I mumbled something about a lifelong interest in UN affairs.

Oscar didn't say anything, but his laugh let me know that he didn't buy a word. By the time he was paged to carry tables upstairs for a luncheon hosted by the ambassador's wife, I felt jolted awake realizing that work just might, after all, be exciting.

WHEN KUMUD INVITED me to lunch with her, since Guru was out of town and wouldn't be at the UN for a meditation, I declined, not wanting to leave my desk in case Oscar dropped in en route from removing an old filing cabinet or changing a fluorescent lightbulb. I sat fiddling with paper clips, staring out the window.

"Busy day?"

I hadn't seen Oscar approach. He carried a clipboard with work orders and a pencil rested behind one ear. I flung my paper clip chain into a drawer and flipped my hair over my shoulder.

"If you need a box of jumbo paper clips to work with next, I can arrange a delivery," Oscar whispered, as though he were a special agent.

The phone rang, and I wrote a message. Oscar stood waiting, amused, as I filled out the official message log, pressing hard into the four sections of colored carbon paper.

"I see why they pay you the big bucks," Oscar said, when I hung up.

Before he left, he asked me to hang out that night.

Later, I worked up a raspy, cloggy throat voice, then called Apala, the head of the singing group that Guru had assigned me to join, to let her know I wouldn't be able to make practice since I felt too ill. When she wished me a speedy recovery and even offered to drop off some soup, instead of feeling guilty for lying, I congratulated myself for being such a good actress. The lie came easily, and I thought that as long as I did it well, I could outwit everyone.

Since many disciples worked in the United Nations complex, it was common to bump into sari-clad devotees while waiting in line at delis or crossing the street. To be safe, I told Oscar I'd meet him by the subway, which was a few blocks away. While I scanned the crowds merging down the stairs into the subway station, Chandika, my father's sister, a disciple who worked at UNICEF, collided with me. She wore a bright pink sari and had large headphones over her ears, as she practiced out loud one of the hundred Bengali songs that her singing group had to perform. Without taking off her headphones, she yelled for me to join her, so we could rehearse on the ride home. She had moved into the first floor of our house. Loud and known for her drastic mood swings, Chandika reveled in being bombastic and quirky. After Guru told her that she had been a duck in her animal incarnation, she started collecting ducks, and her apartment was a shrine to the aquatic bird. I spotted Oscar in the distance, at the top

of the stairs, searching for me. With my best dramatic performance, I suddenly clutched my purse, panicking that I had
forgotten my keys at work and needed to rush back to the
office.

Oscar waved to me. I hesitated, scanning the throngs of
commuters for disciples. I knew that all my hopes for a ro-
mantic adventure would end if I got caught and reported to
Guru. Besides Chahna, there was not a single disciple I could
trust who would not have been thrilled to turn me in for
cavorting with a boy. Until we were safely on the subway
headed downtown, I didn't even look at Oscar or risk standing
too close to him, but he was oblivious, chatting and joking.

Strolling through Washington Square, Oscar wandered to
a bench, brushed off an old newspaper, and asked me to sit.
Oscar smelled like sawdust and soap, and I breathed it in
deeply, entranced by my first real date. Dusk was settling in,
and joggers, students, musicians, and tourists cruised the
park, each subtly checking out the person who had passed,
each more hip than the next in rainbow hair, dashikis, and
carefully ripped clothes. I learned that Oscar the janitor was
twenty-four, had a degree from Columbia, and was working
at the U.S. Mission to save money before going to law school.
He had applied to Yale Law and was only days away from
hearing if he was accepted. Wearing an old German army
jacket over his black T-shirt and black jeans, Oscar was crush-
ingly handsome.

After dinner, we wound through the streets of Greenwich
Village without a destination. He filled me in on his post–law
school plans for returning to Brooklyn as a lawyer who could
defend immigrants against discrimination. His own father,
a Chilean immigrant whose English was poor, had been

swindled by predatory landlords and bosses alike. He spoke about visiting a ranch owned by his distant relatives in Colombia that was taken over by drug lords, and of his dead mother. I continued asking him questions, listening to his past, the stories of struggle and hardship. The more questions I tossed him, the longer I could postpone having to reveal anything of myself or Guru. Why risk losing the way that he lowered his chin and lifted his espresso eyes at me? I feared if I confessed that I wasn't even allowed to talk to him, let alone be on a date, he would view me as an oddity, a freak. All of the magic would vanish, and I'd be left with nothing.

I artfully dodged his questions. When he inquired about the origins of my name, I laughed, claiming my parents were eccentrics. When he asked about my childhood, I shrugged, saying I was raised in Connecticut, what more needed to be said? When he hinted about past relationships, I blushed, stammering that I couldn't remember any. My aloof mysteriousness intrigued him. At the end of the night, when he insisted on accompanying me on the F train to Jamaica, we no longer needed to talk. His hands held both of mine, and as he rubbed his thumbs over my fingers, my entire being tingled. It was so perfectly simple—a Friday night, coming home from a date. So this was what the rest of the world had. Suddenly, it all made sense to me. I understood why out of the billions of people on the planet, only a few thousand had been able to resist these exquisite pleasures. Even Guru's divinity might not be able to compete. To have experienced having true companionship and then be told for the rest of one's life it was forbidden might be too great a sacrifice. It seemed to me then that Guru's relentless railings against the evils of human attachment was a misguided enemy. As I clutched Oscar's hands, Guru's blockade against human relationships felt absurd and utterly incorrect. How was this undivine when it felt absolutely celestial?

Oscar leaned his head against mine. I, Jayanti, finally had an ally. Someone had selected me and me alone. Oscar's focus wasn't on Guru—Guru who? What I had or had not done for Guru, my expectations and failures, didn't matter here.

In this foreign world of the normal, nothing felt remotely normal—it was extraordinary. With Oscar, I wasn't lonely, a solo act. I was part of, for the first time in my life, a couple, and I was not about to let go. I wanted this, and I was going to do whatever it took to keep it a secret.

When we exited the subway and ascended to street level, the boldness I had experienced while safely encapsulated on the train instantly vanished. We were now back in the disciple zone, Guru's neighborhood. Passing in front of houses rented by disciples, I moved away from Oscar and sped up, walking a few feet in front of him. He called out for me to slow down, but without turning to answer him, I mumbled that I wasn't feeling well and needed to get home quickly.

I couldn't take a chance of being spotted.

When we arrived near my house, I decided I would just whisper good-bye before darting inside, but Oscar jogged a few paces to catch up to me, then asked if he could come up to make sure I felt all right. I saw the lights were still on in the second-floor apartment. Since I lived on the third floor above two disciple women, any movements and sounds could have easily been heard. I said no. Oscar placed both hands over my ears and drew me in for a kiss. My body shook from the impact. This, I decided, is what I wanted. At that moment, I didn't care who had seen.

THE NEXT MORNING Guru was back at the tennis court. When I arrived late, Guru already had the disciples form lines and slowly, in procession, soulfully walk up to Guru's throne area and then back across the court in deep meditation. I knew the importance of maintaining the appearance that everything was normal, that I was Guru's first-class disciple, so I smoothed back my hair and clutched my folded hands upon my chest with utter devotion. Yet all I could visualize was Oscar's face, hair, eyes, and hands. I found myself veering away from the line and nearly collided with a woman in the next row who gave me a puzzled look. I slowly sidestepped back to my spot, as though I had been in a spiritual trance. When I was at the front of the line, facing Guru, I tried to block Oscar from my thoughts, but the remembrance of his lips, his smell, filled me. I couldn't extinguish him long enough for the three seconds it took to walk past Guru and turn away. Instead of shame, my failure triggered defiance. If Guru knew about Oscar, so be it. I was in love, and it didn't feel wrong.

After the meditation, Guru called for prasad, then he tapped on the microphone. We sat on the grainy clay of the tennis court in a half circle around Guru's raised, carpeted throne area that had been built into what now resembled a large outdoor bungalow.

"Dear ones," Guru said. The microphone squealed with feedback.

"Oi."

Gagan, a balding thin disciple who was always seen chatting and playing with the children and who used to chase me around when I was little, tickling me until I cried for him to stop, was the official high-tech sound person. He darted up to Guru's microphone, switched on a button, then tampered with endless knobs at his station in the far right of the court, where black wires and speakers clotted together. Guru waited a minute, then started again in a low voice, which always signified a serious matter. When Guru was joking or telling stories, he spoke in musical tones interspersed with grand hand gestures.

"Beware," Guru warned. "Boy disciples, girl disciples, beware. Your lower-vital lives are destroying your spiritual lives. This free mixing, boys and girls, is inviting temptation, which is poison, only poison. To mix openly about rubbish is forbidden. To be a true disciple, you must protect yourself. Be vigilant against the vital life. This type of interaction, mixing together, is dangerous, dangerous, dangerous. Boys and girls should not mix unless it is absolutely necessary. If it is manifestation work or a Center activity, then, and only then, should there be talking. Otherwise, boys stay with boys, and girls stay with girls. When boys and girls must be together for Joy Days or other activity, do not, do not, do not look directly into the eyes. Look at the third-eye area. Look at the feet. But do not look directly into the eyes. This is for your own protection. The hostile forces, the lower-vital forces are powerful, most powerful. You must be always on your guard. Pray, pray to the Absolute Supreme for purity, for protection. Keep your spiritual life always guarded as the most important jewel." Guru stopped talking and slipped into meditation.

I knew what this was about. A local male disciple had run

away with one of the women in Lalima's singing group, the elite group of disciples, which included both Prema and Isha. The pair's secret affair and subsequent elopement had outraged Guru, because after interrogating all the disciples who had interacted with them, a few had spotted the two chatting together at the back of the tennis court or in front of the divine-enterprises. Guru's rules against socializing with the opposite gender and encouraging reporting on delinquent disciples had clearly broken down, and Guru was determined to revive them.

"When you see your brothers and sisters harming their own spiritual lives and that of the disciples that they are throwing their vital-poison into, then it is the duty of all to help by reporting them to me. Before it is too late, and they have drowned in the ignorance-sea, you can save your dear ones, your spiritual brothers and sisters. All of you must report to me if you see this kind of thing. It is to save the lives of your nearest and dearest ones." Guru stood up and slowly exited.

I felt exposed. Somehow Guru knew. My enthusiastic defiance now deflated, I scanned the rows, trying to ascertain how I had been found out. As people shuffled out with downcast eyes and great despair at having disappointed their spiritual master, I reviewed all events since having met Oscar to pinpoint a moment when I might have gotten caught. As I remained seated, it finally dawned on me that Guru could not have been talking about me. His grim focus had been on scandalous relationships between disciples, and for that, I was one hundred percent innocent. I had never tempted and lured another disciple away from Guru and the spiritual life.

I quickly stood up, brushing the dirt off my sari. I could

proudly admit that I had never, not even once, imagined one of the disciple boys as a potential boyfriend. To me that was incest. They were brothers, uncles, and cousins in what felt like the truest sense. Over the years, many disciples had fallen in love and run away. To me, they were traitors, abandoning Guru and stealing disciples' spiritual life. I promised Guru that I would be on the lookout for any such perversity perpetrated by those around me. I hadn't caused this problem for Guru. On this count, I rationalized, I was clean. I was safe. I nearly skipped home to lie in my bed and think about Oscar, counting down the hours until it was Monday morning.

AT WORK, I couldn't concentrate. Documents were shoved into the wrong files, phone messages were lost, and envelopes were mislabeled. I didn't care. When I wasn't writing Oscar's name over and over on my lined manila pad, I was planning how I was going to meet him for lunch or after work. By Thursday, I invented excuses to leave my desk for errands, and I headed into the storeroom in the basement, where I'd sit on top of dusty rolled carpets and make out with Oscar. I confessed my love to him, feeling glamorous and worldly, like a character from a film. When he asked to come over to my apartment Friday after work, I said yes without hesitation. Only later I contemplated the sticky logistics of trying to bring a boy into a house full of disciples in Guru's neighborhood.

Since Guru's lecture about boys and girls not mixing, disciples patrolled the neighborhood seeking transgressions to report—a female and male chatting at the Laundromat or grocery. All interactions not specifically limited to a brief update about Center business or manifestation plans threatened both perpetrators with the risk of being thrown out of the Center either temporarily or permanently. The tennis court guards, the majority of whom had known me nearly my whole life, no longer joked, looked me in the eyes, or even waved hello to me. Once when Ketan drove me home from Guru's house, we passed a newer male disciple, who, after seeing Ketan in the car with me, reported him. Guru's messenger, Romesh, had to explain that Ketan had a sister, mother and aunt in the Center, and that interacting with family members of the opposite sex was still permissible and did not yet merit reporting.

In this climate, it was too dangerous to have Oscar inside my disciple-packed house. If I continued to restrict my dates with Oscar to areas like Greenwich Village where disciples never went, and if they did, it might be a case where I could end up reporting them, then everything would work smoothly. I convinced myself that having Oscar wouldn't be a problem if I kept clear boundaries that separated my Oscar-life from my Guru-life—neither would have to know about the other. I refused to admit that I might have to choose, that I was creating an impossible reality. Instead, I focused all attention on continuing to reap the benefits, the fantasy of having both.

When I called Oscar, instead of retracting the invitation to my house, I ended up confirming the time and date. It wasn't fair that we could never meet in private. Traipsing through the West Village provided a colorful backdrop for dates, but we needed time alone. Since Oscar lived with his father in Brooklyn as a way to save up money for law school, and his father rarely left the apartment except for doctor visits, his home could not serve as an intimate retreat for us. The more

I was with Oscar, the more I craved. I wanted to make up for everything I didn't know about men, for all the missed flings, dates, and romances. I did not want to settle. I didn't care. I was going to find a way.

When Ketan told me the next day that he would be in Minneapolis until Sunday because he was involved in organizing one of Guru's massive public concerts—Guru now only wanted to perform in filled halls of seven thousand or more attendees—I had my solution. It was perfect—Ketan's place. Ketan lived in the two-car garage behind my parents' house in Queens that my father had transformed into an illegal dwelling—a loftlike cottage. It was secluded, separate, and private. Perfect.

That evening, I carefully lied to my parents that the meditation was canceled, so they would stay in Connecticut. I then called Sarisha with the news I would be in Connecticut visiting my parents, which excused me from both the function and the subsequent gathering at Guru's house. I parked my car at the far end of the block to aid my alibi of being out of state. Before making my way down to Ketan's apartment, I called his phone to double-check that his place was empty. Occasionally he had visitors, mostly devoted tennis court guards who popped over to watch endless trashy videos on Ketan's massive surround-sound entertainment center that he had bought for working on special projects for Guru. When no one answered, I peered out my window that overlooked the garage. Everything was dark. Not wanting to risk making multiple trips, I lugged all I needed in one wobbly effort, looking wildly in all directions to make sure I wasn't spotted. I shut the blinds, pulled the curtains across the windows, and silenced the ringer to Ketan's phone. I hid Ketan's piles of clothes and clutter into garbage bags and shoved them inside his single bulging closet. I showered, overdousing myself with new perfumes and lotions, and wore my favorite purple silk dress.

When Oscar knocked on the garage door, a candlelight pasta dinner was prepared and incense streamed from the base of one of Ketan's dead plants. Oscar laughed, taking in the surroundings, asking if this was my private love shack. I fumbled a response about having ongoing remodeling construction inside my apartment, making it awkward for guests, and he nodded as though he knew I was fibbing. Barely touching his meal, Oscar ushered me to the couch.

"So. What's your secret?" he asked, tucking my hair behind my ear.

To end all further questions, my lips smothered his. I was happy, I realized, fully content to burrow in this hidden space with him. Although outwardly he didn't know my situation and the risk I was taking at that very moment, nothing mattered. I had a partner, a mate. Never had I allowed myself to think of a real relationship, a marriage, but here I dared to pretend that this was our apartment, our life. Oscar lay on top of me, holding me tightly, kissing my neck and collarbone. He whispered that he loved me, and I knew it was true.

While his hands slid down my body, mine stayed locked around his back. Kissing was one thing, but sex was quite another. Once in a lecture on purity, Guru warned that sex was so bad and it brought on such dire karma that it would include the karma of all other sinners that the offender had had sex with as well. Guru's doomsday predictions on sex in conjunction with the barrage of public service notices about its dangers in the height of the AIDS crisis made me petrified.

Kissing and hugging were risky enough, but I knew that if I crossed that line and had sex, Guru and my soul would never forgive me. I would be irreparable.

Oscar escorted my hand to the zipper of his jeans. I tensed and stiffened. He sensed my fear.

"It doesn't matter," he whispered. "Only you matter."

It was early morning when Oscar left. Dazed and light-headed, I attempted to erase any signs that I had been in Ketan's apartment. Looking in all directions, I darted inside my parents' house, dragging bags with uneaten desserts up to my third-floor apartment, and collapsed in my bed, not bothering to listen to the two messages from Sarisha inviting me to Guru's house.

The next afternoon after the meditation at the tennis court had ended, I debated returning to Ketan's apartment to check if I had left any incriminating evidence of my rendezvous, but I decided against it. Instead, I asked Chahna to go to a diner for a late lunch. I needed to reveal my news, to have the pleasure of describing my very own boyfriend aloud. My mother was out of the question, my father was even more impossible; Ketan, I knew, would have reported me in an instant with glee. The other disciples were not to be trusted. Friendships in the Center were fragile creations formed by convenience or profitability. Aware that at any point Guru might sever the alliance depending on the changing status of both participants, many friendships remained loose and easily detachable. But that was not the case with Chahna. Though we never discussed it, it was always understood that our bond didn't fit into the normal Center protocol. Even though Chahna and I were different ages, lived in separate states, and held dissimilar positions in the Center, we loved each other completely, without effort. Since Guru often spoke about past incarnations, Chahna and I decided that over the course of many lives we had been sisters and best friends. The one time, however, when I had written a letter to Guru, asking him to confirm this, he never responded. Chahna and I, though, took his silence as an affirmation of what we already believed to be true, and we vowed to always remain sisters and best friends, no matter what happened.

Struggling through high school, Chahna had started writing bleak poetry and wearing black combat boots under her sari. Still thoroughly devoted to Guru, Chahna, now more than ever, didn't fit into Guru's inner elite. Even as a small child, Guru rarely paid attention to her unless it was her birthday, when she, like all disciples who had been in the Center more than a certain number of years, had the blessing to stand before Guru with a small cake as we sang Guru's own version of a Happy Birthday song. However, unlike me, she neither expected nor required outer recognition from Guru in order to feel complete. But when Guru gave me special prizes and gifts, she delighted in sincere happiness for me. Sometimes, in private, when I would ask her if she ever felt sad that Guru didn't talk to her, she'd gaze at me with utter disbelief, as if she were unable even to imagine feeling sorry for herself when, by the mere fact that she was Guru's disciple, she had everything she needed.

Playing with the paper from my straw, I jiggled my feet against the diner's booth, excited to unburden my exuberance about my true love. In between the busboy filling our water glasses, I confessed to Chahna everything that had happened in the two weeks that I had known Oscar, including the most recent news that he had gotten accepted into Yale

Law School for the following September, and he wanted me to go to New Haven with him. As she sat motionless, I saw her take in the new breathless, transformed Jayanti. The way she looked at me made me feel older and wizened. She was quiet as I spoke incessantly. After I had started my job at the U.S. Mission, Chahna had told her parents that when she graduated from high school, she, too, wanted to get a job with the UN. She also said she wanted to live full-time in Queens. And now she listened, as though peering in on what else might be in store for her future. Instead of addressing the un-spoken reality of why I was doing this and how I expected this to continue and when would I face the fact that this would not and could not work, she stared at me from her side of the booth, which felt at once too close and too far. As we walked home and I continued to elaborate on Oscar, re-tracing my earlier story for omitted details, I was relieved and unburdened.

Prideful of my stellar ability to maneuver successfully be-tween the realms of my boyfriend and my guru, I hadn't a clue that there might be a problem until, less than twenty-four hours later, I was summoned to Guru's house and, as I approached his front door, I understood something was wrong. The door, normally shut, was wide open. As I entered the porch, Guru immediately emptied the space, casting every other person out of his house. After a one-minute rush of dis-ciples, squishing on sandals and running shoes on the front stoop, a shock of silence filled the porch. No one even looked at me in their haste to leave. Inside, Guru scanned me for a moment, as though he needed to be sure I was the person he was expecting, the soul he had selected to be his stead-fast and most obedient disciple. Finally, he told me to sit in a disgusted tone that made it instantly and dreadfully clear to me why I was there.

It was all over.

My stomach swirled in anxious dread, and my cheeks flared. Busted, I now had to confess everything to Guru. I could not dare sit before him and make excuses or lies. How had it come to this? Rather than humbling myself and accepting the responsibility for betraying Guru, I felt angry. The sting of being caught overrode everything. I had been so careful the entire time, slinking around like a secret operative. I was meticulous in tending my undercover life so that it wouldn't leak back to Guru, but I had been outwitted. In dates with Oscar, if I had spotted a man in white, I had ducked into stores, feigning sudden interest in hardware or fishing poles. Even speaking to him on the telephone at home, I always made sure to stay in my carpeted bedroom and talk in a low voice, so my conversations didn't seep through the ceiling boards into the apartment below. Nobody knew anything, except Chahna, and I couldn't imagine her ever betraying me. Then I remembered my negligence of not returning to Ketan's house for dropped clues, but I was certain that I had been careful and not left anything behind.

"Your disobedience is absolutely attacking me, giving me such physical pain, such suffering. Your soul wants to punish you mercilessly, ruthlessly. I have to intervene. This kind of life you are living, Jayanti. Oi. Oi. Oi. Your soul knows and your heart knows that the Supreme is your one and only boyfriend. It is your vital, your mind, your body that fight against divinity. In the past, I have prevented your soul from inflicting severe harm, severe punishment on you, but I cannot continue. Very, very serious consequences will occur. Physical danger can come. Karmic punishment for this wild, vital life you are leading." Guru shifted, pushing a pillow behind his back. "Such pain you are causing me. Such physical suffering."

Lately, he had been limping severely, in obvious and constant pain. What was Guru going to do to me? What would this mean for my entire family? Was I now cursed? Were they cursed too? In his public teachings, Guru endorsed loving compassion, but often in private he advocated severe justice. I pictured a massive cave leading to the center of the earth with a plank for a one-way entry. He had no reason to use compassion with me now. I just hoped he would spare my parents from the endless pit of his justice. They were oblivious to my faults. They didn't deserve it.

"The outer life, the ordinary, vital life is not for you. No married life. No children. No negative trappings. You were chosen by me to be my nearest and dearest disciple to achieve victory here on earth." Guru's voice then turned milky and tender, but still edged with his own pain. "You can still be my victory, my Jayanti. You can still achieve the highest here on earth on my path, in my golden-boat. But your vital-life, your boyfriend, is killing both me and you."

"Yes, Guru," I said, my eyes filling with tears, preparing myself for punishment.

"To run faster than the fastest in your spiritual life, to be your Guru's divine victory, you need to tell your guru if you love him." Guru opened his eyes, wide. "Do you love your guru, your Absolute Supreme?"

"Yes, Guru," I said, crying. Of course I loved Guru. He was

the reason for my existence. He was my family and my God. He was the root of everything. Seated in front of his divine presence, I loved him more than anything in the entire world. In an instant, he had the ability to refocus my heart, my life.

"Do you want to please the Absolute Supreme?"

"Yes, Guru," I answered. How could I not want to please the Supreme?

I slunk my shoulders, suddenly overwhelmed with shame for my arrogant and undivine self.

"Then do the right thing, Jayanti, my Jayanti. Give up your boyfriend. Take the Supreme as your only and beloved boyfriend. He will never leave you, never disappoint you. You listen to your Guru, and he will tell you what is best for your inner life. I am one hundred percent responsible for you. You surrender to your guru, and I take one hundred percent responsibility for your inner and outer life."

"Yes, Guru."

"You know Lalita?"

Lalita was a French disciple in Montpellier, a university town in the south of France.

"Yes, Guru."

"You will go to France and stay there."

The rest of what Guru said vanished into the porch and beyond. I knew Guru was right. He was always right. My feelings for Oscar were wrong, delusional. I had not been happy; an outer life with Oscar would never make me happy. The only true path to happiness was with Guru. Time and again Guru told me what I already knew—without Guru, I was nothing. I belonged to him, to his path. I had strayed, nearly too far. I did not deserve Guru's forgiveness, but I would subsist on it. Time and again Guru told me he was the only one who could save me from myself and the wrath of my own soul.

According to Guru, Romesh had a ticket for me to leave for France in two days. Guru handed me an envelope bulging with cash. I dried my eyes and nodded. I would take Guru's endless compassion and not abuse it, promising not to break his trust.

Guru instructed my father to inform my job on Monday that I was not returning, and that I should not go back and "not talk to or see that boy again."

When I returned from Guru's house and I heard Oscar speaking into my voice mail, I numbly picked up the phone and told him that I was going away and wouldn't be back. From my tone, he knew I was serious. Frantic, he demanded to see me, but I told him he couldn't. He insisted that I tell him where I was going, and when I finally admitted it was France, he vowed if I didn't agree to meet him before I left, then he would fly there and meet me. His passport was ready, he said. I told him that was blackmail, utterly unfair. If he turned up in France, I worried, Guru's entire plan and my sincere promise could fail.

As I sat stunned and exhausted on my floor, Oscar negotiated a deal—I meet him the next day and he would stay away forever.

"I promise," he said. "No funny stuff," he added.

I didn't know what he meant. Nothing felt even remotely funny.

My mission was pure. To prevent Oscar from going any further, I needed to see him. Wanting to handle this myself and not cause alarms, I worried that maybe Oscar could not be trusted and felt I needed a chaperone, maybe even a bodyguard. The only person whom I could have dared trust for this most delicate and monumental task was Chahna. When I urgently called her to relay the news, she was numbly silent, but I made her promise to be my strength, my blockade.

Without knowing the full story, my father obeyed Guru's request and, on Monday morning, awkwardly explained to my colleagues that I was offered a "once-in-a-lifetime opportunity to go abroad" and would not be returning to work. Meanwhile, Chahna quietly accompanied me to meet Oscar. Avoiding my direct gaze, I thought she was trying to refrain from being too emotional, and I appreciated her giving me the support yet the distance that I needed.

When I first saw Oscar waiting in the agreed-upon café in Forest Hills, all of my hardened resolve to Guru disappeared. I wanted to grab on to him, hop inside a cab, and disappear forever. But that was absurd. I had promised Guru, my soul, and the Supreme, my life. There was no place for Oscar. I forced myself to pause, breathe, and invoke Guru's presence. I remembered Guru telling me that Oscar was poison, pure poison. I looked at his poisonous body, face, and eyes, wanting to examine them closer, much closer, but Chahna positioned herself directly in between Oscar and me. He kept sweating, even though it was cold at our table near the door. Glaring at Chahna, he stammered with the frustration of being unable to talk to me alone. Chahna, with her eyes lowered, stirred her black coffee. He had frantic questions, and I was determined to block all of them. It was self-defense. The more information he had about me now, the riskier it would be later. I was here only because I was trying to fulfill my commitment to Guru. That was it.

"Will you tell me where you'll be staying?" Oscar begged.

"No."

"Can I get a phone number to reach you?"

"No."

"Do you know when you'll be back?"

"No."

He wiped his hand across his sweaty forehead, and his chair scraped the tile floor. He took a few seconds to regroup.

"Can I get a minute alone here?" He snapped at Chahna.

A minute alone couldn't do any harm. If that was what it took to finally say good-bye and be done with the entire episode, to break free of him once and for all, then I could do it. I nodded to Chahna, assuring her that this was fine. I would walk him the half block to the subway alone.

"I can't believe you're just taking off and are leaving me," Oscar said, still sweating, the moisture now filling his eyes as we descended the stairs into the station.

I didn't know what to say, so I remained silent, which made him shake his head in disbelief.

"This is, this is, complete bullshit," he shouted, then took a few quick breaths.

He grabbed my hands, urging me toward the turnstiles. Inwardly I chanted to Guru for strength. I was doing the right thing. This was the right thing.

"I can't let you go," Oscar said with a weak smile, trying to pull me toward him. "I just don't understand any of this," he said, exasperated.

I knew it wasn't fair. I hadn't told him anything, and now I was abandoning him. No reasons. No explanations.

He slipped two tokens into the machine and whisked us through the turnstile. The squealing raspy engine of an approaching train echoed through the tunnel. He tugged me, with increased urgency.

The E train skidded to a stop where we now stood. The doors opened.

"Come with me. We'll escape together."

He backed into the subway car, still clasping both my hands, pulling me inside.

For a moment I visualized our perfect future together, burrowed in the comfort of a domestic oasis. With him I would gain a loving partner, but I would lose my holy trinity— Guru, my soul, and the Supreme. My life with Oscar was impossible. I was Guru's Chosen One, and because of that, Guru left me no choice.

I took a decisive step, backing out of the door's threshold onto the platform as the doors snapped shut. Oscar pressed his face against the glass and his hands frantically clawed at the doors, attempting to pry them open.

I studied his face, absorbing as much as I could to store away with me.

"Jayanti," Chahna called from a few feet away. "We need to go."

With his mouth open, Oscar's words were gone as the train vanished into the black tunnel. I watched as my once-possible future sped deep underground and away from my life forever. Feeling empty, sick and cracked, I walked over to Chahna, who waited for me with her arms open wide and squeezed me so tightly I couldn't catch my breath. When we steadied ourselves, we ascended from the darkness up the stairs, to the streams of brilliant and aching light from the world above.

7

Exiled to France

WITHOUT INTERROGATING ME AS TO THE FULL REA-
son why Guru was airlifting me out of New York,
my mother and father dutifully helped me pack.
Ketan, sensing juicy scandal, doggedly scrounged for more
information, but I remained quiet. Any attempt to explain
what had happened only made things feel worse, until everything hurt. Each time an Oscar memory began to form, I dug
my nails into my arm to force it to stop. I unplugged my telephone. I threw away my cache of perfumes and oils purchased to entice Oscar. All the outfits that I had worn with
him, including my favorite purple silk dress, I gored with a
scissors before dumping them into the garbage. From movie
stubs to his phone number written on a napkin, I systemati-
cally eliminated all physical reminders of Oscar.

Before the drive to Kennedy Airport, Guru invited me to
his house. With a blessingful letter, explaining how proud he
was of me, and another wad of blessingful cash as parting
gifts, Guru pressed both hands upon my forehead, covering
my third eye. His touch was forceful, as if embossing his protective imprint for my long journey ahead. He beamed a wide

smile, proclaiming his eternal love, pride, and joy for me. I consciously worked to preserve Guru's dousing of sweet affections, knowing I needed his affirmations to be even functional. I felt unsteady and weak, as though I was in the fragile stage right after a serious illness, and Guru sensed this. Without a single scolding or warning, Guru became once again the doting grandfather who years past had beamed while his dearest Jayanti climbed upon his lap or delivered to him a bouquet of hand-picked dandelions. I was reminded of his transformative love, and by the time Guru waved his final round of farewell blessings, I felt strengthened by his enthusiastic confidence in me.

When my father pulled up to the departures area at the airport, I feared that Oscar might be waiting for me, that despite his promise, he could have bought a plane ticket. I scanned the chain of people waiting to check in—every man with dark hair and jeans caused me an anxious jolt. At the security screening, where passengers without boarding passes said their final good-byes, I barely flicked a farewell gesture to my mother as I squinted through the knots of people in case Oscar was entangled with them. At the final boarding call, long after all the other passengers were seated and safely buckled for the long flight, the overrouged ticket collector, impatient at my refusal to budge, snickered, inquiring if I were expecting a Hollywood last-minute movie airport reunion scene. Her comment broke my vigilant stake-out. I surrendered my ticket, while wondering if somehow Oscar would already be on board, relaxed and smiling, waiting for me.

After a sleepless flight, Lalita greeted me at the arrival's gate. Tall and slender with gray hair swept off her heart-shaped face, Lalita was practical and kind. An original member of the Paris Center and an insider to Guru's inner circle, Lalita was the eyes and ears from France to Guru. Fluent in English, she breezily chatted, careful to avoid any mention of why I was suddenly in her charge thousands of miles away from Guru and New York.

After staying a few days in Paris at her elderly father's elegant apartment, we drove through the core of France to Montpellier. From my first sighting of the Eiffel Tower to the endless stretches of countryside blanketed with van Gogh's sunflowers, France felt too rigidly perfect. Its carefully aged villages, complete with faded hand-painted shop signs, felt staged. I waited for the wash of sprawling used-car dealerships, strip malls, and graffiti-covered underpasses, but I never saw them. Queens now seemed farther away than ever. My new terrain was not remotely comparable. Jamaica and Montpellier did not seem to share a single common feature. Outwardly, nothing overlapped.

Quaint pedestrian cobblestone walkways streamed into Montpellier's grand squares filled with outdoor cafés and markets. Ancient Roman aqueducts, now groomed into chic parks, braided the edge of the city. Its university, founded in 1220, seventeenth-century Arc de Triomphe, and eighteenth-century ornate opera house nonchalantly boasted Montpellier's permanent reputation as a cultural bastion of the south. Artisans, students, entrepreneurs, and tourists flocked to Montpellier for its coastal setting and carefree lifestyle. I, undoubtedly, was the only person for whom it was meant to serve as a rehabilitation facility, to break my addiction to boys. The orders came from Guru that Lalita was meant to be my counselor and guard. She did not hover over me, and I was grateful for the respectful distance that she afforded me. Never once did I catch her snooping through my bags or bursting into the small room inside her apartment that she had designated as mine. Cheerfully inviting me to help her give meditation classes or shop for supplies from the market for her divine-enterprise restaurant, Lalita presented the perfect facade that I was a normal guest on a normal visit. I figured if she could pretend, then I could, too.

But I wasn't happy. Inwardly I questioned my rushed evacuation from New York. Being so far away from Guru felt too risky; I needed to be in Guru's constant presence for my recovery to keep me focused on the right path. France was confusing; it lacked Guru's rigid structure, his protective grip. Since I did not want to disappoint Lalita in feeling that her kind efforts were magically working, I smiled, pretending I was in the process of being spiritually reborn, but inside I felt the same rumbles of uncertainty and desire. I had not changed nor was I transformed. Occasionally, if I suspected a phone call from Guru was approaching to check on my progress, I'd casually mention how happy I was, which I knew was better than any type of payment I could offer her. Reporting positive, tangible results was a sure way for her to please Guru, and, as a devoted disciple, that was priceless.

Feigning contentment, I surmised, worked to my advantage, as well. From observing the promotion, demotion, and expulsion of disciples my whole life, I understood the more a disciple showed outer signs of struggle, the more scrutiny the person received from both the genuinely concerned and the predatory opportunists. Unchecked displays of enthusiasm or devotion counted as normal acts, but absences or visible sulking only exaggerated and heightened the troubled disciple's state. It was safest to affix a smile, blending into the throngs to divert attention. Outwardly, when I was with the Montpellier disciples at meditations, the restaurant, or just alone with Lalita, with staged joy I'd mention postering for an upcoming meditation class, or I'd arrange a fresh bouquet of flowers upon the shrine. These small markers were more than enough to divert attention and provide cover for my frail and feeble reality.

As POSITIVE REPORTS stretched back to New York that the initial toxins had been flushed from my system, Guru commanded that I stay in Montpellier to ensure a full and healthy rehabilitation, but I felt isolated in a way that I had never imagined. In Montpellier, Lalita was the closest I had to a friend, but even with her, I was fully aware of the clear boundaries of our friendship. Lalita was busy, and I already took up way too much of her time. Besides Lalita, the other women, all much older than me, were disciples I didn't know well. They all had their own agendas, and I didn't want to seem too needy.

With patchy, fragmented French left over from high school, I was excluded from the ordinary ease of daily small talk and jokes. I stuttered, mispronouncing wrong words, while flicking through a dictionary. The disciples were courteous about switching to English or downshifting to basic greetings when I was in their company, the remainder of the city did not have the time or patience for me. Bus drivers blurted out their annoyance when I tried to cram bills into the automated ticket stamper, and waitresses rolled their eyes when asked to repeat the plat du jour for the third time. I had never appreciated the luxury of living in a society where I was in control of the language. Even when we had traveled with Guru through countless countries like Indonesia, Malaysia, and Japan, where we could not speak the language, there was never a sense of exclusion, of being invisible, since we were just tourists, dropping in for a week or two. Locals who wanted our business, whether it was for a taxi ride or an elephant ride, catered to us, cutting deals in botched English phrases; we were the guests, the special ones. Now, without the padding of a group, I was the single outsider, who appeared both deaf and dumb. Achingly conscious that as a disciple of an Indian guru exiled for rehabilitation, I already occupied a solitary position, but having the extra separation of language heightened my sense of loneliness. When I tried to flood myself with French by tuning in to talk radio, after a few minutes my head felt waterlogged. Nothing stuck. I tried to convince myself that maybe it was better this way, that I could remain aloof, unattached, which might help me jumpstart my Guru-revival, but no matter how hard I pretended that being tuned out from the noise of the outside world was a spiritual boost, it just made me feel more lonely.

Used to having my family as filler between Guru's schedule, without them and without Guru, the fat lumps of unscheduled time in my days and evenings felt ominous. I didn't know what to do with my time, and even if I did, I didn't have Chahna with whom to explore. I both missed and worried about Chahna. She had seemed so harried and torn over my sudden departure. When we had said our last goodbyes, Chahna sobbed, unable to finish a single sentence, as though she sensed our separation would be as final and permanent as I had experienced with Oscar on the train platform. But Chahna, like Oscar, was thousands of miles away.

Enough time had passed, and it was clearer to me than ever that my pining to return to New York was not just because of my yearning for Guru's peace, love, and bliss; I could no longer deny that it was really because I missed Oscar. I imagined meandering through Montpellier with him, arm in arm, using up entire days in one small neighborhood. He would be my companion in a country filled with couples in love who roamed the streets, proclaiming their amorous affections under the brilliant public stage of open squares and street corners. I watched pairs of lovers seated upon the city's marble monuments, embracing tightly, ruffling each other's hair, biting each other's necks. Remembering Guru's proclamation that he had used repeatedly since junior high that the Supreme was my boyfriend, I'd look around, still hopeful to see if maybe, just maybe, the Supreme would actually turn up.

Since the Supreme was an aloof boyfriend, absent and uncommunicative, I turned my attentions back to Oscar. While walking around the city, I pretended I held his hand, experimenting with grips, knitting intricate combinations of fingers, palms, and thumbs. Setting the tables in Lalita's restaurant or chopping fruit to garnish her dessert tortes, Oscar was always with me, my hand skimming his cheek, softly landing in his hair. I secretly searched for Oscar, hoping that he would not have given up on me so easily. I fantasized about him hiring a private eye in a room with thick blinds and hazy smoke, intricately describing the details that led up to my last appearance. When the detective didn't produce any tangible leads, Oscar devoted himself full-time to rescuing me. Vowing never to cease pursuing the love of his life, sooner or later Oscar's trail, perhaps beginning in Paris, would land him in Montpellier. In anticipation of his impending arrival, I carefully checked the mirror before retrieving the mail, just in case Oscar was waiting for me in the lobby of the apartment building. Anytime and anyplace, without advance notice, he could appear. I needed to be prepared. As I waited, peering over the tops of my sunglasses in large crowded areas, I often rehearsed our reunion, imagining a tight embrace, as pedestrians strolled past with knowing smiles.

By inwardly doting on Oscar, I rationalized, I wasn't doing anything wrong. If Guru inquired as to whether I had contacted Oscar, I could honestly answer him that I had not. Even though I wanted to, I restrained myself, so I could, on some level, try to please Guru and do what he wanted. I was still obeying Guru, even by a thread. I wasn't technically breaking my promise to be faithful to the Supreme. After all, I kept telling myself that Guru was the only person who really mattered, that the rest was an illusion, a trap, and I wouldn't allow myself to be carried away again, but it wasn't easy.

Sitting in the sun in the main square writing postcards to my parents and Chahna, I composed postcards to Oscar, but as I dropped the others in the post box, I cast his into the garbage can. When I was alone in Lalita's third-floor apartment, I dialed Oscar's number numerous times but hung up before it connected. Still, I knew that these dangerous indulgences were not what Guru, my soul, or the Supreme expected from me. Being aware of my disobedience made me feel worse. Each time I scurried off to call Oscar seemed like I was being twice as deceitful. Knowing it was wrong and yet deliberately pursuing it was a confirmation of my spiritual sickness. The last time I dialed his number, I looked at a framed photograph of Guru smiling with the sun illuminating the back of his head, creating an aura of white light. Guru's divinity, relaxed and utterly easy, felt like a slap. Again and again, I was not worthy to be the recipient of Guru's compassionate smile, his love. I disgusted myself. Seated before my shrine, I ripped up the one photo of Oscar that I had smuggled with me, and begged Guru for inner assistance.

Assistance came in the form of the Montpellier disciples, my new spiritual compatriots, who showed me a way to be quietly at peace. Long before I had arrived in their city, I was known to the group of twenty-five disciples from Center legends. I had not noticed any of them when they pilgrimaged to New York twice a year for celebrations to honor Guru's birthday and his anniversary of arriving in America. To me, the majority of the thousands of visitors who arrived in Queens from all over the world blended together simply to cause long lines, fewer seats, and general gridlock. Very few visiting disciples emerged from the masses to capture Guru's personal attention, and those who did were either well-connected, rich, or celebrities. With few exceptions, the rest of the international visitors came and went without notice.

Lalita was the only Montpellier disciple who stood out. Having joined the original Paris Center in the seventies as a young engineering student, her unflustered, fearless determination to spread Guru's message in every province of France had quickly earned her Guru's counsel. With much of her initial grunt work now passed on to the next generation of eager new disciples, her position was Guru's unofficial leader of

France. Attending Guru's concerts and trips abroad, she left her crew of workers to the arduous labor of running a restaurant. As in most divine-enterprises, disciples believed it was a privilege to work in a spiritual atmosphere and avoid the dreaded outside world. Their privilege most often included twelve-hour days, no benefits, and subminimum wages. At the restaurant, I was given the light and clean tasks, but I was still relieved when my few hours were over. In contrast, I noticed that the women disciples who labored for hours seemed joyful and content. Because Guru's laws prohibited men from working with women, the men who toiled the overnight shifts of dishwashing and cleaning did so happily. With Guru's music on an endless loop, and pictures of Guru plastered on all the walls, they worked without a hint of a complaint. Twice a week they met together for a one-hour meditation followed by a short singing session, and sometimes on the weekend they ran along the beach. Their lives seemed private and peacefully contemplative.

Though Lalita was always in the loop, up on what Guru said or did at the last function, the majority of disciples were removed from Guru as a personal adviser and didn't seem to mind. Most were drawn to Guru's extended philosophy of meditation and service. Guru himself was not what they chose. Having a personal relationship with him was not what they had expected or, I suspected, what they wanted. They had a deep reverence for Guru, but their lives did not revolve around needing Guru's daily affirmations. Their days and nights weren't composed of sitting at the tennis court wishing Guru would acknowledge them. They understood that Guru did not know them personally, but that did not seem to bother them. They attended weekly meditations and made the biannual pilgrimage to New York, but the rest of the time was theirs to spend as they chose.

In this serene and independent climate, disciples didn't eye each other, waiting for acts of disobedience to call and report to Guru. I doubt anyone had reported another disciple. Beyond the handful of disciples in Guru's top clan, the rest labored hard and lived simple, quiet lives apart from the tension and intrigue of being first-class disciples. To me, this was a revelation. I had no idea that there were alternatives to the kind of discipleship that had been expected of me since birth. Had my parents known about these more-relaxed approaches to Guru's path? If they had, why wouldn't they have selected a calmer, more balanced life in which to raise Ketan and me? I realized that in all the blurry years of sleep-deprived nights, my parents never suggested we stay to enjoy the quiet pleasures of an evening at home. I wondered, if I had been allowed some independence, some freedoms and flexibility, would I have been a better disciple and a more balanced person?

After months in Montpellier, with Guru's full permission I drifted across the great capitals of Europe, visiting the various Centers. Though I always stayed with disciples, I didn't have any set schedule or timetable. If I wanted to work at a divine-enterprise I could, and if I wanted to head off to another city, I could do that as well. Armed with a Eurail pass, I was free to decide where I wanted to be and what I wanted to do. Not having to be at the tennis court or a meditation, the pressures of Guru's tight grasp loosened and dropped. For the first time in my life, I was in charge.

The evenings I spent at various centers for meditations, but the majority of my days I spent alone idling through ancient palaces transformed into museums, cinemas, piazzas, and monument gardens, acquiring a self-guided cultural education. Guru never endorsed visiting art museums or cultural centers. Even though I had traveled extensively on Guru's Christmas trips, Guru did not encourage us to absorb the local culture and rarely wanted us to venture beyond the meeting room of the hotel. Though Guru wrote songs and plays and painted, he had no interest in the works of anyone else and didn't expect his disciples to either. As far as devout disciples were concerned, Guru's creations were the highest, greatest, and would prove to be the most significant in the future—forget the Renaissance masters, Sri Chinmoy was better.

Without a regular routine, I ventured places alone but had a built-in network of disciples who were only too eager to extend their homes and hospitality to me. In Vienna, I stayed with a female disciple who had a framed picture of Guru holding me as a baby on her altar. I had never seen this woman before, and when I tried to introduce myself, she gushed that of course she knew who I was. Prior to my visit, she, like so many other visiting disciples, was a nameless, faceless seeker who worked in one of the divine-enterprise stores in Vienna that sold discounted items imported from China. Daily, she took three trams to work a ten-hour shift in the store. She was always smiling and cheerful, and I was again struck by how different the path was of a "visiting disciple."

As the months accumulated, I, too, found myself slipping into their Zen-like ease. Even with regular phone calls and letters from my mother about Guru's latest news, like the Sri Chinmoy Peace Blossom site, a program to rename major

landmarks in Guru's honor, I received the reports from Jamaica with a newfound sense of distance. In laboring to re-
strain my thunderous longing for Oscar, I had managed to
train my emotions to be muted and still, even those for Guru.
The source of my life, the reason for my being, Guru, like all
of my former attachments, was no longer something I actively missed.

One crisp morning, as I was about to depart for Barcelona,
Lalita called with a desperate request, urging me to Paris. As
an offering to France, Guru bestowed upon the French disciples the opportunity of arranging a free public concert for
ten thousand people. From the raspy sound of her voice, I
could tell she had been on the phone for hours. With the
event only weeks away, she was staying at her father's apartment in Paris, transforming his study into a makeshift concert command center. Accommodations were arranged for
me. I would be the guest of a new dynamic disciple named
Josette, and the sooner I could arrive to help, the better. After
all that Lalita had done for me, and the fact that I didn't really
have a legitimate excuse with which to decline, I reported
for duty.

Guru's public concerts, billed as the "Peace Concert with
Sri Chinmoy," were the supersized version of Guru's original
humble lecture series from the early seventies. He was no
longer content to play in classrooms and gymnasiums for
small crowds; for Guru to perform, the venue needed to be
impressive and the audience overflowing. Visiting Centers
that had produced concerts to Guru's satisfaction received a
boost in their standing. For the disciples of the Cologne Center in Germany, the first international Center successfully to

fill a concert hall with ten thousand, their rewards included many disciples receiving their official "spiritual names." To outshine the Cologne Center, the stakes were raised. The British Centers booked Royal Albert Hall; the Australian Centers countered with the Sydney Opera House. Guru had recently scolded the French disciples for not adequately aspiring, and he offered them the chance to produce a concert for ten thousand in Paris as a boon to rekindle their weak inner lives. Lalita, although she no longer lived in Paris, raised her hand and gratefully thanked Guru, promising him the French would victoriously succeed. Uttam, a well-known composer of contemporary classical music, was the Parisian Center leader. An effete man who carefully guarded his delicate piano fingers, Uttam had discovered Guru through the music of the legendary guitarist John McLaughlin, when McLaughlin had been one of Guru's devoted disciples. Hailing from an aristocratic Parisian family, Uttam was more than pleased when the new crop of hungry disciples clamored to become more involved in Guru's mission. As Uttam's role became more of an honorary position, he gratefully watched from the sidelines, letting the others run around until exhausted.

When I arrived at the Center meeting in Paris, Uttam sat at the back of the room, using the wall as support, with his legs outstretched, while Lalita, from her seat closest to the shrine, read out the long list of volunteer duties required in planning for the mega-concert. I was expecting the disciples to be superenthusiastic, but I noticed not many people were signing up to accept tasks, and the time in between her calling out jobs and the responses grew ever longer. Finally, when the volunteering completely stalled, Guillaume, a grasshopper-thin man with round oversized spectacles who worked as a chef, finally called out, "Pourquoi pas?" The whole meditation room, except Lalita, burst out in whistles and cheers.

With most slots left unfilled, I felt I needed to scribble my name in as many as I could. I figured it was high time that I started to work for Guru, and I hoped my lead would be contagious for the other disciples. It felt like for the majority of the one hundred Paris disciples, the once-in-a-lifetime opportunity of presenting Guru to ten thousand people in the largest, most prestigious concert hall in Paris, while très chic in theory, was an obtrusive, expensive reality that interrupted their daily Parisian rituals. If they weren't prepared to manifest the absolute Supreme, I felt obligated to pick up the slack. I crammed hundreds of leaflets inside a backpack and headed out to the metro station at Les Halles, a bustling district known for hip dining and endless nightlife.

"La Concert pour la Paix." I smiled with leaflets in both of my outstretched hands.

Dressed in jeans, a purple cardigan, and reflective sunglasses, I might as well have had my head shaved with orange robes and a tambourine from the hostile reception I received. Pedestrians who saw me looped in elaborate circles to avoid me. Those who were too preoccupied to notice me until the leaflet appeared directly before them either shrugged me away with a turned shoulder or shooed me away with a flick of their hand. Passersby who felt either vague curiosity or pity snatched the Guru-blue rectangular paper with a central photo of Guru seated cross-legged holding a flute poised upon his lips. Across the bottom half, in compact script, the date, time, and phone number urged an immediate call to reserve free tickets before they all disappeared.

"La Concert pour la Paix," I announced joyously, like I was handing out free round-trip airline tickets.

After one second of inspection, the flyer was crumpled. Comments flew at me—some, luckily, I couldn't translate—ranging from lack of interest to visceral anger. People shouted at me about "la culte," which easily translated; I knew Guru's Center had been placed on the French government's official list of cults. Many shoppers handed the flyer right back, indignantly. I nodded politely, understanding none of this was personal. As the afternoon sun was muted behind clouds, the nearest garbage pail overflowed with my flyers. When I took a moment to replenish my stack from my backpack, I found myself stranded in a sea of Guru-blue papers littering the sidewalk with Guru's holy form tread upon by thousands. The trail of flyers continued like a small river for a few blocks, until they eventually dried up.

In this city of millions, certainly there were at least ten thousand seekers who longed for the experience of an authentic spiritual master. Though Paris was a voluptuous mecca where the finest of everything was up for sale, a single evening focused on inner peace was not too much to ask. Since the concert was only a few weeks away, with my backpack still heavy with leaflets I prepared for my second round. I moved to the top of the metro stairs, aiming to hit the afternoon commuters.

Smiling, I looked at the image of Guru I held in my hand. Surely people would feel what I did when they glimpsed Guru. They would recognize his divinity. For years, perhaps, they had been searching for a spiritual master, waiting for a sign—*when the disciple was ready, the guru would appear*—and behold their Guru-blue sign. My exigent role as their intermediary between seeker and messiah jolted me into action. Each person I accidentally missed could have lost their sign, delaying their encounter with Guru for decades, even lifetimes.

"La Concert pour la Paix avec Sri Chinmoy," I bellowed, thrusting the flyers into as many hands, closed or open, as I could.

One man wearing a New York University sweatshirt, after scanning the leaflet, stopped.

"Sri Chinmoy?"

"Yes! Oui!" I cheered joyously.

"Sri Chinmoy?" he asked again, waving the flyer.

Here was the seeker's moment of awakening, hastened by me. My heart galloped during this transformative miracle. I had discovered a future disciple. I couldn't wait to relate my triumph back to Lalita and even to Guru himself. Why not? It was time that he knew his Chosen One was manifesting his mission, awakening the spiritually slumbering country of France.

"That guy who does all the weight-lifting scams in Queens?" he asked in a thick New York accent. "He's nuts. How much are you getting paid to do this? He brainwashes people. It's crazy shit. Don't you know that?" The man crumpled the leaflet and rejoined the moving masses.

Everything fell. I couldn't scrape up a single word to respond. I stood immobile in the pool of new flyers splayed upon the dirty sidewalk. I knew Guru had vocal critics and enemies. Often outside his concerts, anticult groups protested with pamphlets and signs, and once, during a public meditation at Columbia University, a man burst down the aisle toward Guru screaming threats, before being subdued by Guru's guards. I remembered at the time wanting to dash up and physically defend Guru. I would have done anything to ensure that Guru was shielded and safe. But now, this was different. Instead of rushing to defend Guru, I had been silent, and instead of refuting the stranger's blasphemous claims, I had absorbed them.

THAT EVENING, AS Lalita drove me to yet another strategy session for concert publicity, she was particularly buoyant, eager to share the exciting news that one Paris disciple's elderly relative had died, and the disciple had donated her entire inheritance to cover concert expenses. Giving Guru money to be utilized as divine kindling to help spread his mission was a great honor for disciples. Over the years as disciples posed for pictures with Guru after signing over their inheritance check, I marveled at their good fortune. When my grandfather Charles, my mother's estranged alcoholic father, died he left only a tiny inheritance to my mother, but she tucked the check in an envelope, giving it all to Guru. Elderly disciples were fortunate to will their property directly to Guru. From real estate to cash, disciples, long after their physical death, found ways to continue to serve and support Guru. Although I was without any real estate holdings, stocks, cash, or even a car to call my own, I, too, planned to leave everything to Guru. It was the least I could do.

When the number of concert reservations barely climbed past two hundred, we needed ways to heighten the public's enthusiasm. We heard that for the big Australian concert, the Aussie disciples leafleted on stilts, dressed in clown costumes. Never having mastered riding a bicycle without slamming into the sidewalk to stop, I dreaded the thought of teetering six feet in the air on wooden stilts. Luckily, that was voted down. When someone suggested being clowns without the stilts, I imagined myself on the Champs-Élysées in a striped jersey, white face with a single tear dripping from my eye, and a beret. Since no one else volunteered to back the idea, my immediate future as a Marcel Marceau impersonator was dropped. After proposals of giving out balloons—too environmentally destructive—chocolates—too expensive—or flowers—too hippie—were vetoed, the focus returned to leafleting. Marie, who as far as I knew had not given out a single leaflet, suggested that everyone distributing flyers should wear a massive sandwich board and carry a tape player with Guru's music on a constant loop. Everyone agreed, and when two people finally volunteered to make the sandwich boards available for the next day, the room relaxed with congratulatory praise all around for a job well done, as though the concert hall already exceeded its maximum capacity.

For the next two weeks, with waning enthusiasm, I trudged through Paris's districts, germinating seeds for ten thousand seekers with a plywood sandwich board hanging around my neck. Instead of luring the spiritually inclined, the oversized close-up of Guru standing in meditation with both hands clasped atop his heart worn over me acted like a detour sign, giving people plenty of time to swerve and find an alternate route. When the only person who stopped long enough to read both sides of the sandwich board was a man who scribbled his phone number across the leaflet while asking for mine, I found more reasons to delay my mission as the public's harbinger for Guru's impending arrival. Instead of connecting with the morning commuter rush, I'd sleep past it, figuring I'd catch the evening one instead. Rather than standing on duty for an entire afternoon, I unharnessed the heavy board, propping it against a wall or store while I stopped for lunch, a café au lait, a shopping excursion, or even a movie or two or three. When I returned to discover that the bulky sandwich board hadn't been stolen, I was greatly disappointed. I wanted to abandon it, and sometimes I did, only circling back later through some sense of guilt, and dragging it back home.

As my evenings were spent with crews of two to three women illegally slopping glue onto posters at construction sites, empty billboards, and phone booths while hiding from the police, I questioned the entire manifestation process. The other great saviors of humanity did not have to rely on stilts, mimes, and sandwich boards to find their disciples. When Christ was on earth, his original disciples never leafleted Jerusalem to bring a crowd to his sermons. The Buddha's first followers never dodged the cops while illegally plastering the forests of northern India with posters for the Buddha's upcoming meditation. Why was Guru's manifestation so laborious? How come rather than having seekers stream to Guru as if following an instinctive inner radar, hundreds of thousands of dollars, phone banks, mass mailings, and media blitzes were deployed and still did not seem to be working? Guru's official worldwide disciple count—fastidiously tracked by Guru through mandatory progress reports from Center leaders—was only in the thousands. That left the majority of the globe still needing to magically sense Guru's light. Not knowing Christ's and Buddha's disciple count during their lifetime, I imagined Guru was already well ahead of both, but for the constant effort Guru thrust into spreading his name, the results, I figured, should have been a lot more impressive.

Two weeks before the big event, Uttam solemnly announced that because they had procured barely one thousand reservations, Guru had canceled the concert. It was over. Guru blamed the French disciples' lack of aspiration and dedication as the cause of their abysmal failure, adding that he refused to travel to France until they could prove themselves worthy of his visit. Because the cancellation was so close to the event, the concert hall and all the rental equipment suppliers, including lights and sound, refused to refund a single franc. Hundreds of boxes of full-color posters sat in a garage along with thousands of leaflets. While I was now permanently relieved of flyering and postering duties, the fact that I was partly responsible for yet another fiasco only confirmed what I had achingly suspected my entire life—the impossibility of trying to fulfill Guru's demands.

I didn't want to be in Paris anymore. I decided to resurrect my Eurail pass and head somewhere, anywhere, maybe Switzerland or Scotland. I quickly packed, wanting to evacuate the site of this latest wreck, leaving others to clean up the mess. I had lost only a few weeks, but for others the loss was much greater, like Lalita, who had lost the chance to please Guru, or like the disciple who had lost her entire inheritance. For all of the effort and sacrifice, again, there was nothing to show for it. Guru was an expert at manipulating those who loved him the most to get what he wanted, but his tactics didn't seem fair. While Guru changed his mind on a whim, the disciples silently absorbed the multiple harsh repercussions.

When Lalita asked if I wanted to head to London to assist with the latest project, acquiring for Guru the lofty and revered title "Lord" from the queen of England, without hesitation I declined. Even if Guru had had a vision where Krishna appeared before him and told him that since Krishna was referred to as Lord Krishna, as a fellow avatar Guru should be officially dubbed Lord Chinmoy, I had had enough. I knew Guru had assigned his top British public relations team to begin work on this latest urgent assignment, and even if he had not, I did not care. I was tired in a deeper and more profound way than I ever had been before.

For months, I passed through most of the meditation centers in Europe without becoming involved. I knew I could no longer cheerfully reassume my role as the Chosen One. Not wanting to leak my own punctured aspiration upon the disciples, I was politely quiet. Luckily, in the Center being quiet was often understood as being spiritually absorbed, which held my cover. Volunteering for a few hours in divine-enterprises, I'd then wander around the country that served as my temporary shelter, not bothering to learn even the basic greeting in its language. Instead of feeling isolated by the language barrier, I now welcomed the buffer that it provided me. Not absorbing other people's daily chitchat freed me to dwell solely in my own realm. It didn't matter. Nothing really mattered. I barely contacted my parents or even Chahna. Numbly stumbling from one city to another, I had nothing to report, nothing to tell.

One afternoon I missed my train connection to Italy,

which left me with an unexpected layover in Nice. I checked into a pension across the road from the train station, and then explored the city without any map or guidebook, preferring to blend in, not caring if I ended up lost. It made no difference to me. I had no actual destination. At the end of a narrow, windy street stood an old stone church. I was about to turn and head in the opposite direction, but the fixed structure, weathered and worn, brought me to a stop. Against the conservative gray facade, its stained-glass windows leapt out, their jeweled tones flirting with the few remaining sunbeams. Besides the massive grand cathedrals that bustled with lanes of tourists snapping frantic photos, I had never bothered entering the endless numbers of humble small churches that flanked most of the cities and villages. But with hours to spare and what appeared like rain fast approaching, I heaved open the unlocked carved arched door.

Inside, my own footsteps echoed. Dark and cool with frankincense, the church was empty. I loitered near the door. An invisible organist played minor chords, sustaining notes that vanished through the vaulted ceilings, which convinced me to stay, at least to listen to the music. As I walked forward, I saw that the marble floor was worn uneven from centuries of footprints and prostrations, leaving a visible path to each of the smaller shrines and a direct line down the central nave. Before me the wooden pews stretched vacant. I took a seat in a center row. I imagined that once they were plush with red velvet and filled with the devoted hunched over in prayer. From hundreds of miles away, pilgrims had journeyed for days, sacrificing food and comfort, to crowd inside these sacred stone walls. This was their spiritual center, the essence of their personal connection to the Supreme. Perhaps in a filigreed coffer rested the relic of a beloved saint, a fragment of an elbow, a few threads of a vestment that surfaced to the public's eye but once a year. Without ever even touching the case, they feasted on the glory of being in the same hallowed space as the holy remains. Perhaps hanging from the front altar originally was an elongated Christ, arms spread wide, skin a pale green, head slightly tilted forward, listening to every prayer. In the empty, ancient space, all alone, I felt the company of the seekers who had sought refuge there, chanting, praying, prostrating before the altar, yearning just for one moment for a revelation, a visitation, a vision, or a single whispered instruction from their Lord. Christ had left the earth countless years prior to the church's erection. His own blessed form had never sat at the front of the congregation, and his voice had never reverberated throughout the structure. What would those villagers have given for even a glimpse of their Beloved? If they had had the opportunity, the option of having their avatar alive and teaching, they would never waste a single second. They would have uprooted their lives and devoted the entirety of their existence to him without a second of doubt or delay. And I? My beloved guru was in his sixties, and even though he forbade us from projecting about the future of the Center, in his human incarnation, Guru was mortal. What was I doing? Why was I wasting precious time? And for what? To one day be forced to communicate with Guru as a statue in an empty temple when I had had the rare privilege of daily being in his holy presence and love? How could I have been so careless?

My inner life, so long dead and dormant, felt again multifaceted, burning feverishly inside, rejuvenating, lessening its ache and fatigue. My doubts and anger sloughed off. A vestige of the Supreme, unchanging and unswerving, was what I needed to be. What was I doing, moping and squandering time? I was a seeker. To thrive, I needed to live among a tribe of seekers at the feet of my guru. I looked up at the rose window, realizing that in the future, holy sites would be open for Guru's disciples to come and worship him, and these seekers would yearn to have been among the disciples fortunate enough to have been present when the last avatar walked the earth. Why was I wasting this rare opportunity to be exactly where I was supposed to be? My doubts were erased. I knew what needed to be done. I would immediately return for a life of devotion and service to Guru and Guru alone. I was finally ready to accept my calling.

8

Born Again, Again

MY MOTHER GREETED ME INSIDE KENNEDY AIRPORT'S international arrivals gate with flowers and cupcakes to celebrate my return. I felt myself disarmed in her hug, shutting off my vigil—no more trains, translations, maps—knowing that I was relieved from the duties of taking care of myself. My father, not wanting to pay for parking, looped around the passenger pickup platform, evading airport security, finally slowing down just enough for us to dash inside the car. As my father battled traffic, maneuvering a way through the clogged arteries of Grand Central Parkway, I counted the minutes before I stepped inside my beloved guru's sacred realm once more. My parents' questions at times overlapped, from the current exchange rate of the franc to the comfort level of sleeping in a couchette. They listened to my answers with the respect afforded a world-traveled woman and not the huffish girl they had watched disappear into the departure gate more than one year ago. I sensed we were now three independent disciples, rather than two parents and a child. Their shift in attitude filled me with confidence that returning to New York to begin my new life as Guru's own devout disciple was my sublime mission.

We drove straight to the tennis court, where the evening function was nearly over. Anticipating my first glimpse of Guru, I quickly walked up the driveway and spotted Ketan. He waved me over to him. If he had been the one who reported on me, I no longer felt resentment toward him. My experience, I realized, had made me return to Guru stronger than ever. Filling me in on his newfound duties, from disseminating stories about Guru's weight lifting to news stations to being the chief organizer of concerts from Philadelphia to Minneapolis, Ketan fluffed his new white-blond highlights, while sipping an espresso. As he escorted me through the crowd assembled for prasad, I sensed his pride that I had repaired my life and was fully restored. He had his little sister, once again, along for the ride in Guru's golden-boat.

Prasad was almost over, and I joined the line behind a few new disciples whom I had never seen. They looked at me, eyeing me as a newcomer in my fitted French jeans, then turned their backs quickly to let me know my attire was not suitable for meditation. I smiled at them, finding it amusing that they mistook me for a brand-new disciple. I didn't mind. Older and wiser, I felt generous with the world. I had overcome temptations, renounced the poison of vital-attachments; I had been on the grand tour of Europe, and I had returned to my source, my all. After all of the miles and crossings I had trekked, I could not wait to remain seated in worship at the feet of my master for eternity.

"Jayanti, come, come excellent girl," Guru said, waving his hand at me. The same women who just a few moments ago had snubbed me, now looked at me again, with newfound respect, as I made my way toward Guru's throne. He released a single purple iris from a crowded flower arrangement on his side table and motioned for me to approach. As I leaned before his chair to hold the stem, his hand remained. I once again smelled the familiar, lulling fragrance of Guru I remembered from my childhood, a sweet-tropical perfume, like candied gardenias.

"All my eternal love, concern, and affection. To you, to you, to you, *my* Jayanti."

Tears dripped from my eyes, and I brought the flower to my heart. It was exquisite in its solitude. I understood. I was that same beautiful single flower, whole and complete unto itself, and Guru was the only requirement for my spiritual growth and sustenance. As I bowed to Guru, he tilted his head ever so slightly to the side, his eyes twinkling. I was home.

That night I received an invitation to go to Guru's house. Jet-lagged and still unshowered, I could not wait to be back in the cozy familiarity of all things Guru. Gitali, Vani, and Ushma welcomed me back, inching over to create a space for me on Guru's living room floor, and I stepped through feeling fully entitled to reoccupy my seat, landing back in the exact spot that I had left.

In the crowded room, Guru recounted one of his favorite stories about Krishna. Krishna promised two brothers that he would be the charioteer to the one who ventured around the world and returned first. One brother dashed off on an epic voyage across desert, seas, and mountains, while the other brother walked slowly around Krishna once. Years later when the first brother returned, haggard and depleted, from his epic journey, and saw his brother relaxed at Krishna's feet, he could not fathom how he was defeated. The other brother explained that since Krishna was his world, all he had to do was traverse Krishna, the epicenter of his universe, one time.

Scanning Guru's living room, I suddenly felt foolish. Clearly that story was about me. I wondered if Guru and everyone else viewed me as the living example of the brother who had to learn his lesson through unnecessary efforts and wasted time. While I had nearly drowned in vice, then spent months in restless roaming, the rest of Guru's close disciples were all happily seated at Guru's feet the entire time. I wondered if perhaps there were reasons why I needed the accumulation of those experiences. After all, Guru had reminded us countless times that Buddha himself had spent time as a husband and father before casting off those roles to fulfill his destiny as the Awakened One. The important fact, I decided, was that at the critical moment both Buddha and I turned away from temporal trappings. Even if it took me longer than it should have, I was back to stay at Guru's feet forever.

As I looked over at the doorway from the living room to the porch, there stood Chahna, my best friend. I gasped with surprise, and nearly stepped on Tuhina as I raced toward my loyal sister. I had searched for her at the meditation, but I hadn't seen her. I never expected I would find her at Guru's house. Before I had left for France, Chahna was not on Guru's invitation list.

When I enfolded her inside a big hug, Chahna settled stiffly into my arms, as if surprised by my embrace. I grabbed her hands and plopped her down right near the front door. I saw that her acne had cleared. Her skin looked shiny and nearly smooth. She had lost weight, and her eyebrows had a shaped, higher arch. She looked older, like she too had experienced her own share of travels.

"So?" I asked, tightly gripping both her hands. "I want a complete run-down of everything that has happened in Chahna-land."

She answered politely with vague ramblings about her parents and Puffy, her orange cat, but she didn't mention anything about herself.

Ketan then arrived with the video recording of Guru that had appeared earlier that night on the local news. Before Ketan lowered the lights, Guru asked if Chahna had arrived.

"Yes, Guru," she said from where we sat near the doorway.

"Come, good girl." Guru took a white gardenia, larger than his hand, from the side table. He put it to his own forehead for a few moments as Chahna stood before him with folded hands.

"I am so proud of you, so very proud of you," Guru said.

I watched my Chahna, and I, too, felt proud. Obviously Chahna, like me, had arrived at a critical juncture and solidified her commitment to Guru and to Guru alone. I realized once more how similar we were, how at times in the past we had even shared the same dreams at night, as if our connection had been thickly woven into ancient and lasting layers.

Instead of returning to sit beside me, she found another seat, on the other side of the room. I waved to her to share in the excitement of her blessing, but she didn't look up and stared at the flower with her head lowered.

Guru told Ketan to start the video.

The footage showed a sea-plane, its front propeller whirling, parked on a large platform. Attached to the platform was a calf raise machine that Guru approached, then tucked his shoulders into thick pads that he pressed up against. His thin, muscular legs were braced and slightly bent at the knees.

Guru gave a great groan, and the platform jiggled, then smacked down with a loud thud. The next shot showed the pilot exiting the plane and vigorously shaking Guru's hand.

After a chopped quote from Guru about self-transcendence, the camera returned to the newsroom, where a silver-haired anchorman uttered a rehearsed chuckle, then bid his audience good night.

Everyone clapped loudly when it was done.

"Bah-Bah. Ketan, again, show again!" Guru had sat up in his chair; Amal, the male disciple specially selected to massage Guru's feet, now shifted himself to Guru's new position.

Ketan rewound the tape, and we watched it again.

When the shot of the lift played, Guru said, "Can you all see? See?"

"It's so high, Guru," Gitali said.

"Guru, the whole plane was up in the air!" Bhupal said.

"Again! Ketan, let's see again," Guru said.

Ketan rewound the tape, and pressed play. This time at the lift, Guru told Ketan to pause it, to see the platform move. Ketan backed it up and played it, again and again.

"Very big plane," Guru said, turning toward the girls' side.

"Guru, that was so-o inspiring," Dharinil said.

"That plane was blessed to be lifted by you, Guru," Sarisha said.

Guru smiled, asking Ketan to rewind it, yet again.

I had forgotten about Guru's weight lifting and watching it on the evening news, I found it appeared like a bizarre spectacle. Even after having viewed the tape ten times, I still saw only the front half of the platform slightly tilt, while the back half, where the plane was parked, remained unmoved. I wondered if anyone would be urged to follow a spiritual path after viewing that footage. It seemed neither inspiring or mystical. I wished instead they could have seen Guru as I did, radiating love. I peered over at Chahna, wishing that she were still beside me so I could ask if she had seen the plane lift, but when I tried to signal her, she wasn't looking at the TV but intently staring at the flower in her hands.

I WAS OFFICIALLY a "vagabond," the name Guru affectionately gave to those whose full-time occupation was him. My mother received a message from Guru instructing her that her mission was to support both her children financially so that they could devote themselves entirely to their inner lives. Since my mother thought doing so would make her children happy, she selflessly complied, finding solace in the contentment of her children. When my father grumbled about having to pay for two adults who were fully capable of earning a living to sit around all day, he received a message back from Guru that he was not being receptive to the will of the Absolute Supreme. After that, arguments continued between my mother and father, causing yet another daily source of tension between them, flaring up every time my mother took money out of my father's wallet for her ascetic offspring. With my parents handling all of my living expenses, and extra money given to me periodically in wads of cash from Guru, my finances were taken care of, along with nearly everything else. Not having any burdens or responsibilities for items like rent (since I lived on the top floor of my parents' house in Queens), food, or car insurance, like monks and nuns, my agenda only consisted of one thing: my spiritual life, or, more accurately, Guru.

I woke up at five-thirty for *bhajan* practice at Isha's house, where a select group of women sang songs written by and dedicated to Guru. Following *bhajans,* I scurried home to change into my running clothes to make it to the starting line of Runners Are Smilers, the two-mile road race held every morning around the Jamaica High School track, where I tried my best to avoid finishing in the last handful of panting joggers. Once again, I darted home to shower and arrived at the tennis court at nine, where I sat in the bleachers and watched Guru play tennis, sing, weight lift, draw, eat, meditate, and chat on the phone until dusk, when Guru went home for a brief interval. I, too, returned home just long enough to change into my sari for the evening function. The difference between the day function and the evening function was that at night, the bleachers were crowded with the disciples who had to work during the day, and therefore came to Guru every night eager to soak up as much inspiration as possible. Following the evening meditation came the great honor, when I and thirty lucky disciples were invited to Guru's house, where we sat on the floor of his living room until the early morning. Then I went home to begin it all again.

Guru bathed me in attention and regularly summoned me for gifts of silk saris, tennis rackets, and trophies. He boasted about me into the microphone during functions, praising me for trivial challenges such as catching the prasad orange that he threw or reciting an aphorism. When I wrote a couple simple poems, Guru proclaimed that I was "the poet laureate of the Sri Chinmoy Center." Guru assigned me tasks, such as collecting money for pictures of himself that he sold, the privilege of playing tennis upon his court whenever I wanted, and composing lists of visiting disciples whom I felt should be included in new singing groups. Often he confided in me, revealing secrets such as his increased knee pain was because of other disciples' jealousy of me. Guru had always told me that as the guru, it was his burden to carry all of our ignorance. This colossal weight manifested itself physically, producing a never-ending series of aches and pains in Guru's body. As a result, he now walked with a limp, as both his knees and his back were perpetually in excruciating pain. When I saw Guru limp or rub his hamstring, I felt terrible knowing how much I had contributed to his suffering. I hoped I never again would inflict discomfort upon him. Often during meditations, I cried and inwardly asked Guru to forgive me for having hurt him so much with my years of teenage heresy. But Guru's compassion was endless, and instead of punishing me, Guru offered me more and more kindness.

One of Guru's ways of lavishing blessings upon me was to invite me for car trips. As the disciples lined the lower end of the tennis court and driveway to wave a greeting of hello or good-bye to Guru, his driver would often slow down and motion for me to get inside. The invitation to ride in Guru's backseat was a coveted honor, and as I closed the door behind me, I heard both female and male disciples sigh at my fortune. We never went far, usually to his house, or the divine-enterprises, but sometimes, when Guru was hungry, we went to a diner.

Guru rated the local diners based on the consciousness of the food and the wait staff, and he had his favorite one— Lucille's. Because over the years Guru and his disciples had given Lucille's so much business, they honored Guru by printing a full vegetarian menu named after him. When they hung a framed picture of Guru in the diner, Guru decided that Lucille's had the highest consciousness by far.

When we entered with Guru, the waitresses rushed to the back room to arrange a long table for our feast. Guru always invited at least twenty disciples each time he went out to eat, enjoying the festivities of a table overflowing with steaming dishes.

Engaged in a perpetual war with his waistline, Guru complained that when he had weighed himself in the morning, his scale revealed that he had gained three and a half pounds since the day before. Since he was so disgusted with his weight gain, he glumly ordered only a hard-boiled egg and hot water with lemon. I was nearly finished with my grilled cheese when Romesh, Guru's messenger, interrupted our luncheon to announce that Joideep had died.

Joideep had been a disciple for more than twenty years. A descendant of a southern aristocratic family, Joideep had the mannerisms of a pampered Broadway star. He had been suffering with kidney disease for more than one year, and during that time, he had quietly vanished from view and became a patient at a live-in clinic in Long Island. Joideep had entered the sphere of those disciples who, for one reason or another, became sick, broken, or damaged, and, as a result, were moved to the peripheries and then off the map altogether.

Guru didn't believe in doctors or doctor visits, leaving all medical matters up to the Supreme and the faith of his disciples. According to Guru, none of his disciples could die without having Guru's express permission. As long as someone remained a disciple, they were safe from a sudden death. Since I was little, knowing Guru would never unexpectedly let death snatch away my family members sheathed me with comfort. It was one of his many promises that I relied heavily upon. On many occasions after disciples had survived car crashes or muggings, they would relate their harrowing, near-death stories giving full credit to Guru, who had appeared before them, ensuring their escape from harm and saving their lives. Guru relished these stories, and had them transcribed and published in a book.

"Oi? Tell again." Guru dropped his fork.

"I received a call from the hospital, and Joideep died three hours ago," Romesh said, kneeling on the sticky linoleum floor.

I spotted a wash of panic and shock on Guru's face. Clearly this was unexpected news. I studied Guru's stunned expression. If, according to Guru, disciples had to have his full permission before leaving the physical body, I wondered how come Guru hadn't known or inwardly sensed Joideep's death? Was this an oversight or was Guru just as oblivious to the secret realms of life and death, the inner worlds and karma, as the rest of us?

While Guru never claimed to be immortal, his own inevitable death or the death of his disciples was something he never discussed. He made it clear that the past was dust, and the future was not our concern; all attention must be fixated on the present. Therefore disciples who fretted about notions of health insurance, life insurance, or wills clearly were not full believers in Guru's protective powers. It was evident to all disciples that those who did become gravely ill or died, obviously had not been good disciples and as their lives withered and vanished, they were quickly forgotten.

I had never really known Joideep well. The longest conversation I had with him was when he called our house to tell my mother that he had seen us in the audience of his favorite daytime TV talk fest, *The Phil Donahue Show*. For a limited time, Phil Donahue taped his show in Stamford, and once my mother sneaked off with me to attend a taping. At first, my mother felt flustered by Joideep's phone call, as if she had been caught and was sure to be reported for corrupting me, but when Joideep started gossiping about how he felt that the one guest, the older lady having the affair with the teenage boy, really did indeed love him, my mother figured she would not be receiving a threatening message from Guru anytime soon.

WHEN, WHAT SEEMED like hours later, Guru reopened his eyes, the waitress had silently cleared off and wiped down the table. Guru lowered his voice, so that above the clanking of plates and chatter from the front booths, it was almost impossible to hear him. I scooted my chair in so that my stomach hit the table, and still I leaned in closer to him, needing to hear Guru's response.

"You see," Guru whispered. "This is what is possible when you are not receptive. It was not his time to go. I had a very special force on him. But he was not in the right consciousness and was not receptive to my blessings. He had not been leading a proper spiritual life, and he was unwilling to receive the protective force I had on him."

Guru did not say another word in the car, but instead of going to Guru's house, Asutosh, the driver, pulled over in front of my apartment. The ride was over.

That night at the function Guru taught new songs, sold a book of rhyming aphorisms, handed out the prasad, and even joked with Asutosh about losing to Gitali at that morning's road race. I never heard a single mention of Joideep's death that night or ever again. I was shaken. I saw that Guru had been ignorant of Joideep's death. And whether Joideep had been receptive or unreceptive to Guru, I witnessed Guru's alarmed expression, as though he had just been publicly exposed. Guru had not known about his death, and I didn't believe that it was just a simple oversight. It was larger and complicated. Realizing that Guru's promise of his occult powers to hold us all safe and secure seemed false, I wondered what else about him might be, as well.

A few weeks later, the official story was that Joideep had left Guru's Center a long time ago. Although I knew it was not true, I remained silent.

PERIODICALLY MY MOTHER brought me news from the "outside" world in the form of a home-design magazine, paperback bestseller, or my Connecticut mail, which usually consisted of credit card offerings, discount coupons for roofing materials, or nonprofit membership drives. One Wednesday, my mail contained an alumni newsletter from Greenwich Academy, along with a request for a donation and the completion of an update form. I stared at the smiley photos of my former classmates on a beach standing beside their fiancés, read through news about their acceptance into graduate programs, and their offers from Fortune 500 companies to top managerial positions. Though I certainly did not miss anything about Greenwich Academy, or my classmates, their accomplishments suddenly made me feel deficient. Even when I had been disguised as one of them, I had always understood that I was wholly different, an entirely separate species, and convinced myself of the futility of attempting to compete or even compare myself.

But now as I looked at the empty form, I grabbed a pen to fill it out. *What is your greatest achievement since graduating from G.A.?* I abandoned the love of my life, my Yale Law school–bound soul mate, to be Guru's good little girl and fulfill my destiny as his chosen disciple. *How has your life changed since G.A.?* I now live three blocks from Guru in Jamaica—dubbed the second-highest crime area in New York City five years in a row—and am a full-time "vagabond." *What are you looking forward to the most?*

I stared at the form and felt the question burrow deep inside.

What are you looking forward to the most? Nothing, really.

I ripped the form into tiny pieces. On the alumni newsletter, I crossed out my address and wrote in all capitals, RETURN TO SENDER: MOVED TO UNREACHABLE LOCATION.

THE REPETITIVE LOOP of my routine made each day blur into the next. I was assigned by Guru an endless cycle of busy-work that kept me perpetually serving him. After months spent at the tennis court, listening as the guards counted aloud Guru's stomach crunches and repeating aphorisms about the "compassion-feet" of the master, I felt myself withdrawing from everything around me. It began subtly, as if my eyesight ever so slightly had weakened, and my clear, sharp determination, once perfectly focused, now was slightly blurry. A foggy haze seemed to inhabit my head permanently, making it difficult to memorize new Bengali songs, even when I mouthed the words repeatedly. My ability to understand what I read was also smeared. I read and reread the same page of one of Guru's *Ten Thousand Flower-Flames* poems, and did not have the faintest idea what it meant: what was "oneness-fountain-bliss-joy" anyway?

I descended into a slow, draggy state where I felt tired constantly. It was harder and harder to wake up for morning *bhajan* practice. When I did make it over to Isha's, I sat in the back, leaning against the wall, and dozed in and out of the songs in praise of Guru. Often, I crawled back into bed, missing Runners Are Smilers altogether. When I finally did wake up, it was in the late afternoon. I knew that Guru would still be at the tennis court, but instead of rushing over, I stayed in bed, eventually rising at dusk to make an appearance at the evening meditation, where I would sit in the back, but nothing made me feel awake or inspired. I didn't know what was wrong with me. Something deeply fundamental had changed, and even though I was living in the apex of Guru's ashram, I felt distant and inaccessible. When the gathering ended, I'd squeeze into Guru's packed, overheated living room and numbly watch videos as Guru lay fully reclined in his chair having his feet and legs massaged. Tuhina, as the official videographer of the Center, was given the special task of providing wholesome entertainment for Guru's house. Guru declared many of the old sitcoms that she brought rubbish, but even for the few that Guru enjoyed—a continuous rotation between Hindi films based on the Mahabharata, *Car 54, Where Are You?* or *The Honeymooners*—Tuhina censored any and all objectionable material. On the rare occasion that a movie or show had a scene that passed the censor unnoticed, a near riot occurred.

Once, before Eddie Murphy came to meet Guru, Eddie Murphy's film *Coming to America* was shown at Guru's house. When Eddie's character locks lips with the beautiful waitress, Isha threw her hands over her eyes to block out the obscenity. Imitating Isha's shocked reaction, all of the women sitting behind her followed suit. Some even one-upped her by standing up and storming out onto the porch in disgust. The men's side dropped their heads in shame, all suddenly finding the Guru-blue shag carpet intently interesting. Tuhina, with blaring red cheeks, sprinted up to the big-screen TV, and stood directly in front of it with her arms and legs spread to block out the entire screen. She fast-forwarded until she felt that it was safe once more.

"Oi? Tuhina, all right?" Guru said, twitching his eyes open.

I found myself irritated at the dramatic posturing all around me. Was the spiritual foundation of my brothers and sisters made of tissue paper? Were they so weak that viewing a single kiss would tear apart their twenty-something years of commitment to their inner lives? Their fear of temptation, I found, was a sign of spiritual immaturity, a weakness. If they were true disciples, then they, too, could not only watch kisses but go out themselves and kiss, long and hard, and ultimately still return to their guru. I looked around the living room of the Avatar of the Era, and I suddenly longed for Oscar. I fantasized meeting him for dinner only to pick up where we had left off more than one and a half years ago. In the backseat of my car, in slow motion, our heat would steam up the windows until all of our actions would be concealed.

Although my rendezvous occurred only in my imagination, it felt as though my entire Oscar memory coffer had been, once again, taken out of storage. Days later, I dialed a few digits before hanging up, shaking, from my simultaneous fits of desire and weakness. Each aborted attempt ended with me in front of my shrine, begging forgiveness from Guru. It shamed me that after all my promises, I had regressed to the point where every time I saw a man with broad shoulders and black hair, I'd swear Oscar had tracked me down and was there to whisk me away. But Guru didn't seem to notice; instead, he gave me special prasad and boasted about my spiritual progress, which made me feel worse. As I filled diaries writing poems to Oscar, Guru wrote poems and songs for me. As I longed to take a Greyhound bus to see Oscar in New Haven, Guru flew me with him to Australia and New Zealand, where we met heads of state. Often Guru sweetly reminded me that the Supreme was my boyfriend, and a few times, he inserted the bonus fact that the Supreme was "extremely beautiful," but the only face I'd imagine was Oscar's, complete with his dimple and dark, pleading eyes.

Guru's delight with me bordered on the ridiculous. Either he was utterly oblivious, publicly proving that he hadn't a stitch of inner occult vision, or he was fully aware of all my decrepitude, therefore proving his boundless compassion. Both possibilities embarrassed me. The latter, somehow, made me feel worse. I was his; he had selected my soul, and he had a closer connection to my own soul than I did. Without Guru making me aware of my soul, I would never have believed I had one. I never felt anything bathed in divine light inside me; I didn't even feel anything slightly dampened by the divine. Inside, I merely felt hollow. I wished Guru would call the whole thing off—publicly rescind my Chosen

One status, proclaim once and for all that my entire life had been his error, a mistake. But as I waited to be exposed, Guru continued to praise my high consciousness. And as Guru always set the pace, from Ketan to my parents, everyone seemed filled with respectful awe of me, the supercharged aspirant. I had followers and fans, admirers and well-wishers, but neither Guru's teachings nor his mandated lifestyle felt natural to me. I had everything I didn't want. It was all a sham.

ONE SATURDAY NIGHT it poured, and the meditation was canceled. Chahna's parents returned to New Jersey, and I invited Chahna to spend the night.

She sat with her hands clasped on her lap as I poked about for conversation. The rain slammed against the windows, dripping in from all sides of the skylight. I hadn't bothered to switch on the lights, and now we were in darkness.

"I don't know why I came back," I blurted.

"From France? I thought you . . . aren't you happy?" Chahna hesitantly asked.

"Are you?" I tossed it right back at her.

She didn't answer.

"Everything feels wrong. I don't even want to get out of bed. I have no interest in meditation or the spiritual life, not to mention the Supreme. I'm on an endless loop failing Guru and everything that I can't live up to anymore."

I heard Chahna's feet stop kicking.

"I want something of my own. I want something apart from Guru. Do you know every time Guru tells me how great it is that the Supreme is my boyfriend, I stop listening. I can't stand it anymore. I say to myself, 'Oh yeah, well, where the hell is he? How come he never takes me out or even calls?'"

"Guru's told me the Supreme is my boyfriend too. I think the Supreme is two-timing us," Chahna said.

I laughed, and so did she. It got funnier, and we laughed even harder.

I had my Chahna, and I was so grateful at that moment for her presence, for sharing my life. Without judgment or jealousy, Chahna had and always would unreservedly love me.

"I've missed you so much. And I couldn't even imagine being in all of this insanity without you. You're the only one I can talk to. The only person I can trust to actually be honest with, without fear of not saying or doing the right thing and getting reported."

Chahna suddenly excused herself, and hurried into the bathroom. When she returned she started talking about her cat and her grandmother's fake leopard coat that she now wore over jeans.

"Guru told me my soul wants me to drop out of high school," Chahna said. She was in her senior year.

"And work full-time at the restaurant and share a room in Vedita's house."

We sat in silence.

"I think my soul hates me," Chahna said.

"It's so unfair," I finally said. "It's Saturday night. Do you know that there are people out there who are actually making their own decisions, their own plans? Like hosting a dinner party, or flirting at a bar, screaming at a concert, or dancing at a club?" I started to cry. "Some people get to live real lives. Don't you want that? And here we are. Trapped." I got up, not knowing exactly what to do. I paced around, landing by my kitchenette's single cupboard. I felt my way around the near empty shelf, and grabbed a can.

"Here's what we have: creamed corn. It's you and me on a Saturday night with a can of creamed corn, while the Supreme, our shitty boyfriend, is MIA." I was sobbing.

Chahna had rolled onto her stomach, her face aimed at the floor. When the phone call came later that night, inviting me up to Guru's house, I ignored it.

AFTER THAT NIGHT, Chahna changed. She wore a used army jacket over her Guru-blue sari. Her toenails and fingernails were painted black, and she never seemed to smile so much. Every time I called, she wasn't home. When I cornered her at a function to ask what was going on, she told me to knock off the cross-examination and just be happy for her.

The following month Chahna brought a "seeker" to the public meditation. His name was Rick, and he was a few years older than her, pale with a large nose, and a jagged crew cut. He sat with her father on the men's side, and when it was time for the seekers to go up on stage to meditate with Guru, he went, fully respectful, with folded hands. When I pulled Chahna aside to question her about this "seeker," she just shrugged.

Two weeks later, I was sitting on Guru's porch when I heard Vani whisper to Ushma if she had heard the news about Chahna.

"What news?" I demanded.

"She left the Center. She has a boyfriend," Vani, herself

only nineteen, said, shaking her head in utter disgust at the very idea of such a grotesque act.

Suddenly dizzy, I staggered outside and sat on Guru's front stoop. My own Chahna was gone, jumping ship, without even telling me. I suddenly remembered Rick, the "seeker." But if she had found real love, so urgent, to leave Guru, why would she have kept this, this most critical decision of her life, away from me?

At that moment, Ketan approached the stairs from the sidewalk. He had taken Guru's dog, Kanu, out for his nightly walk. By the look on my face, he suspected that I had heard the news.

"Ironic, isn't it?" Ketan said, tugging on the leash.

"What?"

"You know, don't you see the irony here, with Chahna? After all she did save you from . . ."

"Me?" I snapped. "What does this have to do with me?"

"After Chahna rescued you from leaving the Center by reporting you to Guru, now she is the one who commits spiritual suicide by running off with some ordinary loser. I find it ironic. Don't you?" Ketan bent down and scooped up the tiny white dog. "Come on, Kanu, let's go nighty-night. You already pooped," he said, going inside.

I walked away from Guru's house. I didn't know where I was going, and I didn't care. I wandered block after block not hearing anything except my own storm of thoughts. All this time, and I had never imagined that Chahna, the one person I trusted, had turned me in. I was furious. She was no different from the other poseur disciples, eavesdropping and plotting to get inside Guru's special clan. Chahna, my two-faced friend, had used me to get tenure as Guru's darling, sitting at his house, receiving his flowers and gifts, for having sold me out. I was done with her. I hoped her soul would wickedly punish her. It's what she deserved.

Suddenly, a black van pulled up beside me and beeped. A man with sunglasses leaned out the window, making sucking noises with his mouth. Instead of fear, I only felt outrage. The man tapped his palm against the side of the van, as if to lure me like a dumb stray dog. I bent down and picked up two fistfuls of rocks from the weedy patch between the sidewalk and street curb, screamed and pummeled the rocks directly at the van. Rocks for Chahna's incredulous betrayal and her smug abandonment, for Guru's inability to make me the person I was supposed to be, for my parents' obliviousness to my meltdown of faith, for my brother and his gossipy aloofness, for the clawed and cliquey disciples who smiled while hoping that I would fail again, for Oscar, who never rescued me, for everyone who was living a normal life, and finally for the Supreme, whom I hated and sought a permanent breakup with. The rocks walloped the van and rebounded off onto the street.

The man hollered at me in Russian, then he opened the door and stood beside his van, his arms slapping his thighs.

I screamed back at him in nonsensical globs of consonants and vowels, mashing sounds with shrieks to topple his barrage of Russian curses. At the top of my voice, I shrieked. My voice tore through the dark street, butting the windows of the sleepy residents. A light flicked on from the second floor of the house across the street from where I stood, then the porch light blinked on, spilling light onto our scene.

The man looked up, then back at me, and flicked his hand

dismissively at me, as though I suddenly was no longer worth his time, then scrambled inside the van and hit the gas, leaving behind a long cloud of smoky exhaust.

I roared after him, then refilled my hands with rocks, hoping he'd return. I surveyed both ends of the street, armed and ready. I was not backing down. I had reached my limit, and he had chosen the wrong person. I walked, clutching the rocks, tracing their jagged edges in my palms. I clicked them against each other, and deeply exhaled as I realized that not for one second, even as the man roamed outside the van, had I invoked Guru. I had done just fine without him. I could extend this independence and fend for myself. I determined that I could do without Guru. I had had it.

WHEN I WROTE to Guru informing—not asking—him that I needed to make immediate changes, my fearlessnesses had already receded. Leaving the Center was absolutely terrifying; it meant an irrevocable separation from everything that I had ever known, including my mother and father. I would be homeless and penniless. Though it felt too daunting to parachute into the outside world all alone, I pledged to take small steps away while still grasping the stability and security of the Center. I needed to pace myself, moving slowly toward freedom. To start, I would no longer be a full-time Guru-vagabond.

In order to get Guru's approval of my decision, I knew I'd have to convince him that my actions would ultimately work to serve him, which, to a certain extent, was true. I suspected I would always be serving him, no matter what I did. I pleaded with Guru that I be utilized to help him publicize his activities and recruit new disciples, by becoming a journalist. Guru, as I expected, was not enthused by my unexpected request, and he was perturbed that I wanted to enroll in a few journalism courses. When I was in high school, he had made it very clear that he did not want me to go to college because it was the domain of the mind, and dwelling in the mind, rather than the heart, only led seekers into a forest of poisonous doubts. I persuaded Guru that I would only be taking classes to acquire the tools needed to join his growing public relations team of disciples who gathered in strategizing meetings, toting around briefcases filled with full-color brochures of Guru's meetings with pop stars, presidents, and popes. When I notified my parents about my decision, my father thought it was great and commended me for taking the initiative toward financial independence. My mother appeared neutral, allowing me to negotiate directly with Guru for permission and directions.

To build my case, I wrote an article on Guru's newest project, his Soul-Bird drawings, a series of wobbly pen-and-ink doodles that were meant to represent the soul as a bird. I titled it "A Migration of Art," glorifying his art and playing up the bird metaphor to its fullest. Guru loved it. He published it as a pamphlet and required all of the disciples to buy a copy. He told me I understood the consciousness of his soul-birds, and since he was so pleased, he agreed to allow me to hone my journalistic skills. I was empowered by my own manipulative magic, and it reminded me of the times as a little girl I had charmed Guru into bending the rules for me. Ketan was the only one who seemed suspicious.

"You're going to college? Why?" he interrogated, squinting his blue eyes at me, his blond lashes rapidly blinking.

"You're not going to get yourself all tangled up in something, are you?"

"Oh, please," I said, as if the very question was insulting.

ON THE FIRST day of my classes in Brooklyn, relishing the excitement of my new unsupervised surroundings, I sat next to the cutest guy in the room. I felt instantly energized. After class, Rufus introduced himself and invited me to a party that night. Without a single thought of the inevitable ramifications from the Center, I ended up leaving with Paul, a communist with shaggy black hair and a gap between his two front teeth. We sat at the Dunkin' Donuts on Nostrand Avenue, composing lines of poetry. By the end of the night I wrote, *I think I'm in love with you.*

When I returned home, I had two messages from Sarisha, summoning me to celebrate Vani's birthday at Guru's house. The next day, when Ketan asked where I had been, I told him that I hadn't felt well, and had slept right through everything. When he said that he hadn't seen my car in the driveway, I rolled my eyes, as if affronted by his mere suggestion of a discrepancy.

Suddenly, I no longer missed Chahna or Oscar. I couldn't wait to ride the subway to Brooklyn. It was a safe distance from the eyes and ears of Guru's neighborhood, giving me plenty of space to test out my new self—Jayanti, the dark-arty-writer-communist-lover. With my refusals to answer certain questions about my past or family or invite anyone to my home or anywhere near my neighborhood, I appeared enigmatic and exotic.

After class, Paul and I would make out on the boardwalk

at Coney Island for hours, until I knew I had to return for the evening meditation. Missing meditations was too obvious. In order to maintain the appearance of normalcy in the Center, I needed to be sure to raise the least amount of suspicion possible. I wanted to keep my footing steady between both worlds. Taking the full plunge either way felt too overwhelming. Though I knew I couldn't sustain both equally forever, I forged ahead. I attended *bhajan* practice, ran Runners Are Smilers, appeared at the tennis court before classes, and showered off Paul's sweat and licks by the evening meditation. The difficult part came with Guru's house late at night; I knew that alarms would be sent if I declined his invites, so most nights, I went to his house, then when it was over, I changed in my car at stoplights on my way to Brooklyn, returning just in time to change back for *bhajan* practice at five-thirty.

I thought I was doing great. I felt vibrant and clever, thrilled with my managerial skills over all things me. There was no stopping me now, and why should there be? I felt I could exist this way forever. It suited me fine. I had everything. I inhabited the best of both worlds: I had friends, college, fun, and a boyfriend, while simultaneously, through my continuous presence at the tennis court and Guru's house, maybe could even still inch toward God-Realization. It seemed unfair that the two worlds had to be so distinct; it felt more natural to have both—a rich inner and outer life. I did not understand why spirituality could not be just *part* of a life and why it had to be piously segregated. My family thought I was doing great, and so did Guru. I kept Guru a secret from Paul, and I kept Paul a secret from Guru. Each seemed perfectly oblivious of the other and fully content with my attentions.

One night, I was sitting on the porch at Guru's house, when Fulmala, Vani's mother, who always seemed to be campaigning for Vani to take over my position, sat beside me.

She stared at my face for a few moments, as if she detected the thick black eyeliner and glossy lipstick I had worn earlier.

"You look different," she concluded.

"Oh? My hair's in a bun. Last night I had it in a braid," I said with an exaggerated hand motion to my head.

"Nope. That's not it. It's something else." Her eyes scanned down to my toes and returned to my face. "I know what it is," she said, lowering her voice.

"You do?" I asked, feeling my heart speed up and my cheeks flush.

"Of course. I have intuitive powers. I am a mother, you know."

I sat, afraid that if I even swallowed, I'd be exposed.

"You've been released from Chahna's bad influence. Now that she is finally gone, so are her destructive forces."

I exhaled in deep relief. Of course Fulmala didn't know. Guru didn't even know, and he was supposedly the Supreme of the Universe. Give me a break. I felt suddenly wildly cocky. I didn't care what she thought. Let her report me. Go ahead. I leaned in close to Fulmala, looked her right in her droopy eyes.

"I taught Chahna everything she knows," I said, then smugly walked away.

ONE MORNING, GURU's car pulled up beside me. As I went to open the door to the backseat, Asutosh motioned me away.

This was not an invitation. Guru's window slid down only a few inches, and I leaned in close to hear him through the thick glass barrier. In a low voice, Guru said he had been receiving numerous reports about me from disciples who spotted me sneaking out and returning at odd hours. My deliberate acts of disobedience and lack of aspiration were causing him great pain. Before I could respond, the window shut, and the car pulled away.

My facade as Guru's divine disciple had been exposed. In Guru's eyes I was two-faced and committed to nothing and no one but my own raggedy self, a lying, cheating, pathetic mess. It was all true. I didn't deserve Guru's trust, and I knew that I had deliberately broken all the lofty promises I had made to Guru when I returned to New York to be his peerless disciple. I let down Ketan and my parents, too, who were oblivious to my double life, shoveling blind support toward a false cause. My entire life was a false front. I had no one to confer with, and even if I did, it would expose my ungrateful and selfish self. The only thing I wanted was to be far away from everyone who knew how wretched I was, and to be near someone who didn't know a drop about my spiritual deceits and ineptitudes—Paul.

I invited him to come over to my apartment. I didn't care. Let Sarisha see me answer the door; let Ganika hear us rolling around the floor from the apartment below. I now craved a decisive reaction. Maybe Guru would kick me out of the Center for good, or maybe Paul would permanently kidnap me. The following afternoon, when Paul left with his change of boxer shorts and toothbrush in his hand, I gave him a dramatic farewell kiss in the front yard, wearing only his Che Guevara T-shirt that skimmed my thighs.

The next day, I received a phone call from Romesh with the message that I was breaking Guru's heart and that Guru was asking me to leave the Center for a full six months. When that time was up, he would confer with the Supreme and see what steps would be taken. He said I was doing irreparable damage to my inner life, and he could no longer intervene against the inevitable and dire punishment of my soul. In the meantime, I was not allowed to attend any activities or have contact with anyone inside the Center.

I felt utterly calm. All the crazed turbulence ceased. My mind was in a quiet shock that padded me from thinking or fretting. I sat down and stared at the wall, enjoying its blank whiteness, its lack of complications.

My mother called me five minutes later announcing she and my father were on their way to come see me, and for me to stay still and wait for them. I didn't know what she imagined either she or my father could do for me, but I didn't stop them from coming. We went to a pizzeria, where my mother nervously babbled about planting pumpkin seeds in her garden, while repeatedly interrupting herself to force me to eat. My father remained silent as he ate both his own eggplant grinder and then finished mine. Before they drove back to Connecticut, my mother begged me to return with them for a little rest, but I declined.

A FEW DAYS later, as I walked to the Parsons Boulevard subway station headed to Flatbush to Paul, who remained fully oblivious of the rupture in my life, Tuhina drove past. I waved, but she didn't acknowledge me. On the next block, Vanita cycled by, also without even a nod. Ahead I saw Sarisha jogging toward me. When she came closer, she crossed to the other side of the street. I knew the procedure; it wasn't personal. They were obediently following Guru's orders not to talk to ex-disciples. Guru built an absolute fortress between disciples and ex-disciples. Once a disciple left, all contact with and even mention of the person was cut off. Any exchange with ex-disciples was a serious breach of Guru's rules, and many disciples were asked to leave Guru as a result. I couldn't blame the disciples, but I wondered why they would go to such extremes to avoid me. I wasn't a *real* ex-disciple; besides, I was still Guru's favorite, his Chosen One, so it seemed ridiculous.

When I entered the subway station and waited on line for tokens, I spotted Ketan. It was the first time that I had seen him since Romesh's call. I had suspected that he had been busy on a media blitz for Guru and just hadn't been in town. I walked up to him from behind, placed my hands on his shoulders, and said his name with an overdone French accent. He stiffened, turned around to stare past me as if I were a ghost, then he turned and exited the station.

9

This Is Heresy

"Y OU'RE NOT GOING TO SPONTANEOUSLY COMBUST SIT-
ting on the F train," Chahna said, in her backyard.
After many messages from Chahna, weeks passed
before I eventually returned her calls. Though I was not
ready to forget what she had done, after being suspended
from the Center and having broken up with Paul, I realized
that Chahna was my sole link to friendship. I desperately
needed her. After all, she had only told Guru on me because
at the time she believed she was saving me from what Guru
said would be my "destruction." Now that she was an ex-
disciple, listening to her confidently assure me about life beyond the Center was a jolting shift. Her voice was buoyant,
her sentences uplifted as though, by severing all ties to
the Center, she had gained full immersion in the world. In a
reversal of roles, she had become the older one, more experienced, coaxing me forward. According to the newly authori-
tative Chahna, the outing away from Guru's Queens would be
good for me, and I agreed to visit her in New Jersey.

"I left the Center," Chahna said. "And I'm fine. Safes don't
drop on my head as I walk down the street."

I hadn't thought of that. A safe could drop on my head.

Before I was banished, Guru had told me my soul had lost patience with my reckless life, warning me that he could no longer intervene to save me from its punishment.

"Your soul isn't going to push you in front of a speeding bus," Chahna said.

Maybe her soul was not as spiteful as mine. A bus flattening me sounded more than probable.

"Guru always talks about his path being the Golden Boat, and if a disciple leaves the boat, then the person automatically drowns in the ignorance-sea. Guess what?" Seated in the shade of her family's small yard, Chahna inched her lawn chair closer to mine. "It's a lie."

I looked around, expecting a surge of lightning to strike the aluminum chairs, instantly frying both of us, but none came. Hearing Chahna, the once pudgy, runny-nosed little girl with the greasy hair, brazenly denying one of Guru's chief edicts was a sacrilege. Instinctively, I defended Guru.

"You don't know that."

"Hey. Do I look drowned?"

She certainly did not. Chahna had never appeared so beautiful. With her long hair loosely clustered on the crown of her head and secured by two Chinese-red chopsticks, she was elegantly funky. Her once insecure tics had stopped. She seemed happy, comfortable with herself and her status as an ex-disciple.

For the third time since I had arrived at her house, Rick, her boyfriend, called. Each time, curling the phone cord around her wrist as a bracelet and giggling tightly into the mouthpiece, she finally coaxed him off the phone with a smooch, a rushed iloveyou, and a promise to call him to discuss plans for that evening just as soon as she could. Towering over her at six feet, Rick had enough vintage fashion sense to compensate for his pockmarked complexion and bulbous nose. He had firmly entrenched himself in Chahna's new life, filling every space that might have been left empty from the Center. Even her parents welcomed Rick as an expected fixture in their family. Although both Chahna's parents were officially still disciples, for the past ten years they had been retreating away from the ever-expanding hustle of Guru's activities. From their open acceptance of their only child's curtailed spiritual life to their embrace of all things Rick, Chahna's family life felt alien to me. No wonder Chahna's post-Center crisis seemed nonexistent. Apart from my mother's regular visits with me that made me feel as though I were in hospice care, I felt estranged from my entire family. Ketan shunned me, as did Aunt Chandika; and my father, with his normal cocktail of aloofness and distraction, seemed more concerned about whether the skylight in my apartment leaked after a rainstorm than if I was even there.

Besides my parents, I had not heard from a single disciple. None of the throngs who held me as an infant, played with me as a toddler, or admired me as a child had bothered to phone, write, drop by, or even wave hello. I had been erased. Vanished. Jayanti who? Since childhood, I knew we were supposed to eliminate all traces of ex-disciples from our lives, and I had dutifully done so without much thought. Yet now that I was on the other side, I realized the cruel brutality of the practice.

The silence chilled me. I had never expected Guru to extend the same absolute policies toward me. I believed his tenderness was unconditional, and that soon enough he would nestle me back into his warm care. Never before had he been so severe and official with me. I was banned from meditations, both public and private, and not allowed inside the divine-enterprises. I obediently segregated myself, not wanting to put other disciples in harm's way, even accidentally. Before I opened my third-floor apartment's door for a quick run to the deli, I'd listen to ensure none of the other disciple tenants, including Aunt Chandika, was in the hallway. I wanted to spare both them and me the awkward duties of shunning an ex-disciple in one's own home.

When Chahna announced that we—with her assumed and obvious inclusion of Rick—were going out dancing, I asked why. Dancing, even traditional Indian dancing as a devotional art, was forbidden by Guru. In his belief that the body functioned solely as a vehicle to manifest the Supreme, all other activities involving the body—with the exception of exercise, which was viewed as a vehicle to keep the body fit for manifestation—were lascivious and suspect. Dancing was bad, a lower-vital expression. Even when I was a child, from the Chicken Dance to the squaredance, all forms were condemned.

Before I had time to protest, Chahna raced up to her attic abode, gifted me with two mix tapes of music that she labeled as essential hits played in the club, then flung open her closet and giddily smothered her bed with hanger upon hanger of various billowy and slinky black outfits.

"Who died?" I asked.

"Everyone," Chahna replied, walking toward the bathroom. "It's the look."

Black, Guru declared, was the color of ignorance. It was officially banned from any disciple's wardrobe. Occasionally, while performing one of Guru's plays, disciples cast as hostile forces or demons draped themselves in black cloth, sending the clear signal even before uttering a single line that they represented the bad guys, causing many hisses and boos from the audience as they stood upon the makeshift stage. Now, staring at the black swamp that used to be Chahna's bed, I wondered if one of her first ex-disciple digressions had been to bundle all of her pastel printed saris into garbage bags and replace them with hanger upon hanger of clothes in Guru's ultimate color foe.

Chahna reappeared wearing ripped black fishnets, black combat boots, and a mini black satin vintage slip. White face powder wiped any trace of color or freckle from her skin, giving her the matte finish of rice paper. Around her eyes, black eyeliner flared like the open wings of bats. Caked upon her lips was a coat of black lipstick. The sole touch of color was a red velvet ribbon tied tight upon her upper neck. Dangling from it was a black spider.

"What happened to you?" I asked. She looked simultaneously glamorous and ridiculous.

Ignoring me, Chahna sprayed gel into her wavy hair, then asked why I wasn't dressed yet.

"Do your dad and mom know you dress like this? And where are we going, anyway?"

Before she could answer, Nitya, Chahna's mother, appeared at the top of the stairs, announcing she had just made popcorn. She chuckled at Chahna, complimenting her on the fishnets, reminiscing about how she, too, a long time ago, used to wear them, then she headed back down to the *Twilight Zone* marathon and her bowl of popcorn. Again, I compared this to my own mother, who I imagined upon seeing me cloaked as a black nymphet would have cried, begging me to reconsider my life choices, and I wouldn't have blamed her.

Rick drove us to Manhattan in his massive black truck. As he pulled up to the front of the Limelight, and his muffler snarled exhaust, all heads turned.

We joined the line. Originally built in 1846 as the Holy Communion Episcopal Church, it now served as the Limelight, a nightclub owned and run by the notorious Peter Gatien. Every night, crowds waited hours to enter.

"Hey, Sarah." An Asian boy with a multilayering of chains around his gazelle neck, waved at Chahna to cut the long queue.

I knew Chahna used Sarah, her birth name, at school, but hearing it aloud startled me. It confirmed the current distant divide between her two selves, the disposable Guru-coated entity and her other self. I suddenly envied her for having the option to shed one for the other, to slip into Sarah-mode at will. Since the only name and identity I had were given by Guru, I realized that unlike Chahna or Sarah, I could never switch from one to the next effortlessly, like turning a light on or off.

After squeezing into a parking spot a few blocks away, Rick joined us in the line, wrapping Chahna in his arms and kissing her dramatically, as if he hadn't seen her in ages and desperately missed her.

"You look like a ghost. You look beautiful," Rick said to Chahna, taking small steps toward the bouncer to the right of the door.

"The deader the better," Chahna said in a Bela Lugosi voice impersonation through her lips suffocated under black waxy lipstick.

I walked behind, watching her velvet cape mingle with the sidewalk dirt, feeling anxious and invisible.

The first bouncer spoke with the kind of British accent that made the words "seven dollars cover charge" sound like poetry from Lord Byron.

"Nice dress, love," he added to me.

I smiled at his comment, feeling a little more at ease. I saw Chahna puff up with pride, as if to say I told you so, regarding her choice of clothing. I then watched as Chahna and Rick disappeared arm in arm into the stairwell's mouth that led to the necropolis. They were inseparable, a coupled unit, complete unto themselves. I straggled behind, stumbling in the dark for my footing.

Tuesday nights were called "Communion." The streaky darkness smelled like an incense of manufactured smoke and clove cigarettes. Aching, haunting music pulsated through the room. An opalescent strobe light stabbed through the dark room, and I moved through the crowds. Long-limbed outlines pressed against walls; huddled clumps sat in the corners, lit cigarettes dangling from slim figures. On the dance floor, black forms spun and gyrated like whirling dervishes. A man held a wineglass as he swayed and posed. To his right, a cadaver-thin woman dressed in a corset over a full eighteenth-century hoop-tiered black lace gown and wearing a black wedding veil shimmied to the floor, where she extended her gloved arms as if she were languorously plucking invisible flowers from the tiles.

Someone tapped my shoulder.

"Surprise!"

I looked up to find myself staring at the flat torso of an impossibly tall young woman.

"It's me!"

Way below her belly button, what looked like black Bubble Wrap functioned as a skirt, curtaining off the tops of her bony hips, while revealing black ribbons spiraling up both legs like barber shop poles. Seven-inch black platform heels completed the look.

"Tashvi!"

Tashvi had left the Center not long before me. When, shortly before her departure, her father became gravely ill, Guru had sent her a message that her own bad karma had been the cause of her father's suffering. Tashvi's guilt encompassed her until she was nearly catatonic, then she vanished, fleeing the Center and her parents without a note. Tashvi, a disciple who had been in the Center since she was five years old, now stood before me bare-chested with black electrical tape positioned as Xs that barely covered her nipples. I remembered her at Guru's longest-hair contest, smiling with her rabbitlike buck teeth as Guru announced her the winner. Her hair now was bobby-pinned into clusters all over her head and dusted with a coating of glitter that matched the glitter on her fake eyelashes, cheeks, and lips. I was speechless. My shock only increased when a beautiful boy in a black poet's blouse transparent from sweat and molded against his narrow frame clutched her from behind, enfolding her in his embrace and biting her neck in a sucking kiss. Without even flinching or turning slightly, Tashvi merely rolled her eyes, and when the suction from his lips ended, they didn't even exchange a word as he strolled forward only to be swallowed up by the crowd. This was the same girl who had stood beside me when Guru called the children up to recite his poems, whose nervousness I had seen as her body shook before, during, and after she recited Guru's poem in a tiny cracked voice. Now she was fierce and uninhibited. How had she morphed from the jittery quiet disciple to the vamp in electrical tape?

Soon Tashvi was surrounded by an admiring group. I crossed the main dance floor, discovering a second, smaller, room. Crossing my arms, I felt incredibly alone. Unlike Tashvi, I wasn't sure if I belonged here with the ethereal romantics who donned black velvet and parasols or the harder industrials garbed in black leather and piercings. This was their sanctuary, and I was not an official member of their congregation. Hours passed as I sat on a carved pew listening as the music swirled in urgent rhythms. Beside me, a man wearing a black top hat remained completely still, with his eyes closed. When I glanced at him, he appeared to be meditating. He could have been at a function at the tennis court or at Guru's porch. I wondered what Guru was doing at this exact moment and if he missed me. I, too, closed my eyes, deciding to meditate to create a pocket of divinity. I summoned Guru's compassion, asking him to bless and protect me. When I felt a hand on my shoulder, I smiled, absorbing the weight that I imagined as Guru's confirming touch. I slightly bowed, reveling in its assurance. Suddenly another hand grabbed on to my thigh. I opened my eyes as the man in the top hat hunched over my lap in an attempt to heave vomit on the floor. A splatter of chunky liquid hit my shoes before puddling upon the ground.

The witching hour was over. The music stopped, the lights came on.

"Thank you for coming. Now get the fuck out," the bouncer

with a large purple hat covering half his face said as he opened the vaulted doors and Chahna, Rick, and I stumbled into the street.

It was five-thirty in the morning when I dragged the covers over my head on Chahna's pull-out couch. The sky was already half lavender. I was more baffled than ever. Both Chahna and Tashvi had been disciples, inside Guru's protective cloister, nearly their entire lives, yet they had cast aside their former selves so quickly and with such apparent ease. Where was the anguish and ache for their former lives? Weren't they in fear of their own souls?

I rolled from side to side, vacillating between envy and pity for Chahna, who snored peacefully in her bed only a few feet away. She had her doppelgänger in Rick, a unified family, and acceptance into an inexhaustible social sphere; outwardly Chahna was well stocked with love and companionship. She was not isolated, cowering from a throbbing combination of solitude and fear. I needed to leave. With my hosts unaware of my departure, I headed home.

The familiar comfort of my small Jeep that had ported me in the familiar loop between the tennis court, Guru's house, and my own, with its stains from spilled prasad and a picture of Guru affixed upon the dashboard, held some solace. As I approached Jamaica, I eased my tightened grip on the steering wheel. When I turned onto Parsons Boulevard, the quiet of the early morning was only occasionally broken by a passing car. I surveyed the houses built tightly beside each other with barely enough lawn in front to separate one driveway from the next. Cracked sidewalks with littered patches of discarded bottles, cigarette packets, and escaped garbage can lids marked the seeming outer insignificance of the neighborhood, but inside various homes, disciples were finishing their early-morning meditations and preparing for another day living for Guru.

As I turned onto 150th Street, I saw a man stiffly walking with a limp, swaying from side to side. Dressed in a white track suit and ski hat, it was undoubtedly Guru. I immediately pulled over. For a few years Guru was forced to withdraw from long-distance running due to a nearly crippling combination of knee and back problems, but daily he persisted in logging in miles by walking. Seeing Guru for the first time as a former disciple, I felt undeserving, as though the privilege of gazing at him was an exclusive right reserved for disciples only.

I ducked, peering through the steering wheel. With his arms straight by his sides and his fingers spread open, Guru leaned into the hill ahead of him. From his inchmeal pace, Guru was a worn old man, as though shuffling from his house out to his mailbox, rather than an omniscient and omnipotent avatar who controlled the cosmos. My whole life, Guru's powers over world affairs, forces of nature, and the distribution of karma had made him a massive figure, enormous and all-powerful. Now, trudging up the hill, Guru appeared dwarfed, reduced. When had this happened? Looking at Guru, the same imperial figure who plotted and portioned my entire life from before my birth until the present, limping along the cracked sidewalk, I saw him altered, mortal.

When Guru eventually reached the top, he turned and once again increased our distance by gingerly retreating down the hill. Outwardly he never glanced my way, but I was certain that he had been aware of my presence, and it was his turn to deny me. After he disappeared from my rearview mirror, I proceeded home, convinced that this was Guru's clear signal that it was not yet time for him to accept me back, and that there was a very real chance that he would never accept me.

AS WEEKS CHURNED into slow months, I felt more isolated. Chahna and Tashvi harped that barring myself alone in my apartment served no purpose other than brewing in misery. The longer I spent staring at the famous picture of Guru embracing me when I was only months old, the worse I felt. Of course the oblivious infant was cradled by Guru. At that point, without a formed mind or vital, I was an ideal disciple. In his arms, submissive to his will, he assumed that was how I would always be. The distance between the baby in the photo and my current self was immeasurable. Instead of evolving, my entire life had been slowly and consistently devolving. A spiritual seeker since birth, I was a dysfunctional wreck. I curled up on the floor with my back to my shrine.

When the phone rang, I reached over to pick it up, figuring that it was either my mother or Chahna. After my fake perky greeting, a silence stretched across the line until a man's raspy breath filled the receiver. I asked who he was and who he wanted. He responded only with clumps of deep breaths. I expected he would reveal himself to me, but his panting continued without interruption. I cradled the phone with both hands to decipher his message. The urgency of his breaths increased, getting faster and louder. I listened deeply until I realized that this was the language without words, the primal grunts, moans, and breaths of sex that transcended vocabulary. I had never heard it before. I closed my eyes, hearing him increase his frequency and volume. He sounded near

collapse. When I tried to imagine the way his body was positioned, I thought of Oscar. If I had only chosen to stay with
Oscar, sped off on that subway with him, not only would I be
an insider to glorious fits of passion but I would have someone beside me right now. With a final chalky moan, the man
stopped. The line went dead. I lay on the floor, waiting for
him to return, wishing he would call back.

That night I called Chahna to tell her I was going to the
Limelight. I picked up Tashvi, who marveled at my outfit, a
white sari slip and blouse, declaring my radical inversion of
black was the perfect attention-getter. Entering the former
church before midnight, the crowds were sparse, mostly
clinging to the bar. I stepped onto the empty dance floor and,
for the first time ever, I danced. Without caring about who
was watching my spastic jerks and flails, I soaked up the entire space, thrusting my arms and legs in all directions. I
shook violently, casting away the frigid lockdown on my
body. If this was the vital life, the invigorating movement of
the body, I was engaged in it. I rolled my neck, letting my
long hair drag behind. Inside, I was waking and stirring. The
beat propelled me, and I fastened on to it, allowing it to lead
my explosions of movement and frantic need. When I could
no longer contain my breath, when sweat ironed my slip
against my skin, I leaned against a wall. The first man who
stood beside me, with black pageboy haircut, black lipstick,
and a priest's robe complete with a white collar, tapped my
shoulder and when he asked if I wanted a drink, I shook
my head no, stating I just wanted him. He put his hands on
my shoulders and rubbed my arms. I leaned into him, he
wrapped his arms around me until I was lost in his black
vestments. By the next song, we were kissing frantically, our

tongues racing inside each other's mouths, while our hands rambled up and down, tracing each other's contours. As the club became more crowded, we didn't notice. The lights flashed and smoke spat from the DJ's fog machine. The hazy, streaked light and whirl of bodies on the dance floor made all markings of time and place irrelevant. Imbibing the smooth flawless skin of this raven-haired man, I felt starving, and unstoppable. I needed much more.

"Come on," I said, and tugged him away.

He clutched me from behind as I led him through the tangles of people toward the bathroom. Inside, a black lightbulb barely leaked light. In silence, he slid the bolt into the door and pushed me to the sink's counter. Now that I had him, I let him lead. I decided that I could do anything. I was beyond repair. It only made sense to be fully broken. He lifted up my slip and ripped my white tights. He then hoisted his robe, under which he wore nothing, and pushed aside my underwear. With a few sloppy stabs, he entered me, making me gasp, causing my breath to disappear inside my chest. After violent thrusts, he collapsed onto me, then caught his breath and pulled away, letting his cloak modestly shade him. He pushed his hair off his forehead, nodded, unlatched the bolt, and left. In the soiled, dank bathroom, I slid to the floor. It wasn't until fists pounded against the door that I even remembered where I was.

I kept my eyes lowered as I pushed through the swarms toward the club's exit.

Driving home in the rainy night, my hands and legs shook. The exit for the Brooklyn-Queens Expressway came too quickly, and I veered sharply to the right. Instead of following the curved route, my Jeep skidded across the lane, jerking sideways until it propelled into a spin and whipped into a tight circle while still dragging across the exit. The brakes moaned, as the speed increased. Without any visibility or control, I knew this was it. And I was not surprised. The final impact rapidly approaching was inevitable. Guru had fore-warned me, starting in junior high. Disciples did not betray their guru without karmic retributions. My offenses had been mounting, continually more egregious. Since my only pur-pose for living was Guru, without him I shouldn't be alive. Smashing into a concrete wall or pummeling into a truck—I didn't question my punishment. The soul sent down to serve the last and highest avatar had obviously been given a defec-tive body, vital, and mind. There was nothing left. Rather than fear, I felt relief. I braced for the impact. Everything stopped.

I opened my eyes. I was still inside the Jeep. From a dis-tance, I saw the exit ramp. My Jeep was stalled in the weedy brush well beyond the shoulder of the road. There were no lights. I looked down at myself, checking if I was whole, and I spotted a streak of blood leaking down my thighs.

I could not manage myself on my own. It was clear. Whether it was school, work, Europe, I drifted lost in the out-skirts of those fixed and complicated cultures. Guru's de-mand of unconditional obedience hadn't provided me with the means to navigate those worlds. My only alternative was to return right where I began, to the only realm that I really knew. The retreat back to Guru's path of love, devotion, and surrender was not something I wanted. The end goal of total oneness with God, of God-Realization that kept me awake as a child, was not something that I even believed in anymore. I did not have or long for a spark of inspiration to renew my vows of discipleship, and the reality of spending the rest of my life permanently shuffling between functions with folded hands turned my stomach queasy. It was stifling and repetitive, requiring a level of enthusiasm that I knew I would never be able to fake successfully, but at least it was a relatively safe place to pass a lifetime. While I was a failure at leading Guru's prescribed life, I was thoroughly incapable of being in control of my own. I was better locked up under Guru's constant watch. Even though it filled me with dread, the certain endless future of serving a guru and a mission I no longer believed in, if I begged Guru to let me back inside, as piteous as I was, he could not refuse me. He would have to extend his shelter to me again, sparing me from my own self.

MY LETTER TO Guru asking to return was not long. All linguistic flourishes or nudges toward poetry had long ago shriveled away. I bluntly wrote that my life was not something I wanted. It was the truest letter I had ever sent him. Through Romesh, Guru replied, allowing me to return. Nothing more was offered in the form of a private interview sitting across from Guru in his kitchen or kneeling before his throne inside the pagoda at the tennis court. Guru never gently lent his ear for my confession then blessed me with a sweep of his golden palm. To me, his silence spoke loud and clear—though he had accepted me back, I was less valuable and viable for him to promenade, not only as his model disciple, but as a disciple at all. I understood. I felt the same way. It was an embarrassment that after my whole life as his special disciple, I was not even a decent, average person, let alone a spiritual aspirant. As I fumbled in my twenties, the myth of my birth, now such a vague, past event, stretched back too far to be an all-access pass, granting and guaranteeing me permanent and unchecked privileges. New generations of converts did not scour dusty Center history. What mattered to them and to Guru was what Guru was doing now, and to me, none of that mattered at all.

I rebooted into a sari, feeling the yards of fabric, constrictive and confining. When my mother escorted me into my first meditation, she insisted that I rightfully resume my old seat in the second row, behind Prema and Isha. I couldn't tell her that I didn't want to sit so close to Guru's scrutinizing gaze, where my sloping posture would be read by all those seated behind me as tangible proof of my fall. Instead, I nodded in agreement. Passing the tennis court guards, I caught their surprised faces at my appearance and their subsequent nudges and side-of-the-mouth comments. These grown men, with their receding hairlines and expanding waistlines, acted like catty schoolgirls relishing gossip and glances. When they spotted me watching them, they clumped together in a tight pack. As we walked farther into the premises, a few disciples looked very confused at suddenly encountering someone on the official out-of-the-Center roster at a meditation. Not taking any chances by risking the offense of talking, or even looking directly at an ex-disciple, they turned their backs to me, engaged in a vague object that suddenly held paramount importance. My mother, aware of the growing awkwardness, locked her arm through mine in a tight, protective hold, rambling about how excited Ketan would be to see me. Her clutch tightened as Ketan strode in flip-flops, sipping a coffee. With a wave from my mother, Ketan approached us. It was the first time in months that I had seen him without his dashing into an activity to avoid spotting me straight on.

"You look different," he said to me, attempting to sort out my specific alteration.

I stared back, wondering if he might guess the filthy truth about my changed self.

My mother burst through the friction with an unlinked anecdote about burning dinner. When a young disciple told Ketan it was time to rehearse Guru's play for that evening's performance, Ketan left. While I had been away, a large contingent of new, young, eager disciples, most from eastern Europe, buzzed around, joining the important singing groups, working in the divine-enterprises, and whittling their way into Guru's tightest circle. This new crop of disciples hurried through the crowds, oblivious to me, assured of their important role in preparing for the evening function. Instead of feeling jealous, the shield of anonymity felt fleetingly comforting. For all they knew, I was a nobody, a brand-new disciple.

Moving inside the tennis court, I was not the only changed entity. Any and all signs of the old tennis court had been stripped away, from the net posts to the white lines. The green clay rectangle that for years bounced serves, top-spin groundstrokes, and Guru's famous tricky underspin drop shot, as well as my own practice and play that had soaked up so many endless hours, now was partially covered with a tarp for seating. The clear dismantling of the court felt final, as though another identifiable and concrete feature of my former Center life had been permanently eradicated.

Outside Guru's open-air pagoda, four white chairs were

positioned as seats of honor facing the stage. Flowers flanked the carpeted area, and next to Guru's throne was a massive gold easel with an elaborately framed photograph of Guru bowing and shaking the hand of Mikhail Gorbachev, the former head of the Soviet Union. When I whispered to my mother that I would rather stay in the back, she clamped my arm even tighter, chiding me not to be ridiculous, and escorted me toward my former seat.

Bandhu, the head of Guru's public relations team, and three of Bandhu's assistants accompanied Guru to his throne, talking rapidly. When Guru sat down, he called for different disciples, inquiring if they had all the arrangements ready. Tonight, yet again, was another function in honor of Nadia, a petite Muscovite and high-ranking official in Mikhail Gorbachev's foundation. Ever since Gorbachev's tenure as head of the Soviet Union and lead international newsmaker, Guru had wanted to meet him, but the blockade of Kremlin bureaucracy was impenetrable. It wasn't until Gorbachev left office, opened a foundation, and toured on the lucrative lecture circuit that Guru's public relations team began their relentless campaign to bring Gorbachev and Guru together. Although Guru had always avoided all forms of political activity, even with regard to volunteering or donating to charities, he observed that donations of a certain level proved an expedited invitation into powerful circles. Soon disciples in Centers all over the world were regularly instructed to send money to New York that would be collected and then presented to The Gorbachev Foundation. For disciples, too, the more money they gave, the more it pleased Guru, and for Guru, the more money he transferred to the foundation, the more it pleased the chief fund-raisers. Suddenly a correspondence blossomed, beginning with simple thank-you letters signed by Gorbachev that Guru read and reread aloud at meditations.

After careful research, Bandhu and his assistants homed in on Nadia as an especially close adviser of Gorbachev and the courting began. First-class tickets from Moscow to New York, lavish gifts, and endless flattery, including having disciples serve as Nadia's personal chauffeurs and lackeys while in New York, left Nadia championing Guru to her boss. After hundreds of thousands of dollars, Guru procured his first meeting with Gorbachev. It was in a Manhattan hotel, and the agreement was that one photographer was allowed, but no video cameras. Despite that, Guru told Bandhu to keep a video camera hidden, to capture each and every moment for posterity. Though the meeting only lasted a few brief minutes, enough photographs were taken to document every second of their encounter. The photos and the contraband video were both immediately splashed onto all of Guru's public relations materials, proving Guru and Gorbachev's intimate friendship.

When Nadia arrived with an entourage, Guru stood to greet her, bowed deeply, then walked her to the white chairs in front. I expected Guru to meditate, but that never happened. Instead, I watched Guru's lavish show, a continuous patchwork of disciples to perform songs for Nadia, skits about Russia, and video compilations of Guru weight lifting.

By the end of the function, Isha placed a box in front of Guru for more donations to The Gorbachev Foundation. My mother tucked fifty dollars into my hand for my contribution, and I joined the line of other disciples waiting to have their moment of recognition, of being at the center of Guru's attentions, if only long enough to drop money into a box. I paused before Guru, flaring with the instinctive ache of needing his personal validation of my return, my place, and my attempt to mask my simultaneous dread, but when I dropped my money in the box, Guru still did not look up. I reclaimed my seat, wondering if Guru would ever talk to me again. However, after Nadia was presented with the overflowing cash stash and the function ended, Sarisha said I was invited to Guru's house. Guru had recently changed his house gatherings to be alternative evenings with either women or men as part of his imposed clamp-down against men and women interacting. That night was the women's turn. Lying on his couch, Guru waved to me when I came in, and smiled. And that was enough. The other women, after seeing Guru welcome me, freely motioned me over and offered me a seat.

Guru read aloud his latest thank-you letter from Gorbachev, with the inclusion of thanks from Gorbachev's wife for all the gifts that he had sent their family members. Everyone burst into applause. Clearly pleased, Guru smiled and jiggled his feet while reading it three more times. Guru's insatiable urge for celebrity endorsements disturbed me. As the supposed direct representative of God on earth, why would he possibly need or care about a quote praising him from random people, famous or not?

Bandhu bounded through the door, presenting Guru with updates on his other main target: Princess Diana. According to Bandhu and his contact with Radhika, a London Center disciple assigned to cover all of Guru's public relations work in the United Kingdom, their meeting was officially set. Guru sprang upright, slapping his hands on his thighs. Everyone stood up, wildly applauding the news. I, too, stood up, not wanting to expose myself. I clapped gleefully along with everyone else, but I couldn't help but wonder why Princess Diana, with her chosen charities and protective charge of her children, would want to meet Guru. Wasn't his vision of the world just too different from hers? I wondered if she knew who Guru actually was, and what kind of fabricated presentation she was given that persuaded her to meet him. She didn't seem like someone willing to endorse a group that banned the Internet, TV, movies, music, newspapers, radio, political activism, mixing with the opposite gender, and all forms of free speech. Although I cheered with the others, I wished I could have warned her about Guru and the organization she thought he represented. Princess Diana was a woman with people clamoring to exploit her, and I knew that Guru, in his own way, by sneakily using her quote and image as a public endorsement, intended to do exactly that.

Weeks later, the meeting with Princess Diana was over. Against the express wishes of the princess, Guru had instructed Radhika, the only person at the meeting besides Diana and Paul Burrell, her infamous butler, to record the meeting secretly, as well as to smuggle in a camera and plead for a few photographs to be taken. Diana reluctantly agreed and stiffly posed in her pink suit with her fixed smile as Guru leaned extra close to her, clutching both of his hands against his heart, smiling in wide triumph. Shortly after, Guru's hottest release, a book that included a full transcription of their supposedly private meeting in Buckingham Palace, was on sale for all disciples to buy.

While I slid into my former routine as a full-time vagabond, carting myself to all of the functions, races, and singing practices I could, Guru focused on expanding his Princess

Diana triumph by acting as a go-between for the princess to meet her humanitarian idol—Mother Teresa. Guru's own opinion of Mother Teresa had drastically changed over the years. He initially described her as a charlatan who used food and shelter as bait in order to convert India's suffering masses into surface Christians, but as Mother Teresa's missions gained international prominence, Guru turned off his criticisms and turned on his efforts to meet her. The tiny woman in the white sari and white habit was initially uninterested in Guru as well, but as both became more savvy in their tactics, Guru found his entrance by presenting her with the U Thant Peace Award, an award of his own creation, and a large donation to her Indian missions. In return, Guru added her complimentary quotes and photo to his ever-expanding collection. Still actively pursuing his ultimate goal of achieving the Nobel Peace Prize, Guru's manifestation team sought a letter of recommendation from Mother Teresa for the official nominating committee in Oslo. Princess Diana readily accepted Guru's gesture of arranging a meeting between her and Mother Teresa. I understood that it was all part of his larger plan of establishing more and more publicity-equity for himself.

Now nearly every function was dominated by visits from celebrities, from A-listers all the way to loopy local characters. Most of the meetings were formulaic and quick, centered on the bait that the celebrity was invited in order to receive the Oneness-Heart Award, in honor of the person's achievements and contributions to society. Lulled by accolades and confirmation of their greatness, luring public figures was surprisingly easy. With Ketan heading the team of disciples actively inviting celebrities to receive this award, as part of the endlessly repeated ceremony, the stars climbed up Guru's special one-arm weight-lifting platform that budged up a rickety inch to signify that they had been lifted, and then an award was given, a song sung, and many photographs taken. From Susan Sarandon and Tim Robbins to Jeff Goldblum, Yoko Ono, and Sting, each day heralded a new visitor. The more photos and quotes added to the PR materials, the more convincing and legitimate it appeared to other celebrities. Soon Guru hosted Nelson Mandela and Archbishop Desmond Tutu. I wondered what these men who championed freedom and liberty would say if they knew that Guru praised his devotees for rooting through the garbage of fellow disciples accused of the offense of drinking a bottle of wine or complaining about the Center. I was quite sure that these elements of the Sri Chinmoy Center were not highlighted in the glossily produced materials about the Ambassador of Peace.

For Ketan, the apparent new mission of the Sri Chinmoy Center as a special events headquarters for celebrities was more than he could have ever hoped for. Being sent on special urgent missions from Guru, such as flying out to Malibu to hand the actress Judith Light an envelope inside which contained her spiritual name, was perfect for him. I didn't know how other disciples felt about Guru's new focus. It wasn't something to be openly discussed.

As another birthday approached, I wished I was near the end of my life rather than barely halfway toward middle age. I imagined myself in my thirties, forties, fifties, sixties, and seventies reciting poems for Guru with the rest of the children's group, then shuffling back to my assigned seat. My destined future existence—an exact replica of my current one—was numbing. Caged and kept, I inhabited Guru's exquisite prison. Void of any spiritual drive, any longing for a higher power, I realized that nothing had made me happy. Neither being in nor being out of the Center had offered me a sense of belonging, of comfort. On the day of my twenty-fourth birthday, while most of my contemporaries in the outside world were finishing graduate school, getting engaged, buying apartments, eagerly embarking on life's possibilities, I realized I had already died.

10

Cartwheels in a Sari

"YOUR MINDS ARE POISON. SUCH POISON," GURU SAID, holding the microphone too close, causing it to squeal with feedback.

As soon as Guru spoke, I stopped listening. Undoubtedly, it was to be another lecture about impurity, disobedience, and destruction. After Guru announced his New Year's message, disciples banded together in a sense of panic. Guru's usual New Year's message was an aphorism promising the upcoming year to reveal boons such as elevated states of consciousness and newfound wells of aspiration. The message, read at a final public gathering prior to Guru's departure for the annual Christmas trip abroad, assured disciples and seekers of another year frosted with special favors from the Supreme. This year's message, however, tore off the layer of promised bliss, dunking it instead inside a vat of doom. A warning of possible spiritual obliteration, Guru's manifesto was the first of many scoldings and lectures on the same theme repeated that year. During functions, Guru constantly sermonized on the slothful state of his disciples. Night after night, the disciples lowered their heads, absorbing Guru's poundings on how deliberately disobedient and recklessly negligent they were in all matters pertaining to their inner lives. I believed I was the only person who wasn't rattled to the core. To me, this was not news, and I no longer cared or wanted to even hear about it.

Guru tapped the microphone. After a long pause, he said that out of his infinite compassion, he was giving the disciples the secret to regaining their inner progress.

"Inside your heart, deep inside your heart, beneath its insecurity, there is still hope. That hope is still pure, still good," Guru said.

The audience, after having readied themselves for another barrage about their corrupt vital, body, mind and heart, sat up straighter. I blankly stared ahead.

"You must forget your current age, forget your age. All of you, no matter how old, must be, act, and become like seven-year-olds. Girls and boys. All of you should be like seven-year-olds. Seven-year-olds live only in the heart, the heart. No mind. No mind. Act and be like seven-year-olds," Guru said.

He unzipped his electronic synthesizer from its custom case and taught two new songs: "I Am a Seven-Year-Old Boy," and "I Am a Seven-Year-Old Girl."

I mouthed along. I was past listening, letting his words affect me. I could sit for hours before him as he talked, but it was as though I was far away beyond hearing, beyond his reach. As a child, to fill the uninterrupted hours of silent meditation, I had played games in my head, but now I dwelled constantly inside a dark cavern of quiet, remaining empty and void. Blocking out what I didn't want to hear was easy.

When Guru instructed all the disciples to soulfully sing "I Am a Seven-Year-Old" every day, I dismissed this as just another task to pile onto Guru's litany of mandatory daily duties that would soon enough rot into neglect. If disciples had performed all of the prayers, poems, songs, and chants that Guru had urged as part of their daily rituals, they would never have time away from their shrines to eat or sleep. But this directive was different.

That night when I entered the tennis court, I was shocked when some of the women in their fifties and sixties who brought their own folding chairs and specially designed orthopedic back support pillows had changed the style of their gray hair from an understated bun to pigtails. Other women entered with new pink Hello Kitty backpacks worn over their saris. Groups clustered, giggling together. To my horror, someone carried in a baby doll dressed in a polka-dot sari. The men, too, huddled in circles; some played jacks, cheering wildly. Others held a skipping contest up and down the driveway. This looked absolutely psychotic. I panicked at the spectacle around me.

I sat in the back row and watched Sarisha circulate through the aisle using a high-pitched baby voice to collect money for "a speshwel pwasad in gwatitude to Guwu." Scanning the gathering of disciples digging into their purses and wallets with their smiley excitement, I questioned when this shift of receiving Guru's symbolic words on a literal level had occurred. I knew that in religions such as Christianity and Islam, long-standing debates raged between believers who read their sacred texts literally and those who viewed the same passages metaphorically, but we had understood Guru's messages to be metaphoric directives. How had the disciples collectively decided to turn this into a practical instruction and enact skipping and baby talk as a route to salvation? This bizarre impersonation of seven-year-olds, this mad stampede toward the inner child, made me wonder if it was their defense, protective armor, against the maelstrom of demonic destruction promised by Guru in his New Year's prophecy. If so, then their desperate tenacity felt sad, and the idea of joining or even supporting them repelled me.

I now understood that by rejoining the Center I, too, lived like a dependent, mindless child. Until that moment, I had not witnessed the absurdity of my lifestyle. Stripped of all pretenses, the reality horrified me. Nothing about being a seven-year-old—naive and malleable—felt appealing. I did not want to neglect and shut down my mind, giggling blankly. I had been seven once, and I had no desire to return to that age. My numbness toward Guru and the Center subsided. I loathed everyone and everything around me.

With clenched teeth and my hands in fists, I restrained myself from screaming aloud. Below, the tennis court guards wheeled in various tricycles, motorized carts, and mini choo-choo trains, arranging the brightly colored, shiny vehicles along the court's fence. When Guru arrived, walking with a profound limp in both legs, he inspected his array of new toys. One by one, Guru climbed inside the child-sized vehicles and rode around the perimeter of the tennis court, making sharp turns at each corner as the disciples sat with folded hands in deep meditation, eager for the moment when Guru scooted past their area. Guru's self-indulgence, his ego, sickened me. Getting whatever he wanted whenever he wanted on his own time clearly was not enough for him. To keep up his role as spiritual leader of his flock, he multitasked his personal hobbies, habits, and indulgences into so-called spiritual practice for all his ardent believers who financed and supported him. From munching potato chips to bicep curls, he wrote off everything he did as a meditation, an opportunity for his disciples to be nearer to the Supreme.

Lap after lap, he toured the same small stretch until, eventually like a toddler, Guru moved on to his next toy. With each vehicle, Guru initially jerked the machine into motion, until he found a smooth ride. My whole body shook with restless anger. I hated it. I hated him. I hated every ounce of my entire life as Guru limped over to the vehicle he had saved for last—the mini red choo-choo train. Since his childhood, when Guru's father was an inspector on the Bengali railroad, Guru, like most little boys, held a fascination for trains, and now, as an old, frail man, he had his own with which to play conductor. Even when Guru tooted the caboose's clownish whistle, utter reverent silence continued. For the disciples, this was serious meditation. For me, this was beyond bearing.

As Guru lapped the tennis court in endless circles wearing his conductor's cap, I saddened, terrified that perhaps this *was* normal. Maybe this made sense. It was follow the leader, and didn't everyone follow some sort of leader around in circles? I suddenly remembered, years ago, loving the sickening dizziness of turning circles. One of the highlights of my entire year was performing gymnastics in Guru's Madal Circus. Banned from wearing leotards because they were too revealing, in my circus costume of a shiny sari, fearlessly tumbling, somersaulting, and cartwheeling around the stage to Guru's applause. He smiled and waved and told me to continue cartwheels in a sari as an encore. The inversion of my body, losing track of gravity and direction, was disorienting and delirious. From my vantage point, I saw Guru and all of the disciples upside-down, and no one else had. Their faces blurred past, a rush of nonsensical colors and shapes. By the end of my routine, I didn't know which was the correct way. Both felt as equally unstable then as they did now.

I didn't wait for prasad or for Guru to invite disciples to the microphone to share their profound inner experiences during his meditative joyride. I fled to my apartment, where I decided to stay, taking permanent cover in my bed. I could not carry on anymore to another folded-hand meditation, another aphorism, another video. Other disciples plowed ahead, adapting to Guru's broadening plans, his new adventures, celebrities, peace awards to dictators such as Zimbabwe's Robert Mugabe and Burma's Secretary-1. All of my ability to pretend was spent. Each day when I finally awoke, I was disappointed. I'd stare at the clock, counting how many hours remained and how I could erase them. There was always too much time, too many afternoon and evenings that even with my eyes closed still stretched over me. After sleeping and pretending to sleep, eventually the sounds streaming to my window from the street below—people leaving for work, children biking, police sirens—felt foreign. Their world was reliant on time, squeezing more hours out of the clock, stretching it to fit in more minutes for work or family. They had deadlines and appointments, engagements to uphold. By Guru's design, I had none. Twenty-four hours a day were available to trail Guru, bumbling along, waving and cheering him on, satisfying his needs. I ducked beneath the covers, hoping to fall asleep again, to speed the end of yet another day.

KETAN PILED VARIOUS messages seasoned with judgment on my answering machine. His latest recording chided me for

missing the big celebration in honor of Guru driving. I didn't
return any of Ketan's calls. One morning he banged against
my door relentlessly until I stammered to open it. According
to Ketan, in five minutes Guru would drive around the block,
and attendance was mandatory. Since the weather had been
getting colder, Guru's new hobby was driving in a circle from
his house to the block with the divine-enterprises. A new Center information phone line, with its number safely guarded
from all ex-disciples, posted frantic updates as to the exact
time Guru would motor past for a drive-by meditation. Not
wanting to miss it, disciples began lining the street, staking
their spot with folded hands, waiting for the one-car parade.
Guru splurged on a range of tiny cars, just like his array of
mini-vehicles, to suit his various moods. Garages were rented
throughout Jamaica to store Guru's fleet, and the cars, like the
tricycles and choo-choo trains, were maintained and re-
trieved by the tennis court guards at Guru's whim.

Ketan, sporting a new suede jacket with matching gloves
and perfectly coiffed hair, told me I looked like hell, not having showered for days and wearing stained pajamas. He ordered me to chuck on something decent, claiming there
wasn't time to waste. Feeling lightheaded, I followed him out
of the house into the gusty winds of the cold, dark morning. Even though Guru's route was only two blocks away,
Ketan drove, and we waited inside his heated, idling car
while disciples stood outside, shivering with folded hands as
their saris billowed and tangled from the wind. Without looking at me, Ketan sternly informed me that the ominous year
had already claimed a lot of disciples, dumping them out of
Guru's boat for good. In the past, gossip of disciples getting
kicked out of the Center had been my penultimate news to

savor, as it confirmed what had always been suspected, that the new ex-disciple had never been either good or worthy, and it had left a smug smile of reassurance about the highly evolved state of my own soul. But now these stories felt like testaments to the larger insanity all around me. As Ketan delved into the secret details of one male disciple's being caught with a woman in his apartment, and later when it was discovered that there had never been a woman, and the woman's voice heard by the disciple in the next apartment had been someone speaking on National Public Radio, the accused disciple decided that he would rather be out of the Center than have to live in Orwell's *1984*. I listened to Ketan's disgust with the next offense, a male disciple who called up his friend and sang "Happy Birthday" in a mock-seductive Marilyn Monroe impersonation. That same afternoon, a message came through Romesh expelling the crank caller from the Center for his misdeed.

"It's not a joke," Ketan said defensively.

I never thought it was. I knew far better than to imagine anything could be buoyant and free like a joke. There was nothing humorous in the Center. Nothing over which to laugh, let alone smile. Ketan proceeded to tell me that some traitors, disgruntled ex-disciples, were organizing slanderous campaigns against Guru, claiming Guru had various sexual relationships with former and current disciples. One supposed relationship ended up with the woman pregnant by Guru and Guru's insistence that the woman have an abortion. The rabid group of ex-disciples was contacting the press and maniacally spreading lies about Guru and his mission.

"You don't use a computer, do you?" Ketan grilled me suspiciously.

I shook my head.

"Good," Ketan said. "Guru doesn't want anyone using the computer. Especially for e-mail or the Internet. He's forbidden it."

I nodded. I knew Guru did not allow a computer inside his own house, and told his good disciples they should not have them either.

"All I'm saying is that you better watch it," Ketan warned, pointing his index finger at me. "You need to clean up. You're hanging on by a thread."

He then turned off the car and hopped out, joining the other tennis court guards, who, like Ketan, had been waiting inside heated cars, and just now joined the row of shivering disciples who had been positioned along the sidewalk for hours.

A neighbor woman walking her dog, bundled up in a knitted sweater, tried to maneuver a path on the sidewalk as the disciples self-righteously held fast to their spots. Other outsiders, en route to work, familiar with the disciple blockade, sighed and crossed into the street, glimpsing peeks at the now routine morning spectacle. As I shuffled into the line-up, I imagined the scene looked like a training exercise for boot camp, with the troops temporarily halted by their commanding officer. Or it was a human line of prisoners awaiting execution by firing squad to be knocked off one by one. Either way, saris and whites and Guru-blue parkas splayed across the neighborhood, superimposing private faith onto public property.

Beside me, a short new visiting disciple jumped up and down, maintaining her claim to the line. She had spotted Guru. I watched her bounce in eager anticipation. Still a half

block away, Guru advanced toward his human chain of disciples in a comically small Guru-blue two-seater that looked
like it had escaped from a ride on a fairground. Afraid to
drive anything large, Guru's personal fleet of cars consisted of
an entire motorcade that would have been ideal for children
and dwarfs. Disciples on both sides of the street stood at full
attention, silent with folded hands. It had been hours since
the recorded phone hotline announced Guru's meditative
drive, and these faithful disciples who had been devotedly
standing in one spot were now to get their reward. With a
speed so slow that the wheels barely rolled forward, Guru
proceeded up the block. Not looking at the disciples on either
side of the street, Guru kept his windows tightly shut, not
wanting to expose himself, ever so slightly, to the bitter
temperature outside. As Guru passed where I stood, for a moment, with only his head and neck visible, I shivered, remembering back to my childhood chills of fear of the lifelike Guru
bust that had plotted to strangle me. Back then, it had been
my secret that I was not allowed to tell—no one uttered a
word against Guru, the person or the image. As I stuck my
hands in the pocket of my jacket, the chills I now felt resulted
from waiting, endlessly waiting, in the cold morning. Nothing more. The fear was gone; so, too, was that little girl.

Studying Guru cruising in his playmobile, the absurdity
of the moment, of the massive, elaborately concocted scam,
assaulted me. A myth. A fake. A lie. The truth was that nothing was true. Guru Sri Chinmoy was a fabrication dreamed
and designed by a young and churlish Bangladeshi intent on
hypnotizing the world. He had manufactured his image as a
modern swami, his own presentation, to suit his vision. With
subtle modifications along the way, he molded himself to fit

the story he wrote for himself. If Guru was fiction, an invention, I realized, then so was I, for he had created me. My values and truths were all approved, filtered, then injected into me by Guru. No ethics, philosophy, or ideas blossomed organically by myself. I was the creation of the Sri Chinmoy Experiment. I could not imagine that somewhere inside was a real person who could exist wholly unto herself. A fake, created as part of a larger scheme, for nearly twenty-five years, I had absorbed space, heralding a false life and false creator. Nothing around me was true; the emperor wore no clothes.

I didn't know if I had such a thing as my own will, but I did know that I still had control over my own body, and for the first and last time, I was going to use it.

With my head throbbing, I rushed back and scrutinized my small apartment. I needed a finale. I viewed the distance from my windows to the sidewalk below. Even though I was on the third floor, the drop, I concluded, was not far enough to offer a decisive conclusion. I moved from the windows, forcing myself to think of another plan. As I paced across the room, I veered to the kitchenette, surveying it for sharp objects. Never a cook, I owned one dull bread knife, which barely sawed through bagels. I angrily crossed into the living room, lifting my eyes to the ceiling. But without ceiling fans or overhead light fixtures and with the sloping contours of the dormers, fastening a cord from the ceiling was clearly impossible. There was nothing from which to hang, nothing to hold me as an anchor.

I entered the bathroom, positive I had found my answer. I grabbed a pink shaving razor and swiped it across my wrist. Nothing sliced, nothing cut. The blade was nestled inside its protective plastic. I tried to bend it, snapping the blade free, but it held securely in place. Smashing it against the sink, it nicked my finger, letting out a tease of blood, too shallow for any impact except a small and steady leak. I cursed and threw the razor inside the sink, catching a glimpse of my reflection in the mirror, which made me shudder. I couldn't stand to look at myself. To avoid confronting my own image, I thrust open the medicine cabinet. Surely something toxic, life-threatening, existed inside its shelves. I dumped dental floss, a nearly squeezed-out tub of toothpaste, mouthwash, deodorant, and powder into the sink below. Although the shelves stood bare, I stared into the dusty levels, hoping I had overlooked a perfect potion. I wondered how other people were lucky enough to have vials and bottles of expired drugs at easy reach with which to brew a lethal cocktail. I didn't have a doctor, let alone access to forbidden prescriptions. I grabbed the plastic jug of mouthwash from the sink, hoping to find a warning sign proclaiming its fateful properties, but there wasn't any.

Time was wasting. This was taking too long. I needed something else. Urgently. I needed a gun. All I needed was a gun. I had never seen a real gun and had no idea where to buy one. I split open the phone book, tearing through pages, while my finger left a blood-smeared trail. I followed the prompts from the heading Handguns, to Sporting Goods Suppliers. When I called and asked the lady who answered the phone if they sold guns, in a nasal voice with a thick Queens drawl, she attempted to detail the lengthy process and waiting period required to obtain a gun permit. She was still speaking when I hung up on her. My head boomed with blurry pain. I was soaked with sweat. I could not wait. Nothing could wait. I hurled the fat yellow directory from my lap, its thick stack of pages cushioning its landing.

I had it, a new plan—foolproof and simple. Leaving everything except a single token, I ran downstairs and headed straight to the subway, energized with queasy hope. I didn't feel the cold air; I was still panting, bleeding, and sweating in overdrive. Ushered through the turnstile, I followed the sounds toward the distant puffing of an approaching train. It churned louder and louder. I raced to the platform, checking to find its direction. What at first appeared as a tiny flashlight soon morphed into the high beam of an approaching express train. I walked myself forward, steps from the platform's edge. This would be quick and easy and of my own volition, free of premeditated or predestined design. The hot air swirled dirt and garbage in wild clouds. I felt perversely light, as if I, too, could be lifted into the maelstrom of tunnel winds. No doubts. No highlight reel of my life screened before my eyes. No tears. No regrets. I literally had nothing to regret. Certainly no prayers. I didn't want the Supreme, Guru, or my own soul involved. I wanted all three of them, for once and for all, to stay away, far away. I did not look in any direction, but I moved forward, always forward, to my finale.

Arms jerked me backward.

"You fuckin' sick?" A Hispanic man in his late sixties, wearing a navy blue janitorial uniform, dragged me in reverse, with his forearms pressing my collarbone.

The train streaked past, grinding the tracks, excreting a metallic stink.

"You crazy?" he shouted at me, furious.

He wanted an answer. But that was impossible. Even if I

could have spoken, I could not answer him or anyone. He held me still; his fingers, like pegs, braced my body. I wiggled my shoulders, jutting out my elbows.

"You speak English?" he demanded.

I kicked my legs wildly, and when he released his grasp, I sprinted toward the stairs out of the station. He yelled, but I never turned around. I did not feel my breath, legs, or arms as I kept running. Too stunned for any detours, I ran until I was in my own apartment. There the sounds of the subway stopped. Just an endless stretch of quiet replaced it. Around me, on all the walls, framed pictures of Guru stared mockingly, confirming their smug knowledge that I could accomplish nothing on my own; everything was ultimately decided and manipulated by him. I knocked the meticulously matted and framed photographs of Guru in various poses off my walls and shrine, hurling them into my garbage. It did nothing. Nothing could be done. I sputtered tears at my foolish entrapment, and at this pathetic and utterly debilitating attempt of ridding myself from my fabricated life. I screamed and screamed, until my throat was stripped sore, and I collapsed on the ground.

ONE WEEK LATER, the phone rang. It was Romesh. Without any explanation provided, Guru no longer wanted me to be his disciple. I was permanently banned from the Center. I listened, but I was not sure I understood what he said. I kept the phone to my ear, and he repeated himself. Romesh asked me if I had any message to send back to Guru. I sped through years of aching and exaggerated questions, of messages des-

perate to be sent and received, but I could not think of anything. He quickly hung up, eager to be rid of his task.

Hours later, I still held the receiver to a silenced line. I
peered out my window, expecting a full eclipse or torrential
hailstorm, but the sun filtered through the puffy white clouds,
as though it were a normal Thursday in a normal week. I sat
on the floor, while I tried to remember what Romesh had
said. Part of me was unsure he had ever called, and I wanted
to call him to double-check. My fingers could not read the
numbers on the phone. The digits made no sense, appearing
as squiggly abstract shapes. They were a secret code, untrans-
latable but to all those who were in on the grand scheme. I
wasn't. I hung up. And I waited, waited for something to happen. All my life things happened, blessings, messages, scoldings, invitations, proclamations, and expulsions.

That evening, my mother burst into my apartment. She
scooped me into her arms, hungering for any sign that I
would be all right. I watched her reaction, wondering if I
should be feeling like her, but I didn't feel anything. My father, always quiet, finally asked me what I was going to do
next. The ease and casualness of his question made me stare
at him. Out of everyone, he and my mother should have
known that because of their decision decades earlier to find a
guru, for my entire life I was never asked or allowed to imagine what I was going to do next. I wanted to let them know
that this entire mess was their fault, starting from the day
they went in search of a guru. Why hadn't they, like people in
the outside world, been able to run their own lives and not
need a guru to do it for them? The night, decades earlier,
when they surrendered their lives to Guru, they unknowingly

had surrendered mine as well. And I never asked for any of it. Guru had been their choice. They, not I, had sought him out.

To now hear my father ask me "what I was going to do next," an alien sentiment, as if that question could lightly be tossed to me and fielded back with the ownership of an answer, felt maddening. I wondered if he heard the hypocrisy in what he was asking. There was no "next." There was nothing. In one month I would be twenty-five, and I had no experience with the outside world. Suddenly I was dumped on the side of the road and meant to have prepared a plan?

My father again retreated into silence, as though he had moved on to a new project. My mother implored me to come to Connecticut for a while. I didn't understand how that would make any difference at all.

Tired of my mother's fuss and my father's silence, I urged them on to that evening's meditation. After changing her mind four times, it wasn't until my father was beeping the horn in succinct patterns that my mother finally agreed to leave me. I told her there was no point in worrying now. While I was sure that Guru's standard menacing threats of vicious karmic attacks delegated by my own soul predicted utter destruction for me, I knew I had stepped outside the angle where any of it mattered. I could not look ahead, even to worry about karmic payback. I could focus only on steering my way through the present moment.

When I closed the door behind my mother, I saw that a note from Ketan had been slipped under my door. In his notoriously poorly spelled and sloppy writing, he scribbled enough sentences to inform me that although he was my brother, he could not support me and my evil lifestyle. He wanted nothing to do with me from that day forward. Suddenly my new reality landed. On my first suspension from the Center, I had felt its temporary losses. I now faced a permanent and nonnegotiable severance. Family, church, friends, beliefs, ideals, identity, nothing was spared. One phone message, and forever after Guru and his mission repossessed everything. It all disappeared.

How easy this had been for Guru to leave me with nothing, to terminate me from his existence. I understood that the Center, Guru's system of beliefs, had only served him and his own purpose. The individuals who followed him were ultimately expendable figures, but I wondered, was he always so detached and cruel, willing to cast off the same soul that he supposedly chose as his unique companion and devotee? Even if the entire myth of my birth was his own invention, a convenience to smooth over the awkward transition from his encouragement of marriage and his subsequent eradication, he was still the one responsible. I did not deny that I had shamelessly broken his rules, repeatedly neglecting my promises and exploiting his leniency. But how was it possible that after all these years of Guru's raising me, from his initial greeting in the hospital's nursery, that he could so easily withdraw me from his life? Regardless of whether he was or was not a God-Realized spiritual leader, an ordinary human being would hesitate and reflect before ordering a full disassociation. I wondered at what meditation or during which video night at his house did he conclude me an unprofitable investment and decide to sell at a loss. Was he weary of his lectures to me? Or had I just utilized too much of his precious time?

For years, I knew I hadn't behaved as Guru had wanted or expected, his shining jewel, a model for other disciples new and old to emulate. Rather than being his obedient apostle, I had thrashed and torn through his edicts, panting and pouting. Perhaps since Guru had credited himself for my formation, I was now a liability, a public embarrassment, tangible proof of his own false claims. If he was so wrong about his miracle-child, then wouldn't it be painfully clear that he was way off the mark on his other visions and prophecies? It was better to dispose of me now before I caused him further public disgrace. For a moment, I understood his position. I, too, felt embarrassed by my own self. For someone who was reared by the supposedly highest spiritual avatar, I was as far from a Yogi as possible; I was an immature, emotional infant—certainly not a highly developed spiritual being. But I never claimed to be his perfect disciple, and unlike Guru, I never boasted endlessly about possessing infinite compassion, claiming limitless and boundless forgiveness. I realized there must have been a specific moment when Guru decided to repossess his compassion and forgiveness from me. At what hour did Guru decide I was beyond compassion, beyond salvaging?

THE NEXT EVENING, lacing my boots on my bottom step by the door, I heard my mother enter the house, followed by Romesh. I listened as he told her that Guru wanted her to do the right thing and evict me immediately. Having an ex-disciple living in a house filled with disciples, Romesh explained, placed all the disciples at risk.

"That's my daughter. Guru wants me to kick my own daughter into the street?" Rage swelled in her voice. It was clear that Guru had gone too far. Banishment from the Center was one thing, but instructing her to evict her daughter confirmed Guru's deliberate and malicious intent.

"Calm down, Samarpana," Romesh said, with an attempt at a lighthearted laugh.

"You tell Guru that I will never do any such thing. Don't you ever, ever threaten me about my children again," my mother barked through clenched teeth. "Get out of my house. Get out now. GET THE HELL OUT and NEVER EVER STEP NEAR ME AGAIN!"

Without a reply, Romesh backed out, retreated down the steps, burdened with the awkward task of formulating a return message to Guru.

Being deeply entrenched in Guru's path meant basic forms of survival, home, and job were all reliant on it. In an instant, those, too, were snatched away, leaving one homeless and penniless, in addition to being without family, friends, or any thread of support. It was all part of a larger system of control; the longer one stayed in the Center and the deeper they rooted themselves, the more impossible it was to leave. That fear, deeply submerged and never discussed among disciples, was always present, privately emerging at moments of doubt, panic, or rare clarity. I wanted to run downstairs and hug my mother, grateful that unlike countless other parents who had ceased all contact with their own children after their children left or were told to leave the Center, my mother had resisted Guru's pressure. In that moment she proved her loyalty to her family and the priority of her family over Guru. Yet, instead, I remained fastened to the step, unable to act.

The next day my mother received phone messages from

all the disciple tenants insulting her ruthlessly and informing her that they were moving out as soon as possible. This
included Aunt Chandika, who, after leaving her message,
aborted all contact with my parents. From a full house, including basement, the house was instantly vacant, except my
apartment. In addition to the lost tenants, my parents lost
their invites to Guru's circle of favorites. While they remained
disciples, I watched as they slid further into the periphery,
silently loosening their ties to the Center and to each other.
Although I was well aware that I was the cause of the uproar,
I was unable to offer an apology or to help.

I WAS NOW alone. Guru's terse rejection did not include any
suggestions or advice. As far as I knew, no manuals or instruction guides were readily available on how to create a life
and how to function in a post-Guru world. I knew hundreds
of Guru's Bengali songs, poems, and aphorisms; I'd memorized endless classic Indian tales about masters and disciples
that Guru narrated over the years. I could sit still, never
budging, with my hands folded, for hours. Those were my
skills and background experience. I doubted any of it qualified me for anything. Positions required experience. Mine
didn't translate.

When I called Chahna, my only friend who had smoothly
transitioned to the outside world, she was heading out to a
party with Rick and a group of friends. She was busy, engaged in the fullness of her life. She promised to call me back
as soon as she got home, but after a few days passed, I understood that she had forged on and was reluctant to regress

back to where she had been, even if it was for me. She was constructing a new life complete with a boyfriend, college, job, and friends, and she was too far ahead of me for me to ever catch up. I had to let her go. I then thought of trying to find Oscar, but years had passed. Even if I could have located him, I cringed, imagining the awkward embarrassment of trying to explain to the established lawyer and family man who I was and why I was calling. Nothing from my past was available for me to rely on—I was on my own.

I decided I had to begin. Somewhere. With something. These new steps were all mine. I was not shadowing or being shadowed. I asked myself what I wanted to be when I grew up. It was finally time for me to seek my own answer. Guru's invisible ashram walls had barricaded me my entire life, but I was only a few miles away from Manhattan, the epicenter of commerce and chance, the destination for life makeovers.

I left my apartment and began walking down the congested lanes of Queens Boulevard, absorbing the signs, smells, and noises. Crossing the bridge to Manhattan, the water linking the boroughs reflected the sun in thin strips like tinsel. Once in Manhattan, I wandered uptown, passing parks with nannies and the elderly dozing. I crossed corners where vendors sold gyros and pretzels, and businessmen hollered into mobile phones. Midtown, at Times Square, I followed a class of high school students from Kansas dressed up for a Broadway show as they walked with their mouths open in disbelief. I wound my way downtown past pizzerias and movie theaters. Couples holding hands, students walking dogs, police writing tickets, everyone was busy. I looked up; the endless floors above me that lined the avenues pulsated activity—the doing and the getting, the achieving and the losing. New York was in motion, as was the world. Millions of people actively erecting their lives. Sri Chinmoy who? Never heard of him. They were independent contractors reporting to themselves. I could grab anywhere and anything—no limitations. Everything was here. Whatever I wanted was available, I was sure of it. No one or nothing could tell me the opposite. The steaming manhole covers, broken traffic lights, and perfectly picked tiers of fresh flowers outside the delis were all part of the vast rich possibilities. I was free.

I decided to start college as a full-time student. With the support of my parents, who anxiously awaited signs of my stability, I called Queens College, close enough to walk to, and spoke to an admissions counselor. Even though I registered for college, I needed to learn subjects and skills about the outside world that would never appear in their course catalogues. Timid and uneasy, I had switched from being the Chosen One, the bold, confident leader, fully comfortable performing onstage before hundreds of people, to a shy, back-row observer. Watching the natural interactions of students and faculty, I was jealous of their seeming unity. They shared a background and culture of American normality. After time, I discovered that Queens College had a large percentage of recent immigrants enrolled, eager to begin their American experience, and it was with this group of students that I felt the most in common. However, my Connecticut accent didn't convince others that I too was a newly arrived foreigner. I excelled in my coursework but failed in making friends. For a while it felt easier to avoid people altogether than to risk having to reveal anything about my past. Although the faculty were gracious and encouraging, I guarded my privacy. I planned on keeping all traces of Guru locked away in permanent storage. Except that wasn't so easy dwelling in Guru's neighborhood.

I became skilled at dodging in and out of my apartment, avoiding the throngs of disciples out for their daily run sporting Sri Chinmoy Marathon Team T-shirts, or not looking closely at the cars that drove down my block, the normal route taken by both Guru and disciples due to the pattern of one-way streets from Guru's house to the tennis court. I never drove the section of Parsons Boulevard where the divine-enterprises clung together. Since Queens College was more than two miles from the tennis court, I thought I was in a Guru-free zone, but soon enough, one of the disciples opened a divine-enterprise, a printing press, only two blocks from the college, and then almost next door, another disciple opened a vegetarian restaurant. Their unusual manners and habits drew attention, and I overheard students talking about the blue restaurant where the drugged-out waiters invited them to cult ceremonies. When I finally began joining campus activities, like going to the student center for poetry readings, I found posters for Guru's upcoming public concert as well as for the formation of a new meditation club on campus. I wanted them to go away—how dare they encroach on my space. When Guru's April and August parade route changed, the jumbo floats and contingents of marching disciples, distributing leaflets about Guru, rolled past the college's front gates. It felt like Guru kept circling in, closer to where he knew I was.

When the regular facility where Guru's biannual circus

took place banned disciples from renting it again, sure enough, as I crossed campus en route to a world literature class, I saw swarms of Europeans in saris and running shoes rushing with their clown costumes draped over their arms toward the college's gymnasium. For a second I panicked, wanting to dart into the Social Sciences Department to hide, but I stopped myself. I watched the steady progression of disciples on foot, Rollerblades, and bikes, migrate to where Guru would be. Some faces I knew, disciples still committed, permanent back-row disciples, hoping for Guru's blessings, his favor. A contingent of men from Germany crossed the quad in matching Guru-blue shorts and shirts. Perhaps they would juggle, wrestle, or whistle, adding to the hours and hours of humble acts designed to please Guru. I shook my head at the utter futility of their efforts, the impossibility of surrendering their lives to a human who stands in for God. I could have told them to run far away, but their smiles and sure-footed march toward the gymnasium made me realize their absolute belief was their gift and their burden. It was not up to me or anyone to puncture or unravel their faith. Unlike me, as adults, they had chosen Guru themselves and followed a set of teaching that satisfied them. To them, I was the piteous one, eclipsed and swallowed by ignorance. I would not debate them. Who could possibly win? I knew what I wanted, and it was not contained inside the gym at Guru's circus. I would never go there again. I was through tumbling for him, done cartwheeling, dwelling upside-down.

The clock tower chimed. I hooked my backpack over my shoulder and turned in the direction of the English department. I had a class to attend. I couldn't be late. I had wasted enough time.

ॐ

News of Sri Chinmoy's latest escapades, stunts, and scandals continued to flow to me, mostly from my father, who remained a disciple for seven more years, until he was officially asked to leave. After involving himself with a group of ex-disciples who posted online testimonials regarding a range of alleged improprieties committed by Sri Chinmoy, my father's public questioning among new and old disciples was the breaking point of an increasingly strained relationship. Perhaps it took my father years to process all that he had personally witnessed and knew from his decades in the Center, but he didn't tell me until much later any of the doubts and suspicions that he had secretly harbored. In an attempt to grapple with his conclusion that he had been duped, spiritually swindled, he finally revealed to me that at Sri Chinmoy's house on the night of the 7,000-pound "miracle" one-arm lift, when the disciples present were instructed to meditate with their eyes closed and backs facing the barbell, my father disobeyed. He witnessed that Sri Chinmoy never lifted the weight. I had had no idea at the time, but it seemed, for decades, he had been gathering evidence against the man to whom he had pledged his life. Shortly after Sri Chinmoy severed my father's ties to the Center, my father turned around and severed his ties to my mother, leaving her for another woman.

My mother then soundlessly left Sri Chinmoy's group, requesting privacy from all members, both past and present. Not wanting to devote one more single ounce of energy to either of the men to whom she had surrendered her entire adult life, she neither retaliated nor reminisced. She boxed up all of the contents of her former life, her shrines and saris, her scoldings and servitude, and threw them all away. Permanently free, she was now able to embark on the process of resurrecting her own long-buried needs. Years later, as she shared with me her own painful struggles of her decades in the Center, we began a new relationship of openness and truth. There would be no more secrets, no fear of repercussions.

In contrast to my parents, my brother, Ketan, remained steadfast, firmly committed to serving Sri Chinmoy, obediently shunning his family members—except my Aunt Chandika, who remained a disciple—from all visits and communications.

As for Chahna, despite trying, we couldn't assimilate our unique relationship into the new world from our old habitat, and we sadly drifted apart, until we both understood it was only fair to finally let each other go.

According to information leaked from disciples, the Sri Chinmoy Center lumbered along. Alo Devi was still planning trips to villages tucked into remote lands. New legions of fresh-faced devotees joined as many of the original disciples left, including Prema, my former meditation idol. After Prema's exit, Isha promptly cemented her title as the official number one disciple, and others began greeting her with folded hands and reverent bows.

As for Sri Chinmoy himself, it took years before I finally understood that the reason I had a new and richly fulfilling life was because of him. He had released me from his elaborate shadow box when I was too afflicted, too weak, to have done it myself. His freeing me was his greatest unwitting act of compassion.

As I receded further and further from my prior life as his disciple, my awareness and remembrance of Sri Chinmoy shrank until I thought of him only on rare occasions. It was, therefore, unexpected that news of my former Guru returned to me as I lay in a hospital bed recovering from the birth of my daughter. Only a few hours prior to my daughter's entrance to the world, Sri Chinmoy had exited the world, dying of a heart attack on his front porch. While I had long ago dismantled him as my god and savior, his very ordinary, mortal death shocked me, as though a small part of me had still expected him either to be immortal or to ascend toward the heavens. I was sure that he, too, would have wanted something more visionary and celestial than a mundane cardiac arrest. As my husband nestled beside me, and I cradled my fragile, tiny daughter upon my chest, with wonderment I thought of the story of Sri Chinmoy's first visit to me as a newborn in the hospital, where he welcomed me with my name, blessing, and the myth of my birth. In between my birth and the birth of my own daughter, I had lived what felt like many lives, and I sensed Sri Chinmoy had as well. I suspected that he had secretly kept informed about me, following from afar rumors about my life, and I wondered if he knew I was having a daughter. His death made certain that my daughter would never meet him.

But I knew that one day I would want to tell her about him. Maybe I would describe to her the golden early days of the Center, when it was a small circle, a loving family with idealistic dreams to transform the world. Perhaps I would share with my daughter Sri Chinmoy's lasting impact on me—the vacant, permanent clearing of my faith and belief, and the amorphous, empty, and luxuriously open area that filled its place. I thought of the word *Guru*, teacher. He was no longer my guru and would never again be my teacher. I was no longer his Chosen One and would never again be his victory. In the end, we had known too much about each other for false labels. But for my daughter, I realized, I would need to start at the beginning, with the wistful tale of a girl whose soul, years earlier, had been specially chosen to serve her guru.

ABOUT THE AUTHOR

JAYANTI TAMM is an English professor at Ocean County College, where she teaches writing. She lives in New Jersey with her husband and daughter. For more information, visit her website, www.jayantitamm.com.